Geneieve

Tom, Becky, ⟋⟋⟋ ⟋⟋⟋ ⟋

MORE
Strong-Minded
WOMEN

Other books by

LOUISE R. NOUN

published by Iowa State University Press

Journey to Autonomy: A Memoir

Strong-Minded Women: The Emergence of the
Woman-Suffrage Movement in Iowa

MORE
Strong-Minded
WOMEN

Iowa Feminists Tell Their Stories

LOUISE R. NOUN

Iowa State University Press / Ames

Louise Rosenfield Noun, a distinguished feminist, is a member of the Iowa Women's Hall of Fame. She is a graduate of Grinnell College and holds an M.A. degree from Radcliffe/Harvard. Noun was a founding member of the Des Moines chapters of the League of Women Voters and the National Organization for Women. She is the author of *Strong-Minded Women: The Emergence of the Woman-Suffrage Movement in Iowa* and *Journey to Autonomy*.

Authorization to photocopy items for internal or personal use, or the internal or personal use of specific clients, is granted by Iowa State University Press, provided that the base fee of $.10 per copy is paid directly to the Copyright Clearance Center, 27 Congress Street, Salem, MA 01970. For those organizations that have been granted a photocopy license by CCC, a separate system of payments has been arranged. The fee code for users of the Transactional Reporting Service is 0-8138-1819-2/92 $.10.

⊛ Printed on acid-free paper in the United States of America

First edition, 1992

Library of Congress Cataloging-in-Publication Data

More strong-minded women : Iowa feminists tell their stories / [edited by] Louise R. Noun.—1st ed.
          p.   cm.
     Includes bibliographical references and index.
     ISBN 0-8138-1819-2 (acid-free paper)
     1. Feminists—Iowa—Biography. 2. Women social reformers—Iowa—Biography. 3. Women political activists—Iowa—Biography.
     I. Noun, Louise R.
HQ1438.I7M67   1992
305.42′09777—dc20   92-23124

Grateful acknowledgment is made to Routledge, Chapman and Hall for permission to reprint extracts from *Pleasure, Power and Technology* by Sally Hacker (Boston: Unwin, Hyman, 1989).

The cover symbol is from the original state ERA flag (1977), courtesy of the State Historical Society of Iowa.

No matter whether life be long or short—the important thing is to hold one's banner high and to fight in the struggle. For without struggle there is no life.

—KÄTHE KOLLWITZ, 1943

Contents

Foreword

More Strong-Minded Women is a powerfully affecting book. It is history and sociology, biography and drama. It is a primer, a tonic, a reawakening, a reminder of all that has changed and all that has not as women have sought to live full and unfettered lives.

Here Louise Noun, who chronicled Iowa's previous wave of feminism in *Strong-Minded Women,* looks at the second wave of women's rights activism in Iowa, from about 1960 to 1980. What she could not do before except in limited fashion—tell the story in the individuals' own words—she is able to do now. The result, the pleasure of direct communication with all these remarkable women, is richly rewarding.

These are the personal stories of twenty-three Iowans who participated in a period aboil with change, prodigal with questioning, astonishingly vibrant with hope and energy. Surely Iowans will be amazed to see, or to see anew, the remarkable intensity and complexity of the second wave of the women's movement in Iowa. For Iowa truly was a pioneering place in this era.

A reminder of this pioneering comes with the description of the founding of the Emma Goldman Clinic in Iowa City in 1973, "the fourth feminist clinic to open anywhere in the United States" as one of its founders writes here, and the first outside of California. Another reminder comes with the description of the four collectives in Des Moines alone, not to mention the stories of activism in Cedar Rapids, Iowa City, Dubuque, Waterloo, and elsewhere.

More Strong-Minded Women is full of the singular spirit of the time. Like a movie rich with period detail, this book will stir the memories of all who lived through the era—and inform all who did not. Take the roots of growing feminist awareness, for example. Some of the subjects here trace their receptivity to their mothers,

others to their education, others to activism in the civil rights or antiwar movements.

Some recount particular incidents of being wronged, from not being able to wear culottes to junior high school, to having to do all the housework after a full day at work, to having been victims of incest. Others talk of a single rally that moved them, or of a single book. Again and again, Betty Friedan's *The Feminine Mystique* is cited.

The slow raising of consciousness, complete with resistance, is painfully clear. "*The Feminine Mystique* was published in 1963 when my daughter was very little," says Ruth Cotter Scharnau of Dubuque. "At the time, we were living in graduate student housing at Northern Illinois University in DeKalb where my husband was working for his Ph.D. A woman in our dorm kept urging me to read the book, and I just wouldn't. I knew that it would open a Pandora's box and I was afraid I would never be able to close it. Of course you heard things on television and read about events in newspapers and periodicals, things that were happening in the cities, but I always thought, They are so radical. I bought the line of the media, as I am sure many women do."

Beyond the resistance is the thrill of discovery. Deborah Nye speaks of a Grinnell College class in which she was exposed to the works of Friedan, Kate Millet, Germaine Greer, Simone de Beauvoir. "The class was small and experimental. Although I was reading these works for the first time (many of them were newly published works), the basic ideas had been inside me like a gray fog. Reading these works gave form to this fog."

There followed the search for like minds, and then the inspiration of early activism in all its varied guises: opening the door for girls on school safety patrols or as newspaper carriers, getting working women into schoolbooks, or working on better health care for women, political activism, sex education, reproductive freedom.

And always the worry as to how one was coming across, the painstaking care to do something just right, to present something palatably yet with courage. Here is Ginny Benware discussing the 1976 founding of the Des Moines bookstore, A Mind of Your Own. "We didn't want to be too offensive but we certainly wanted to stand by our principles. We decided to call the project a nonsexist bookstore as opposed to a feminist bookstore because even in 1976 too many people were threatened by the feminist label. Nonsexism seemed the less threatening term."

Here is Bev Mitchell, an organizer of the Cedar Rapids Women's Caucus, on the group's response to speaking invitations. "People who invited us to speak often looked at us as freaks who were there to be looked at and have their prejudices confirmed. So we developed a thing called the 'token lovelies,' two squads of women that were outstandingly good-looking. Those were the ones that we sent to all men's groups. . . . This was awfully sexist of us but sometimes it was whatever works. . . . At least the audience came away with, 'My God, you know, these women are not as freaky as I thought.' Hopefully, that allowed the message to be heard."

This is a book that brings memories rushing back: the soulful talks, the health-care gatherings complete with vaginal self-examinations with a speculum, the sense of history changing swiftly around one. Here is Nye describing the readying of the house that would be used for the Goldman Clinic. "I spent the summer of 1973 doing things like painting, laying linoleum, cleaning and scrubbing the house, all the while listening to the Watergate testimony which was going on before the Senate investigating committee."

All of this was representative of the movement throughout the nation, but—as this book amply reminds us—Iowa had its own special flavor. There are many stories here from small towns and from farms, as well as out of the cities. There is sturdiness and solidity, the tenacious and the temperate, even when the topic was revolution and courage was the requisite.

The goals, the particular visions, the specifics, were as widely varied as the women themselves. Here is Mary Garst, of Coon Rapids, telling of her hopes that she could hire cowgirls as well as cowboys, and make it work—and of the pain and frustration the quest brought. And Garst again, being put on corporate boards because, she was told, she was seen as a woman "who won't cry at board meetings."

And from the many stories, the larger themes emerge, from

reproductive freedom to personal freedom to equal pay for equal work. And gradually, out of the early flush of enthusiasm comes the awakening sense of the complexity of the issues—and then of the cost and pain of the fight. How high were the hopes, how overblown, it came to seem, were the expectations. And how hard came the sense of loss. As farm activist Naomi Christensen says, "I thought it was all going to happen in ten years and now I realize that it is not even happening in my lifetime."

There is wistfulness at the lost sense of engagement. Here is Nye again, describing how she felt after ending her association with the clinic to finish her law studies. "I am never able to reproduce the feeling I used to have when I left a hard day's work at the Emma Goldman Clinic. I always left the clinic feeling I had helped to empower some woman or many women, no matter what service I participated in, or whether I had only gone to staff meetings that day. This feeling comes from doing what you believe in."

There is puzzlement at today's young women, who don't seem to understand. Says Barbara Mathias, who was director of the YWCA on the campus of Iowa State University in Ames and now lives in Des Moines, "In the middle 1970s we at least knew we didn't have it so good and it seemed like more of the young women were in touch with that and were willing to work for some changes. Now it seems almost as if the younger women think that the women over forty were kind of foolish to have worked so hard when we were going to get our rights anyway. In fact, we don't have them yet."

In her introduction Louise Noun writes, "Feminism remained at a low ebb from the time of the ratification of the Nineteenth Amendment in 1920 until its reemergence in the 1960s." That's forty-plus years, and countless women's lives, that were not all that they could have been.

Iowa in the 1990s cannot afford a like hiatus. The state's need for the vision and leadership of all of its citizens is too great. A rekindling now of the energies and hopes that ring through these stories could brighten Iowa's future immeasurably.

This is a book that could help. By chronicling such an important era, with such human warmth and poignancy, it can teach us, and help us remember, and give us hope, and inspire us.

GENEVA OVERHOLSER
Vice President/Editor, *Des Moines Register*

Preface

WHEN I CONDUCTED these interviews during 1989 and 1990 I asked each woman to begin by telling me something about her childhood and how she became a feminist. Other than this request there was no set formula for the interviews. My questions were framed to bring out important elements of each woman's story. Sandra Roehrick transcribed the interviews and after I edited them they were sent to the women interviewed for correction and approval.[1]

I have tried to include a variety of activists in these interviews; rural women, labor union women, and professional women. They represent varying political views: Republican and Democratic, socialist and anarchist. I regret that there are not more minority women. This failure can be attributed to the failure of the women's movement as a whole to attract minorities, a situation caused in large part by differences in perception and needs between middle-class white feminists and minority women. As Kesho Scott points out, "While many white, middle-class career women [the backbone of the women's movement] have experienced work as liberation from traditional sex-roles (grounded in domesticity), black women—like other oppressed and poor ethnic women—have for generations been forced to work outside the home so that their families could live and develop economically. . . . Black women have almost always operated outside of traditional and middle-class white sex-roles" (Scott 1991). I also regret that no lesbian or bisexual woman was willing to talk about her struggles with sexual orientation. Unfortunately, societal attitudes are still so hostile that these

---

1. Due to travel difficulties, I did not interview Deborah Nye in person. She wrote this account of her life.

xii

women are reluctant to suffer the consequences of going public with this aspect of their lives.

Gathering the material for this book has been a pleasure because it has brought me into contact with many women with whom I worked in the 1970s as well as giving me the opportunity to meet others whom I had not known before. All these women were most willing to talk about this exciting time in their lives and I am very appreciative of their cooperation. Many other Iowa women, with interesting stories to tell about their involvement with the feminist movement in the 1970s, are not included in this book because of space limitations.

Sally Hacker died before this project was begun, but I was fortunate in locating an interview with her that Dorothy Smith conducted shortly before Sally's death. Dorothy has generously shared this with me. I also interviewed Bart Hacker, Sally's husband, about her life and philosophy. Jean Lloyd-Jones and Mori Constantino gave me valuable information about the 1977 International Women's Year meeting in Des Moines. Linda Yanney shared her information about Iowa City activists and Margery Wolf gave me encouragement when this project seemed stalled. My thanks to all these people. The Des Moines Public Library reference department has cheerfully answered countless queries, and I am most appreciative of this service.

REFERENCE

Scott, Kesho Yvonne, *The Habit of Surviving: Black Women's Strategies for Life* (New Brunswick, N.J.: Rutgers University Press, 1991).

Landmarks

OF IOWA'S SECOND-WAVE FEMINISM

1961 • President John F. Kennedy appoints National Commission on the Status of Women.

1963 • President Kennedy's Commission on the Status of Women issues *Report on American Women* documenting the problems of discrimination in employment, unequal pay, and lack of social services. • Governor Harold Hughes appoints Iowa Committee on the Status of Women. No funding provided. • *The Feminine Mystique* by Betty Friedan published. Three hundred thousand copies sold within a year.

1964 • Governor's Committee on the Status of Women issues report. • Congress enacts Title VII of the Civil Rights Act outlawing discrimination in employment on the basis of sex. Administered by the Equal Employment Opportunity Commission (EEOC).

1965 • Conference on the status of women at the Des Moines Young Women's Christian Association (YWCA) sponsored by the Iowa Committee on the Status of Women.

1966 • National Organization for Women (NOW) founded in Washington, D.C., by a small group of women attending the third national conference of state commissions on the status of women. Purpose "to take action to bring women into full participation in the mainstream of American society now."

1967 • President Lyndon B. Johnson issues Executive Order 11246 prohibiting discrimination on account of sex by the federal government or federal contractors. This order goes into effect Oct. 13, 1968. Administered by the Office of Federal Contract Compliance (OFCC) of the Department of Labor. • First attempt to modify Iowa's restrictive 100-year-old abortion law defeated in committee.

1969 • Students at Grinnell College remove their clothes at a meeting addressed by a representative of *Playboy* magazine in protest of the magazine's treatment of women as "lapdog female playthings." • Rapid growth of loosely structured radical women's liberation groups throughout the country, including groups in Iowa City and Grinnell.

1970 • *The Dialectic of Sex* by Shulamith Firestone published. • *Ain't I a Woman* begins publication in Iowa City. Said to be the first radical feminist paper in the United States. • On the fiftieth anniversary of the ratification of the Nineteenth Amendment thousands of women throughout the country march in a protest called the Women's Strike for Equality.

1971 • National Women's Political Caucus founded in Washington, D.C., by author Betty Friedan and congresswomen Bella Abzug and Shirley Chisholm. Bipartisan organization to increase women's visibility and participation in the political arena. • Des Moines chapter of NOW organized. • Cedar Rapids Women's Caucus (later Cedar Rapids NOW) organized.

1972 • Congress enacts Title IX of the Higher Education Act outlawing discrimination on the basis of sex in federally funded education programs. Administered by the Department of Health, Education and Welfare (HEW). • Iowa Commission on the Status of Women, a statutory body, replaces Governor's Committee on the Status of Women. • First statewide meeting of Iowa NOW chapters.

• Conference of Iowa union women organized by Betty Talkington.
• Congress submits the Equal Rights Amendment (ERA) to the states for ratification. Iowa fourth state to ratify.

1973 • First convention of the National Women's Political Caucus held in Houston. • Iowa chapter of the Women's Political Caucus organized under Roxanne Conlin's leadership. • U.S. Supreme Court in *Roe v. Wade* rules that women have a constitutional right to abortion during the first six months of pregnancy. (This ruling nullifies the Iowa abortion law.) • Emma Goldman abortion clinic opens in Iowa City.

1974 • Coalition of Labor Union Women (CLUW) founded at a Chicago meeting attended by three thousand women. • Margaret McDowell appointed first chair of the Women's Studies Program at the University of Iowa.

1976 • International Women's Year meeting in Mexico City.

1977 • Fifteen hundred Iowans attend state International Women's Year meeting in Des Moines. • National International Women's Year meeting in Houston. Iowa sends twenty-two delegates.

1979 • Iowa General Assembly approves a state ERA.

1980 • State ERA defeated in a popular referendum.

1982 • Time limit for ratification of federal ERA expires. Measure dies because of failure of three-quarters of the states to ratify.

1991 • Iowa General Assembly again approves a state ERA to be submitted to a popular referendum in the fall of 1992.

MORE
Strong-Minded
WOMEN

Introduction

THE WOMEN who were interviewed for this book played a variety of roles in the rebirth of the feminist movement in Iowa in the 1970s and together they give a vivid overall picture of feminist activities in the state at that time. This picture is also representative of the activities and struggles of feminists elsewhere in the United States and therefore serves as a microcosm of the emergence of the movement throughout the country. It is important that stories such as these be preserved.

These second-wave Iowa feminists join a long line of dedicated Iowa women whose struggle for equality began in the mid-nineteenth century. A quick look back will help set the stage for the emergence of this second wave.

EARLY SUFFRAGE EFFORTS

In 1855 when Amelia Bloomer, dress reformer and editor of a temperance and woman's rights paper, settled in the rough frontier town of Council Bluffs, her efforts to promote the idea of woman's rights in her new community were greeted with ridicule. When Annie Savery delivered the first lecture on behalf of woman suffrage in Des Moines in 1868, her primarily male audience was decidedly hostile to her message and she was criticized by both sexes for her boldness in daring to lecture in public.

It was not until after the Civil War ended in 1865 that Bloomer, Savery, and other feminists throughout the state found hope for their cause when there was a move to revise the state constitution to allow African-American men to vote. Woman's rights advocates saw no reason why women should not be enfranchised at the same time and they urged that the constitutional provision limiting the right to vote to white males only be enlarged to include all women, regardless of color, as well as African-American men. However, Republican politicians who were leading the fight for African-American suffrage over Democratic opposition responded by telling women their turn would come as soon as African-American men were enfranchised. This is the "Negro's hour," they said. The "woman's hour" would be next.

The question of African-American male suffrage in Iowa was settled in 1868 when an amendment to delete the word "white" from the qualifications for voting was given final approval in a popular referendum. Consequently, Republicans in the next session of the general assembly meeting in 1870 were faced with the problem of making good on their promise to women. Goaded by Democrats, who accused them of favoring black men over their own wives and daughters, Republicans with the help of tongue-in-cheek Democrats approved a woman-suffrage amendment that in hindsight had little or no chance of gaining the required second approval by the assembly at its next biennial session in 1872.

Suffragists, however, were so optimistic about the prospects for legislative success for the Iowa-suffrage amendment that they organized a statewide woman-suffrage association in June 1870 to assure victory when the measure was submitted to the required popular referendum after its approval by the 1872 general assembly. In the interim, however, the woman-suffrage movement suffered a barrage of unfair and vicious criticism. Suffragists were accused of being an influence that would break up the family by promoting divorce and advocating free love. Male legislators, who had no desire to share their power with women under any circumstance, were very willing to listen to these accusations and accordingly failed to approve the amendment a second time. It was now necessary to start the amendment process over again.

The 1874 Iowa general assembly again raised suffragists' hopes by approving a suffrage amendment, but it was defeated by a small margin two years later. Thus began a pattern, which the state legislature followed with few exceptions until 1915, of endorsing a woman-suffrage amendment at one session and then defeating it by a small number of votes at the next. National suffrage leader Susan B. Anthony called this the "cat and mouse game," and it required the utmost dedication for suffragists who continued their fight year after year in the face of so many defeats.

INTO THE TWENTIETH CENTURY

Finally, in 1915 a state woman-suffrage amendment received the necessary second legislative approval and was submitted to a referendum at the primary elections the following year. Suffragists were hopeful that at last success was imminent, and they mounted a well-organized campaign for their cause assisted by Carrie Chapman Catt, president of the National American Woman Suffrage Association, who had begun her suffrage career in Iowa. Alas, suffragists once again were destined to suffer defeat. The amendment lost in an obviously dishonest election in which suffrage ballots were handed out indiscriminately at the polls. The final tally showed that there were 29,000 more votes cast on the woman-suffrage amendment than the total votes cast for all candidates for governor. There was no remedy other than to start the amendment process all over again. Meanwhile, Iowa women finally received the right to vote in 1920 by means of the Nineteenth Amendment to the U.S. Constitution.

After ratification of the Nineteenth Amendment the National American Woman Suffrage Association, at Chapman Catt's suggestion, transformed itself into the League of Women Voters. The league's purpose was to educate women in how to use the franchise for the common good. High on the league's legislative priorities were progressive reforms affecting women, such as regulation of child labor, protective laws for working women, and provisions for maternal and child welfare. The Iowa League of Women Voters, organized in the early twenties, was headed by Flora Dunlap, a social worker and former president of the Iowa Woman Suffrage Association.

The National Women's Party, an outgrowth of the radical wing of the woman-suffrage movement, took issue with the league's reformist efforts to ameliorate women's situation. This group saw protective legislation as working against women's best interest.

They believed that the only solution for women's problems was in legal equality through an equal rights amendment to the federal constitution. The National Women's Party was successful in securing the first congressional hearing on an Equal Rights Amendment (ERA) in 1923 but there was little support for this legislation due to the opposition of reformist women's groups and the almost total lack of public interest in women's rights at this time. (The first I heard of the ERA was when I joined the League of Women Voters in 1944 and was told that the league opposed this legislation because it would do away with protective legislation for women. In 1972 the league reversed its position on the ERA.)

1960s REEMERGENCE OF FEMINISM

Feminism remained at a low ebb from the time of the ratification of the Nineteenth Amendment in 1920 until its reemergence in the 1960s. As late as 1964 Alice Rossi, a noted feminist scholar, commented that "there is practically no feminist spark left among American women." This situation, however, was rapidly changing. A major catalyst for the emergence of contemporary feminism was Betty Friedan's book, *The Feminine Mystique,* published in 1963. Friedan, addressing primarily college-educated, middle-class women, pointed out the discrepancy between the reality of women's lives and the image to which they were trying to conform. *The Feminine Mystique* was an immediate success and within a year more than three hundred thousand copies were sold. Many of the women interviewed for this book indicated the importance of *The Feminine Mystique* in developing a feminist consciousness.

The year 1963 also saw the publication of the *Report on American Women* by President Kennedy's Commission on the Status of Women (a group appointed by Kennedy two years previously). This report documented in great detail problems of discrimination in employment, unequal pay, and lack of social services for women. On October 11, 1963, the day that this report was issued, Iowa Governor Harold Hughes announced the appointment of a Governor's Commission on the Status of Women patterned after the Kennedy commission. It was Hughes's hope that this commission (which was unfunded) would "focus attention on the changing role of women in our state's society and on the remaining inequities they face." The report of the Iowa commission issued in September 1964 documented a number of inequities suffered by women in the work force and in educational institutions but its findings were necessarily limited because of lack of finances. The commission's recommendations met a deaf ear in the Iowa legislature. According to commission member Betty Talkington, the commission's biggest success was in getting the requirement for "earth closets" in the Iowa Code changed to "water closets."

Talkington, women's activities director of the AFL-CIO, represented the governor's commission at annual meetings of state commissions on the status of women in Washington, D.C. At the 1966 meeting in Washington, Talkington was one of a small group of delegates who met informally in a hotel room where they founded the National Organization for Women (NOW) because they saw the need for a civil rights organization to prod the government into stronger support of women's issues. NOW was the first activist feminist group in the twentieth century to combat sexism on a broad front. During its early years NOW had a slow growth but by 1970 it was well established with affiliates throughout the country, although none as yet had been established in Iowa.

1970s FEMINISM—NATIONAL ORGANIZATION FOR WOMEN

To mark the fiftieth anniversary of the passage of the Nineteenth Amendment giving women the right to vote, NOW in 1970 called for a Women's Strike for Equality. Thousands of women throughout the country responded with marches and demonstrations, especially in communities where there were NOW affiliates. Sarah Hanley and her two daughters went from their home in Cedar Rapids to Boston where they marched in a large demonstration. (Hanley still cherishes the "Ain't I a Woman" poster that she carried in this parade. This poster was inspired by the words of Sojourner Truth, the nineteenth-century African-American feminist.)

In 1971 Hanley, along with Bev Mitchell, was instrumental in organizing the Cedar Rapids Women's Caucus, the first mainline feminist organization in the state. Two years later this group affiliated with NOW. The Des Moines chapter of NOW was organized by Virginia Watkins in 1971, and Sally Hacker helped organize an Ames chapter at about the same time. In 1972 some Dubuque women who called themselves the Feminine Equality Movement began meeting at the University of Dubuque. This group became a NOW affiliate in 1973. The first state meeting of NOW chapters was held in Cedar Rapids in 1972, but for a number of years NOW had no state organization other than the volunteer services of a peripatetic state coordinator.

NOW chapters in Iowa generally worked on a broad agenda to

change societal attitudes toward women educationally, legally, economically, and socially. Their activities ranged from supporting the ERA to fighting sexist practices in the public schools, desegregating restaurants, protesting sexist advertising, and calling attention to how the United Way discriminated against women and the poor. High on the NOW agenda was the issue of reproductive freedom, but when the U.S. Supreme Court legalized abortion in 1973 the question of abortion rights was generally put on the back burner for the rest of the decade.

In 1972 Congress at last approved an ERA and feminists throughout the country were jubilant. Due to pressure by Minnette Doderer and the handful of other women in the state legislature, Iowa became the fourth state to ratify this amendment. During the protracted fight for ratification in Illinois, Iowa NOW members went to Springfield by the busload to support Illinois feminists in their losing battle. By 1982, when the time limit for ratification of the ERA expired, only thirty-five of the necessary thirty-eight states had approved this measure and Congress refused to extend the time limit. Meanwhile, feminists increasingly looked to their state legislatures to insure women's rights through the passage of state ERAs.

WOMEN'S POLITICAL CAUCUS AND UNION ORGANIZATIONS

As the feminist movement gained momentum in the late sixties and early seventies other feminist organizations emerged. Among the strongest of these was the National Women's Political Caucus, which was founded in 1971 by congresswomen Bella Abzug and Shirley Chisholm, and author Betty Friedan as a bipartisan organization to increase women's participation in politics and to encourage women to run for office. The Iowa affiliate of the caucus became the strongest in the nation after its organization by Roxanne Conlin of Des Moines, a lawyer and an active Democrat.

The first convention of the national caucus, which was held in Houston in February 1973 was attended by only two Iowans—Mary Lou Houston, who was sponsored by the Dubuque chapter of NOW, and Conlin, who went independently. Conlin was so impressed "with all the wonderful people in the same room at the same time" that soon after her return home she set to work to organize an Iowa Women's Political Caucus. The first state caucus convention, which was held in Ames the following September, was an enormous success. While a few hundred women were expected, almost a thousand showed up. Great care was taken to include both Democratic and Republican women in the Iowa Caucus, the most prominent Republican being Mary Louise Smith, a member of the Republican National Committee.

The caucus adopted an ambitious nine-point legislative program that included

1. Providing state-funded comprehensive child care.
2. Prohibition of discrimination on the basis of sex in educational institutions.
3. Prohibition of discrimination on the basis of sex in housing, in benefit systems, and in retirement plans.
4. Giving the Iowa Civil Rights Commission authority to deal with sex discrimination in credit policies and practices.
5. Elimination of sex discrimination in insurance.
6. Valuing in-home labor at its fair market price for inheritance tax and legal purposes.
7. Providing adequate financial resources for welfare recipients.
8. Elimination of the requirement of corroboration in cases of rape and sexual assault and prohibition of inquiry into the past sexual conduct of the victim.
9. Allowing enforcement of child support for children through the age of eighteen.

The caucus was a congenial home for feminists who were put off by NOW's confrontational tactics. Several local caucuses were organized during the summer of 1973 prior to the Ames convention and others were organized soon after. The caucus "was very effective," Minnette Doderer comments, "because that was the first time a group of women who had standing in their communities were working for a common goal of improving the legal and economic status of all women." This action was in contrast to individual women working through churches or other benevolent organizations.

In addition to its ambitious legislative program, the Iowa caucus was active in its early days in teaching women about the political process and in encouraging them to run for office. During the 1974 session of the general assembly the caucus successfully backed three pieces of legislation: (1) elimination of the requirement of corroboration in cases of rape and sexual assault, (2) revision of state inheritance tax laws to eliminate provisions discriminatory to women, and (3) legislation permitting cosmetologists to cut men's hair. Laws passed in later sessions of the general assembly can be attributed to the seeds of reform planted by feminists in the early seventies. These include prohibiting sex discrimination on the basis of sex in housing, in work-related benefit systems, in credit policies, and in state-supported schools. The legislature has also provided for comparable worth pay for state employees.

In 1972 Betty Talkington organized the first of several statewide conferences for union women, which met an enthusiastic response. Delegates were inspired to work for positions of authority in their male-controlled local unions. In Cedar Falls, Kay Stone organized a women's caucus in her Communications Workers of America (CWA) local which had no female officers. Within two years 50 percent of the officers were women.

Union women gained further solidarity through the Coalition of Labor Union Women (CLUW), which was founded at a nationwide meeting in Chicago in 1974. Only a few hundred women were expected and two thousand showed up.

"This conference was very special," Talkington says. "At the end we all held hands and sang solidarity. Everybody had tears."

RADICAL FEMINIST GROUPS

In addition to feminists associated with mainstream organizations such as NOW, the Women's Political Caucus, and labor unions, there were also more radical, often loosely structured groups, that helped leaven the feminist loaf in the late sixties and early seventies. Perhaps the earliest feminist action in Iowa occurred in February 1969 when six members of a Grinnell College women's liberation group along with four men removed their clothes at a meeting of about seventy-five students gathered to hear a representative of *Playboy* magazine explain the publication's philosophy. The purpose of the students' action was to protest *Playboy*'s treatment of women as "lapdog female playthings" and to affirm "the dignity of each human body, and each person who occupies it." The students' message was lost in the furor that followed this demonstration. Photos of the naked students appeared in newspapers and magazines throughout the country and even as far away as Thailand. Charged with indecent exposure by Richard Turner, Iowa's attorney general who had no use for unruly students, they were ultimately convicted. Deborah Nye tells how this same liberation group distributed birth control literature to each dorm room at a time when the college offered no birth control services and town physicians were loathe to serve single women.

According to Clara Oleson there was a radical group in Iowa City, the majority of whom were lesbians, whose revolutionary issues were gender politics, socialism, day care, and rape. They had no interest in working against employment discrimination, which they considered a reformist effort that would only help perpetuate a bad system. Bev Mitchell recalls that this group refused to help picket a Cedar Rapids company that was laying off female employees. In 1970 the Iowa City group began publication of a newsletter called *Ain't I a Woman* which is said to be the earliest radical/feminist publication in the country.

The Feminist/Socialist Group was organized in Des Moines in 1972 by Karen Johnson and two other recent Coe College graduates. Many of this group lived in communes. They spent a great deal of time studying alternative political systems and searching for a way to a more just society. Unlike the Iowa City radicals, the Feminist/Socialists were willing to join picket lines and work with other community groups to improve conditions for low-income people.

FEMINISM AND SEXUAL ORIENTATION

The 1970s brought many feminists into contact with lesbians, who were an integral part of the feminist movement. This resulted in new friendships with people who had acknowledged their struggles with sexual orientation, and a greater understanding of the problems faced by homosexuals. National NOW at its 1973 convention pledged to seek legislation to end discrimination based on sexual orientation and in 1977 the International Women's Year meeting in Des Moines endorsed gay rights as part of its platform. Peg Anderson was subsequently defeated in her campaign for mayor of Cedar Falls because she supported the International Women's Year platform.

"One of the chief virtues of the movement," says Sarah Hanley, "is that we didn't allow anybody to divide us up along any lines whether they were political . . . or whether they were sexual."

1977—INTERNATIONAL WOMEN'S YEAR

The feminist movement in Iowa reached a crescendo in 1977 with the three-day International Women's Year meeting, funded by the federal government, which was held in Des Moines in early June. Similar meetings were held in every state preparatory to the nationwide International Women's Year meeting to be held in Houston in the fall. Fifteen hundred women from all walks of life participated in the Iowa meeting where a wide range of issues were discussed. There were ninety workshops on fifty-six different subjects such as the one titled "City Women–Farm Women" in which Naomi Christensen participated. Roxanne Conlin led a workshop on "Homemakers and the Law," and Betty Talkington headed a workshop on "Practical Advice on Job Hunting." When this author spoke to a plenary session on the ERA she was so sanguine about it soon becoming law that she warned the audience that law alone was not enough to free women; that changes in societal attitudes were equally important. Dozens of recommendations to benefit women were adopted by this meeting, the two most controversial being support for reproductive freedom and the passage of state legislation to prohibit discrimination on the basis of sexual orientation.

The Des Moines meeting elected twenty-seven delegates to the International Women's Year meeting in Houston. Among them were Peg Anderson, Ginny Benware, Roxanne Conlin, Minnette Doderer, Mary Louise Smith, and Betty Talkington. Naomi Christensen was later appointed a delegate to the Houston meeting by the national International Women's Year Committee.

Despite the enthusiastic response to the International Women's Year meetings the year 1977 proved to be a kind of watershed for the women's movement in Iowa. The original vigor and excitement of the movement was beginning to wane as feminists were coming to realize that there was a long, hard road ahead to reach their goals. The comparatively easy job of consciousness-raising had been accomplished but internal frictions were hampering the movement nationally and although there had been legislative successes on both the national and state level, only a few inroads had been made into the deeply imbedded sexism in society.

In January 1977 Louise Swartzwalder reviewed the state of the movement in Iowa in a series of four articles in the *Des Moines Register.* She began by pointing out that since the organization of the first NOW chapter in Iowa six years previously, "Iowa has been in the front line. The feminist effort here has been among the largest, best organized, most active, most effective, and most sophisticated of any state's." But then she went on to point out that the tide seemed to be ebbing and that some observers were saying that 1976 might be looked back on as the year of the death of the modern women's movement. For example, nationally, the drive to add the Equal Rights Amendment to the U.S. Constitution was stalled four states short of ratification and was facing increasingly bitter and well-organized opposition. The national leadership structures of both NOW and the National Women's Political Caucus were reeling

from internal disputes. The Iowa caucus was having difficulty getting its priority bills passed by the legislature and it had annoyed
some politicians with its policies on supporting candidates.
Swartzwalder wondered if these difficulties were the death knell of
the women's movement or merely growing pains.

Swartzwalder interviewed me as president of Des Moines NOW
and I assured her that current difficulties were only growing pains. I
said that NOW was still doing important work by continuing to
make the public aware of sexist advertising and employment discrimination and that it was also taking on new projects such as
exposing the problems of battered wives. I was frank in admitting
that national NOW had a "terrible" president but said that she
would soon be out of office. I can still remember the sense of be-
trayal I felt that Swartzwalder would even question the viability of
the women's movement.

Peg Anderson, president of the Iowa Women's Political Caucus,
admitted that her organization was having less legislative success.
She explained, however, that the issues the caucus backed in 1974
had been around for a long time and were ripe for passage. The
caucus was now backing bills that dealt with economic issues,
which required legislators "to put the taxpayers' money where their
sympathetic mouths were." Anderson said the caucus was starting
a drive to interest women in running for school boards and city
councils as an extension of earlier efforts to get women to run for
the legislature.

RIGHT-WING BACKLASH

State legislator Minnette Doderer told Swartzwalder that there
was currently no hard-core opposition to the women's movement.
This statement typifies the blindness of most Iowa feminists to the
rising tide of national opposition led by Phyllis Schlafly, a right-wing
lawyer from Illinois. Schlafly, both glib and persuasive, was an ada-
mant opponent of the ERA and the 1973 Supreme Court decision
legalizing abortion. She and her cohorts had managed to dominate
the International Women's Year meeting in Missouri and several
other states, and Iowa women took great care to see that they didn't
take over the Des Moines meeting. In Houston the Schlafly forces
put on a countermeeting and its delegates refused to vacate hotel
rooms promised to the International Women's Year delegates.
Naomi Christensen was a victim of this action.

Two years later Iowans were to witness Schlafly's effectiveness
when she came to the state to campaign against ratification of an

equal rights amendment to the Iowa constitution. This amendment, which was approved by the legislature in 1979, was submitted to the voters at the general election in the fall of 1980. Under Peg Anderson's leadership feminists organized a coalition of forty-five groups of widely varying interests and raised more than $160,000 to support the campaign for ratification. Governor Robert Ray supported the measure and there were good prospects for success. Public opinion polls consistently showed that the majority of Iowans supported the ERA but in the end this support turned out to be very shallow. During the last two weeks of the campaign Schlafly came into the state with her message that the ERA would do away with protective legislation for women, force men and women to share rest rooms, sanction monosexual marriages and, in general, destroy the traditional American family. She spent $25,000 on television ads showing men kissing each other during a gay rights parade in San Francisco. Schlafly turned the tide against the ERA and the measure lost by vote of 55 to 45 percent.

The defeat of the ERA in 1980 marked the end of the first decade of the rebirth of Iowa feminism. It was a period of excitement and hope, expressed by Barbara Mathias who recalls, "We truly believed that all things were possible and that it would only be a few years, maybe just a few months, before women had a more equitable situation."

REFERENCES

Rossi, Alice S., "Equality Between the Sexes: An Immodest Proposal," *Daedalus,* Proceedings of the American Academy of Arts and Sciences, vol. 13, no. 2 (Spring 1964):608.
Swartzwalder, Louise, "Whither the Women?" *Des Moines Register,* 16–19 January 1977.

Irene Talbott

Virginia Watkins

Louise Noun

Ginny Benware

I *Community Activists*

Sally Hacker

Karen Johnson

Bev Mitchell

Ruth Cotter Scharnau

Deborah Nye

Naomi Christensen

THE WOMEN whose interviews appear in this book are multifaceted in their activities and therefore difficult to categorize. In general, however, they can be divided into three classes: (1) activists whose feminist activities were separate from their usual occupations either as paid members of the work force or as homemakers or students, (2) women who promoted the feminist cause through the political process, and (3) activists whose feminism was expressed through employment-related occupations.

The majority of the community activists in this section were members of NOW, which provided a support system for women to spread the feminist message in the early 1970s when feminism was still a pejorative word.

Irene Talbott served as the first state coordinator of NOW and was president of the Des Moines chapter in 1974. Talbott tells about the consciousness-raising activities of NOW in its early days such as leafleting bridal fairs to warn of consumer-oriented myths about marriage, and protesting an ongoing "big tits" contest sponsored by a local bar. She also worked as a volunteer for the first rape crisis center in the city and edited the NOW newsletter. Talbott was one of the NOW members who formed the Motley House feminist collective.

Virginia Watkins was responsible for the organization of the NOW chapter in Des Moines at a time when it was difficult for her to locate even ten women as charter members. She tells the story of how she went about finding these women. (I was one of the charter members of this group and I include myself in these interviews so that the readers of this volume will know something about its editor.) Ginny Benware and Sally Hacker were other Des Moines NOW members whose stories reflect the breadth of feminist activities at this time.

Benware tells of her efforts to organize clerical workers in Des Moines and of her initiative in founding the feminist bookstore, A Mind of Your Own.

Sally Hacker was the dominant influence in the Des Moines chapter through her enthusiasm and her daring in challenging entrenched sexism with humor and a sense of fun regardless of her establishment position as a professor of sociology at Drake University. Hacker's radical political philosophy stretched the thinking of many of us who worked with her.

Karen Johnson was a member of the New World Collective, a group of men and women who were dedicated to the idea of doing away with sexism in their personal lives and to the idea that communal living could be an alternative to the traditional family. This group joined with other radicals in Des Moines in forming the Feminist/Socialist Group dedicated to feminist ideals and the need for a more just alternative to our current political system.

Bev Mitchell was a leader in organizing the Cedar Rapids Women's Caucus, which later affiliated with NOW. Mitchell took part in activities such as desegregating lunchrooms and challenging the lack of athletic opportunities for girls in the public schools. The newsletter, *Lilith Speaks*, which Mitchell edited for the Cedar Rapids chapter, was (and still is) the liveliest feminist newsletter in the state.

Ruth Cotter Scharnau tells about the organization of the NOW chapter in Dubuque, a conservative community where even desegregating school traffic patrols was a challenge. She also recalls how the friendships she developed with lesbians whom she met in the feminist movement helped in her acceptance of her daughter's lesbian orientation in later years.

Deborah Nye was still in school when NOW members were first challenging sexism in society but she took time out from her study of law at the University of Iowa to help organize the Emma Goldman Clinic in Iowa City after the U.S. Supreme Court legalized abortion in 1973. Emma Goldman was the first clinic in the state to provide abortion services and Nye continued to work there for the next thirteen years. She tells about her particular interest in health care for women, stemming from an illegal abortion she had while she was still in high school.

Naomi Christensen, who lives on a farm in southwest Iowa, is an example of how rural women find an outlet for social action through their churches. In Christensen's case, her religious-oriented activities led to contact with other feminists in the state and her participation in the International Women's Year meetings in 1977. She is now chair of the Iowa Commission on the Status of Women.

Irene Talbott, known to her
friends as Tally, was a member of the Motley
House women's collective in Des Moines and a
president of Des Moines NOW. Tally was one of
the organizers of the feminist book store, A
Mind of Your Own. She now lives in New York,
where she is a financial planner specializing in
retirement plans.

*"We were concerned that efforts of
volunteer charity applied mere Band-
Aids to really major wounds in our
society and allowed people to
postpone facing and solving these
issues head-on."*

Although my name is Irene, everyone calls me Tally. I
was born during the first year of the baby boom in Basin, a Wyoming town of 1,200 people. Both sets of my grandparents had left
the comfort of the South and the Midwest to buy land out where it
was cheap, to become farmers in Campbell County, near Gillette,
Wyoming. My mother and my father lived with their respective parents until they were in their late twenties; this was a lonely life
because it was a ten-mile ride by horseback to the nearest neighbor.
My dad, being the youngest son and the only one still at home when
this farming—he called it homesteading—idea had struck Grandpa
Talbott, took the responsibility of caring for his parents. So when
my parents were married they moved in with the Talbott elders. By
then it was the late 1920s or early 1930s and, in a land where it
never rains anyway, an additional drought hit. Much against my
grandfather Talbott's wishes, my dad finally carted up the oldsters
and Mom and moved across the Big Horn Mountains to the Basin

side of Wyoming, where Buffalo Bill Cody had started an irrigation system. However, Dad very soon forsook farming and got a job with the highway department, which he held for about thirty years until his death in 1968.

Grandpa Talbott was much older than Grandma and was dead before I knew him. But I have some memories of Grandma. She had married what she thought was a middle-class candy store owner and dance-band musician who was twenty years older and had gone to live in Missouri from Illinois. Then when her husband is about sixty-four and she about forty-five, this guy uproots her and her two youngest sons and hauls them all out to the Wyoming desert. Meanwhile, he became a religious fanatic—certainly no more dance bands. Talk about false advertising! Grandma did not get what she bargained for, but of course, in those days women went along with it.

My mother's father had been a railroader in the South, then came to Wyoming originally to work in a sugar beet refinery. They lived in Sheridan, until my mom, by then about twenty years old, saw an ad in the newspaper for cheap land in neighboring Campbell County. So that's how their family became hard-trying farmers.

My sister, who is about eight years older than I am, had a great influence on me. I always tried to imitate her. Since my parents were so strict and rarely let me play with other kids, I would try to tag along with her and her friends. Watching her struggle through some very tough years taught me a lot. She had her first child just after turning seventeen herself. Her husband was a mean and violent man (I realize now that he was just a boy), and by the age of twenty-two with three young children, and not having been allowed to finish high school after motherhood, she was stranded in our isolated little hometown. Somehow she managed on the low wages she could earn to provide financial support for her children and to finish what today we'd call a GED. I saw that marrying young takes away one's own childhood and makes for big struggles prematurely.

While I did not have a label of "feminism" to use while growing up, my family role models were a pretty graphic example of what not to do. I saw an uprooted grandmother; a mother who never seemed happy but who remained a homemaker for her in-laws, her children, and her grandkids; a sister who really had to make her own way; and an aunt who had an invalid husband to support and care for. So I did NOT learn that a Prince Charming would smooth life's wrinkles out for me.

The minute I was through high school I left for Des Moines to attend Drake University. I had won the Betty Crocker Homemaker of the Year scholarship which, along with my savings from having worked in the county library through high school, saw me through my first year of college. My friends love to tease me about this award because I am emphatically not the type one thinks of as a home-maker. But this scholarship is awarded on the basis of a written test given nationally with two winners in each state. For the essay question they happened to pick my area of expertise. The question was, "Why is maturity an important prerequisite to parenthood?" Having watched my sister, I was a shoo-in for this one. Drake was really a shot in the dark for me. I knew nothing about it, but as I looked on a map, it seemed about far enough away that I could get back to see my family when I really wanted, but I wouldn't be expected to be there every weekend. Des Moines was a big city to me after living in a town of 1,200.

After I graduated from Drake in 1967 I went on with their economics program for my master's degree. Starting in 1969, I worked as a social worker and public relations agent for the Iowa Commission for the Blind, traveling statewide three or four days a week. One day early in 1971 Peggy Leonardo, a friend of mine from Drake dormitory days, called me to say she had heard about this feminist movement she thought I'd like. She invited me to a NOW meeting, and I instantly felt I had found a home.

After a NOW meeting one day, a group of us discovered that we would all welcome a change in living arrangements. Kay Plymat was separating from her husband. Sally Hacker wanted to live in Des Moines near where she taught at Drake rather than staying with her husband in Ames. Vicky Ness was a "youngster" of eighteen or nineteen who had been living on her own, marginally, for three or four years already and had asked Kay to be on the lookout for a stable living arrangement for her. I was attracted to the idea of living with others, both for the personal reason of welcoming company and seeing it as a chance to get better acquainted with Kay and Sally, whom I admired as movers and shakers in this new-found women's movement. I also welcomed the opportunity it presented to share responsibility for Maggie Brown. Maggie was a lonely and emotionally needy young woman who was spending a lot of time with me. As my job took me out of town three or four days a week, I had lots of chores to do when I got home, and I had begun to find Maggie burdensome. Here she had four others to relate to.

We were very excited about the idea of living in a cooperative arrangement and I was flattered to be included in a group I saw as including some of the most insightful minds in the women's movement. We were a varied group, ranging in age from about nineteen to forty, in education from a high-school dropout to a Ph.D. All but the youngest one had professional jobs with incomes adequate to support living alone, but communes were common then. In September of 1972 we rented a house on Motley Street, and since we were a motley group we called ourselves the Motley House Collective.

Kay was the president of the local NOW chapter and Sally was on the national NOW board. With such company, I was quickly drafted. NOW was looking for a chairperson in each state to keep communication going between chapters and individuals in their respective states. Sally nominated me to be the Iowa coordinator since I already traveled statewide. As I would pass through small towns, I'd stop at a phone booth and call individuals living in isolation in towns too small to have a chapter. They would be glad to hear from another member. There were several fledgling chapters, too, in Dubuque, Cedar Rapids, and Davenport, at least.

Our first statewide convention was held in the spring of 1972 in Cedar Rapids. The Cedar Rapids chapter had made the newspapers often, as it had been active in the public school system, especially regarding athletics, pushing for equal sports for girls. It also worked to get rid of blatantly sexist imagery in texts and curricula. The Cedar Rapids NOW convention was such an affirmative gathering of kindred spirits. It was probably a highlight for a lot of people because a lot of these groups had been going for a year or a year and a half, pretty much in isolation, and it was just such a good feeling to all get together and see how many of us there were and how many things we had accomplished. This meeting also meant that some of the people in the smaller towns where there was no chapter could finally get a chance to look at another NOW member. People were so eager to help that anyone who had done anything, we could just call them, and they would be glad to talk about it in a workshop. After that we had statewide camping trips in addition to annual state conventions. We called our outings "Camp Bra-Burn."

Maggie Brown killed herself in May of 1973. Knowing what I know now, we had warning. But at the time I'd never given the idea much thought and just believed the myth that "people who talk about suicide never commit suicide." Also at that time Phyllis Chesler's *Women and Madness* and a number of magazine articles were pointing out that many women are characterized as mentally ill when in fact they simply don't fit some preconceived mold. So I thought if enough people just listened to her, she'd be fine. Actually, Maggie had been in treatment for depression for years and years. All who befriended her gave as much as they could, but it was never enough to lift her self-esteem. Her death came as a bitter shock. The

TALLY TALBOTT, 1980.
*"While I did not have a label of
'feminism' to use while growing
up, my family role models were
a pretty graphic example of
what not to do."* Photo by
Karen Johnson

people in Motley collective were especially undone by this, because we had spent so much energy and had thought it had been helpful. The irrational guilt, "if only I had been a better friend, she would have been happy to live," took a decade to fade.

It was a great boost to Des Moines to have Sally Hacker in our midst. She was in the sociology department at Drake. As an academic, she leaned toward research, writing, and then confronting as an instrument of change. Many times her recommendations for action were more radical and outlandish than the middle-class image of NOW generally would have led one to believe. No matter what authority figure she encountered, she would keep asking and pressing, what does *your* organization do to and for women? What about wage structures? What about child care? No innocent bystander could even say hello to her without getting quizzed about his company's policies on women. She was especially outraged at the job structure for women. Although technology was advancing, women's jobs remained menial and low-paid. As large companies were changing over to computerization and women were being lured into becoming keypunch operators, Sally foresaw that after the transition, they would no longer be needed. Yet they were being enticed into paying for training programs to prepare for these transient jobs. AT&T particularly was a target of hers. She studied the pay structure of women's versus men's jobs there and led a national exposé of AT&T employment practices. At about that time a number of women in Des Moines took training for, and became, nontraditional workers at the phone company. Sally was there cheering them on. I worked with her one year when she had a Ford Foundation grant to study the impact of technology on the women's job market (actually this was the springboard for her deserting us and going to MIT). This was a project she never saw as ended—she devoted endless hours talking to union leaders, everyone she could, about employment opportunities for women.

Sally had a brilliant mind and a wonderful sense of humor, although the authorities she was always quizzing to the point of discomfort probably didn't think so. One example of Sally's humor is that she and Barb Yates and several others cast a witch's spell on the Ames football stadium, saying in essence that the money should be spent on child care and people, not sports buildings. The stadium, which was under construction, did indeed collapse and had to be restarted. We just loved that, of course, and to make it even more dramatic it was coincidentally timed to happen while most of us were in Minneapolis at a regional NOW convention.

Sally's role was to keep the pot of ideas boiling. She often started things, like inviting speakers to town, and let others of us do the detail work. But without her these forums would not have happened, even though her name did not show up as one of the people who brought them about. One example is the way she pushed me into becoming the state coordinator so soon after I discovered the movement. It proved to be good for me, but I would not have sought out the post on my own. Sally challenged everyone to question everything and to give all the energy they had. She talked to everyone leading "the movement" and she was a great believer in picking up the phone at the drop of a hat and calling women all over the country to hear what they thought or were doing on a given topic. She was the master coordinator and coalition builder.

Many of the definable Des Moines NOW activities centered around changing attitudes by way of the education system and the public image perpetuated by the media. There was an education committee that placed much emphasis on the curriculum and textbooks and also on providing equal opportunity in sports. Barbara Burns was the chair of this committee for some time. She not only met with officials to raise these issues but also worked on packets of material they could use instead of the sexist stuff they were using—in other words, she did much of their homework. The promotion of female employees of the school system was also scrutinized and in conjunction with the Iowa Civil Liberties Union, NOW filed charges with HEW [the Department of Health, Education and Welfare] of sex and race discrimination in the Des Moines school system.

Rita Dohrman chaired the media task force for several years.

They monitored ads and TV shows for sexist imagery, as well as monitored local stations' hiring and promotion practices. Challenges were then brought to the FCC [Federal Communications Commission] as stations' licenses came up for renewal. Presentations were made at these hearings or mailed to the FCC. We see now the impact of having let up on that. Many commercials now would have been spurned then, as for a time it went out of fashion to portray women as helpless, or beautiful toys, or dumb housewives needing instruction from an off-camera male voice. Although people may have differed with us or felt unjustly criticized, at least the issues raised were easier to define. At the base of it all were the questions: Do girls deserve equal educational and sports opportunities or not? Should women be portrayed as real people or not? Not that people couldn't cloud these with questions like, "Why do you want girls to act like boys?" Or, "Don't you enjoy sex, that you feel offense at these ads?" The affirmative action concept of hiring and promoting women and minorities was new enough that people were not yet so full of well-rationalized arguments about reverse discrimination as they are today. A few actually felt some slight threat that they should comply, just in case the government decided to enforce these laws. Today it seems there is no pretense at enforcement.

Some issues tackled by the chapter were even harder than these to communicate to the general public. I guess they were labeled the more radical for that reason. Among these were our United Way campaign, our action at the bridal fair, and the "big tits" contest protest, all of which took place during my presidency of the Des Moines NOW in 1974–1975.

Under Louise Noun's guidance a study was done in 1975 of fund distributions between girls' and boys' and women's and men's programs by the United Way. Large discrepancies were found and documented, all the way from the Girls Club versus the Boys Club (forget it, there were no Girls Clubs but a big Boys Club) to the YMCA versus the YWCA. We held many meetings with the United Way authorities pointing out this discrepancy and also pointing out that large numbers of low-paid women workers were being strong-armed into contributing, largely for men's benefit. We also noted that the United Way as an employer had some pay/promotion faults as well. Many no doubt did not understand this and saw our action as an attack on well-intentioned charities.

But an even more basic sacred cow was also being questioned— the time-honored institution of voluntarism. At base was the concept that "women's work" is never paid. Wherever people need care and help, be they children or frail elderly people, confused teenagers, or the destitute homeless, women are expected to do the work, and to do it happily and for free. It is simply part of being feminine to give endlessly of oneself, for others, and asking for something in return is crass beyond words. Sure enough, it was found that more women volunteer than men. One root of feminism is the idea of "women's work" period. We said all people must pitch in to do *both* caring "women's work" and analytical, active "men's work." Perhaps even more importantly, we were concerned that efforts of volunteer charity applied mere Band-Aids to really major wounds in our society and allowed people to postpone facing and solving these issues head-on. Many people in the general public saw this action as challenging basic human generosity. However, among community action groups our United Way action became a model nationally. We printed material describing how we went about our study, and feminists nationwide used it as they sought guidance in approaching their local United Ways.

Another easily misunderstood action was our protests at the local bridal fair. This annual event was sponsored by the merchandisers of products women supposedly need to produce a wedding and set up housekeeping. It was intensely advertised over the radio, with prizes and giveaways for those participating. The NOW chapter leafleted attendees and was interviewed for a TV newscast. This action was ripe for misunderstanding, with surface analysts proclaiming that NOW members are just bitter man-haters who can't find a man to make them a bride, or more charitably, as an attack on the institution of marriage. Many feminists *do* see grave traps in marriage, especially for young girls with little world experience and little sense of self-direction who have been fed all the popular culture's mythology that the only way to live is to become a wife and mother. One role of feminism is to present another view; to point out that almost all women today *must* be employed to support themselves at some point in life, and that self-direction is something nobody gets from being an appendage. We were trying to make points about choice, and about consumerism. The message of the trade exhibitions is that along with the man, these products will make you happy.

A third, hard-to-summarize campaign was our opposition in 1974 to the "big tits" contest operated weekly by a local bar. One night each week, the female patrons would be sized up and the one with the largest bustline would receive prizes. We tried to talk to the owner of the bar, who was very unreceptive, of course. Our line was that any woman who entered the bar was a contestant whether she wanted to be or not, or even if she had not known about this event

TALBOTT, 1974, running off newsletters in her kitchen. *"I did the NOW newsletter so I could stay out of the limelight."* Photo by Karen Johnson

and stumbled innocently in, because the spirit of the evening was to size up the women's bustlines. The blatant public use of such a crass concept, with ads on the radio, symbolized wanton disregard for women's dignity. The owner was saying, this is all in fun and we have a right to do it and the women who are participating are volunteering. Probably this wasn't one of our best-chosen fights. The reason I remember it is that the ambiguity did bother me a lot. Our picketing of the event made national news and my sister called me from across the country and said she'd heard it. Of course, the news stories were so skewed that many of our supporters turned out to be Holy Roller Christian types. I felt we'd really been defeated because of the slanted news reports. In some ways it is similar to the current controversy over pornography—opponents are seen as prudishly favoring censorship or trying to squelch pleasure.

After this confrontation, a group of us went in a camper to the national NOW convention in Houston, Texas. This was my first national convention. After that I went on an extended vacation, never to return to spokesperson role again. I disliked it anyway, being shy.

For many years after that I did the NOW newsletter so I could stay out of the limelight. I had a mimeograph in my kitchen and I knew that if I could sit down and write something, think about it a while, I could do better than standing on my feet refuting arguments in front of the press or confronting the director of some organization.

In the spring of 1974, Anne Schodde and others organized a day-long forum around the issue of rape. A concern for the way victims are blamed, for the assumption that any man who is related to, known by, or married to, a woman, has free license to do as he likes, even against her will; the attitude of courts, police, and her own supposedly loved ones that somehow this only happens to women who ask for it and can easily be avoided if you stay home where you belong unless accompanied by a protective male (even though these are exactly the men who rape most women—men they trust through past association); all these ideas were discussed and a group of representatives from a wide spectrum of organizations was formed to do something about it. Ideas like Take Back the Night marches and self-defense classes were discussed to try to prevent rape. We saw that we could provide comfort to victims while assisting them as they dealt with the police, hospital personnel, the court system, and family and friends. Most of all, we hoped to bolster their self-esteem—help them get angry rather than turning their feelings inward in the form of depression and guilt. A crime was committed against you, we would remind them.

By the fall of 1974, a rape crisis center was established, directed by a one-person staff, Corinne Whitlatch. The hospital and/or police would call her when a rape was reported. She wore a beeper and was constantly on call. I became her volunteer assistant, on call every other night and on weekends. I would go out and meet the victims in the hospital or police station and help them, but Corinne would then do the follow-up and all the daytime work of going to court, etc. Much of the effort went into educating hospital staff and police. Like most people in society they tend to blame or disbelieve the victim, and this shows in subtle but devastating ways to the victim. Without pushing too hard, we encouraged women to press charges, because until rapes are reported and lots of court victories won, the public thinks it is a limited problem and the rapist thinks there's no threat of getting punished. Corinne traveled statewide helping other groups educate their communities about the basics, and we wrote articles concerning attitudes about rape, some of which were distributed nationally. Des Moines had one of the first, most strongly feminist rape care centers, judging from the questions we got from around the country.

As awareness grew, and use grew, formal, permanent funding was sought and the center became part of the county budget. We had mixed feelings about this. On the one hand, getting funding every year by soliciting organizations is an energy-consuming task and makes for difficult planning. It also raised small amounts, so activities were limited. On the other hand, once the center is county-funded, the staff is picked through the county personnel system. Feminists have no real control over what these people say or do. The whole purpose is defeated if the staff have the same attitudes held by the general public. We considered it a big success that we converted a female attorney we dealt with a lot from an attitude of "the victim is probably lying" to, "Hey, if she was a victim of crime, justice should be found." Also, a number of emergency room staff people and some police personnel did gain finesse in using at least neutral terms so victims would not feel so disbelieved and to blame.

In 1975 there was a big Equal Rights Amendment rally in Peoria, Illinois, the hometown of Betty Friedan, one of the founders of the women's movement. Our local NOW chapter chartered a bus for the trip to Peoria. For me it was an emotional high, my first mass rally. I'll always remember how exciting it was to walk over a hill and see thousands of people united in the streets. On the way back from Peoria, a group of us started talking about how great it would be if Des Moines had a feminist bookstore, a place to disseminate educational materials to the general public and to supply ourselves with the latest in feminist reading. At least two avid readers, Mae Green and myself, were in this group, and Mike and Ginny Benware were two of the practical how-to-do-it minds involved. When we got home we began immediately to plot in earnest. We approached a few "investors" for gifts rather than trying to reach hundreds at $10 each, hoping to reach our goal faster. We raised between $2,500 and $3,500 very quickly because ten or twelve people could spare $200 or $500 or $1,000. We rented a storefront on 25th Street off University Avenue near the Drake University campus. We chose the name A Mind of Your Own, built bookshelves out of old high school gym bleachers, and did minor renovation to the space, all with donated time and materials. A committee of us combed through book catalogs and ordered our first stock. We opened in 1976. My particular job was to write a catalog including brief reviews for local use as well as statewide mail order.

That particular year a number of the people involved with the bookstore happened to be between jobs or working part time, and we were able to staff the store with volunteer clerks and with a managing committee to order books, do bookkeeping, etc. Clerks would leave notes about things that happened on their shifts. We tried to operate in a nonhierarchical fashion, reaching consensus rather than voting, and those who had donated money were not given special treatment; in fact they were anonymous.

We carried nonsexist children's books, a fledgling idea then, popularized by Marlo Thomas's *Free to Be You and Me* record and book. There was a special corner set aside where kids could play. We deliberately tried to focus on nonsexist books, not just classics that happened to be nonsexist. We also sought feminist theory because other bookstores in town did not emphasize these books. Poetry and art books were popular, too. Fiction by feminists was not too plentiful then; groups like Naiad Press were just getting started.

The bookstore provided a focal point for community activity. It was a place to post announcements about events in the feminist and political arenas and it was a place open for such gatherings. Cross-country travelers would stop in for camaraderie. The aim was to create a friendly drop-in center atmosphere, and a following was created for whom it served this purpose. Certainly not all feminists were drawn to the bookstore. It served more the people who were looking for a sense of sisterhood or community and who were interested in feminism on a deeper level than the less-controversial equal-pay-for-equal-work level.

As our first year came to a close, and volunteer clerks could not be expected to carry on forever, we applied for CETA [Comprehensive Employment and Training Act] grants as an educational institution, which, indeed, we strove to be. Our longstanding mainstay, Pam Hicks, was paid with CETA funds. She was not only clerk, but also general manager who ordered books, did the bookkeeping, etc., although the board remained actively involved in daily operations as well. From time to time Pam had part-time helpers, also paid with CETA funds.

With hindsight, it is clear that the bookstore was always undercapitalized. At the time we were very proud that we could move from idea to reality so quickly, and, indeed, that speaks well for the wide appeal of the idea. But the shelves were always sparingly stocked because though we managed what resources we had very well, we didn't really earn enough to add to the original base. For one thing, the markup on books is much smaller than on most merchandise. Also, we had never earned enough to pay our employees.

Since CETA has a three-year limit on funding positions with a given employer, we'd always known we were borrowing time. As the deadline drew near in 1980, we were divided as to how to proceed. I was among those who felt that if we had to go back to volunteers it would drain all the energy of the feminist community and nobody would have energy left for other aspects of the movement. Also the financial facts seemed to say that we could bow out gracefully now, but waiting might sink us into debt. Another group thought we could do a big fundraising effort and raise $12,000 to pay staff of the store for a year. We agreed to try that, but with a deadline of spring so that the decision wouldn't drag on and on. Today, as I sometimes stand at my garbage can and throw away fund-raising pleas without even opening them, I'm proud all over again that we raised about $1,500 just by contacting people who enjoyed the store and asking for donations. I think that success was a testimony that many people were supportive. But the long term did not look promising. We did close gracefully in early summer, 1980, with a big party.

For me, personally, the closing of the bookstore just sort of beat my spirit down and I just didn't want to be involved in an activity again for quite a while. I remember during the wind-down period that I'd come home from work and stand at the kitchen counter and try to get some kind of food crammed down my mouth so I could get on to the next meeting. My tension rate was about the highest I ever remember, because I was very sad and I was very conflicted, too. I felt that I was being cast as this nay-sayer for advising that we shut down the store when there were all these people who wanted to keep it going. I just built this up to be a giant event in my life. Probably everybody else has forgotten by now, but I took it so seriously and so personally.

The books from the bookstore went to the Thoreau Center in Des Moines. The money raised became a fund to bring cultural events to the Des Moines women's community, with the understanding that it be used as seed money and that profits from concerts and other sponsored events be used to keep the fund going.

I have lived in New York since 1983 and I presently do financial planning, sell investments and insurance, and teach related courses through an education company. I have tried several feminist groups since moving here but have not yet found a niche. I am moving toward teenage motherhood issues again, in programs similar to those sponsored by the Young Women's Resource Center in Des Moines. I have a deep-seated interest because of my sister's experience, but also because looking at the poverty and welfare and school dropout figures in this city, it is obvious that teenage motherhood is a severe problem here. [Tally currently is a financial planner specializing in retirement plans.]

It is discouraging now to see what has been happening in the Supreme Court with all the civil rights cases and the abortion ruling, but also just feeling the apathy among women. A lot of young women today are, to some extent, reaping what we did because they have been told they can do anything they want with their lives. They've heard a little different rap than we heard growing up. People don't see feminism as an issue now; anything as an issue, really. There's nobody out marching in the streets, but maybe marching isn't an effective tool anymore. Right now we are demonstrating for abortion rights, but it took this big scare to do it. I often think of the remark that since history is a pendulum, when times really seem tough, you always know that probably the pendulum will swing back again. It won't stay this way forever. I find hope in that.

REFERENCE

Phyllis Chesler, *Women and Madness* (N.Y.: Doubleday, 1972).

Virginia Watkins,

a young mother who was inspired by Betty Friedan, founded the Des Moines chapter of the National Organization for Women in 1971. She is currently executive director of the Minnesota Social Services Association.

"It took time to get some know-how and some way of finding other feminists."

I grew up on sort of a farm outside of the small town of Russell, which is near Chariton. My father is a retired hatcheryman; he hatched chickens, a business which at one time was very much in demand by farmers. My mother is a Grinnell College graduate and a former schoolteacher. I have a brother who is four years younger than I am.

Even as a child I can remember having feminist thoughts. I recall thinking it was too bad that women didn't have more important roles and I guess I tended to see these roles as being in the work force instead of being a homemaker. Now I see it a little bit different. Now I know that the important thing is that women have power and respect in the roles they play, which could be volunteer, such as governmental task forces or commissions, or officers of voluntary associations. However, the first thing I could grab onto when I was young was that it seemed that women should be able to be in the work force and have good jobs the same as men do.

During my childhood I did have a few occasions to see women in roles that were unique or even powerful roles for women at that time. Although I did not then conceptualize the idea that women should organize and strive for goals, these women at least gave me the idea that women could be equal. One of the women I recall was a pastor who served for a while at our church, the United Methodist Church, in Russell. This was something pretty much unheard of in the 1950s. I was probably ten or eleven years old at the time. I was also influenced by members of my family who were interested in politics and political issues.

One grandfather had served in the state legislature. Unfortunately, he died before I was born, but I understand that he fought the Ku Klux Klan when it was active in Iowa in the 1920s and hearing about this was something that made a deep impression on me. In fact, both of my parents' families were political people. My other grandfather was a county officeholder. My mother majored in political science at Grinnell College. So the politics part of feminism is something that was very natural to me. After graduating from high school in Russell in 1957, I went to Drake University in Des Moines and was married before I graduated.

One of my first jobs was as a public welfare worker with the Polk County Welfare Department. I was concerned about the punitive ways in which some people, mainly women I worked with on AFDC [Aid to Families with Dependent Children], were treated, in most cases undeservedly. So I started out as an advocate for people on welfare. I was concerned that they have adequate money to live on and were treated in a fair manner. That is what led me to an interest in politics. I became active in the Democratic party and I also got involved with the civil rights movement and the antiwar movement during the Vietnam War.

I had my first child in 1961 when I was an AFDC worker with Polk County. They were so surprised that anyone would come back to work after having given birth that they actually let me have three weeks maternity leave. When I was pregnant with my second child two years later, I asked again for maternity leave but they not only told me I could not have maternity leave, they even took it upon themselves to guess how advanced I was in my pregnancy and I had to leave at six months. This still outrages me.

What interested me in the women's movement was Betty Friedan's [1963] book, *The Feminine Mystique*. In a way, I felt that this book was written for me because at the time I read it I was a homemaker with two children. Frankly, I have nothing against homemaking, but it seemed like that was a role into which women were cast which limited women's opportunities. At least that was the thinking of society at the time, and with reading Friedan's book

VIRGINIA WATKINS, 1970.
*"What interested me in the
women's movement was Betty
Friedan's book,* The Feminine
Mystique. *In a way, I felt this
book was written for me."*

I began to feel not so guilty about wanting some other kind of role.
Friedan's book made me feel better about who I really was and artic-
ulated how I felt. I feel that the basic issue is that neither men nor
women should be limited in the roles that they want to play in life.
Having grown up with the feeling that there should be equality and
fairness and then being active in politics, plus reading Friedan's
book, all combined to make me an active feminist. As a result, I did
go out and get a job and ultimately I also finished my college degree.

I knew that Betty Friedan was organizing NOW and wanted
chapters organized throughout the country. She came to Des
Moines in about 1969 and made such a plea at a talk at Drake University. Even at that point, it still took me another year or two to
work up the courage to try to organize a NOW chapter because this
was something so new and so controversial. It also took time to get
some know-how and some ways of finding other feminists. You had
to have ten people to charter a chapter and I went to work to see if I
could find that many. I had been a member of national NOW almost
from the time it was organized in 1966, so I got the names of other
NOW members who lived in Des Moines. There weren't very many
of us, only a couple besides myself. You, Louise, were one of them;
also Pauline Johnson, who turned out to be a neighbor of mine. I
also drew upon a group of wives of Drake professors who had a
consciousness-raising group I had attended several times. Some of
them became my first contacts. In addition to that, I tried to enlist
some of my friends who were in sympathy with the women's movement, as well as some women whom I knew through my political

contacts. So I developed a little convening group that met regularly at my home and we worked to pull together the publicity and meetings that would attract more NOW members.

Louise Swartzwalder, a reporter for the *Des Moines Register,* was one of the women who met with us. Since she was a reporter she had to be very careful about her association with us and I'm not sure she ever really joined NOW. She was most helpful in reporting our activities. Pamela Cullison, now Pamela Wilson, was one of the original members. She is currently a free-lance editor with Meredith Publishing Company. Pam helped with publicity. She had quite an argument with the television people about getting them to come out when Wilma Scott Heidi, the national president, came to town. I'm not sure what she told them but she got them there. Another charter member was Roxanne Conlin, who subsequently [1982] was the Democratic nominee for governor of Iowa. Then there was Pauline Johnson, already a national NOW member, and Sally Hacker, who was a professor of sociology at Drake University. Sally was also helping organize an Ames chapter. Kay Plymat, a nurse, joined up early on. She succeeded me as president of Des Moines NOW.

In the spring of 1971 we began holding public meetings. They were advertised by word of mouth, by running ads in shoppers, and by hand-made posters we put up in libraries. I remember that you, Louise, and your sister-in-law, Dannie Rosenfield, came to some of those meetings and that you or Danny sometimes came up to me after the meetings and gave me a little cash to help pay for the ads. Our group gradually grew. In June, Wilma Scott Heidi came to Des Moines with Mary Jean Collins, the Midwest regional director out of Chicago. We got good publicity for that meeting. At this point we started our chartering process. Our first officers included myself as president; Pam Cullison, vice president; Roxanne Conlin, vice president in charge of legal affairs; Pauline Johnson, recording secretary; and Carol Hayse, publications. Hayse, a member of the radical community here in Des Moines, also headed a task force to organize a fall conference on women's employment. Kay Plymat was treasurer and Louise Swartzwalder was assigned public relations. The nominating committee consisted of you, Louise, Madeline Kaloides, and Maggie Brown, a Phi Beta Kappa classmate of mine at Drake. In addition, we had committee chairs and a telephone committee. We were too poor to pay postage so we kept in touch with members by phone.

While we were still in the process of finding a permanent meeting place we could afford we held a meeting in one of the labor union halls on the east side of Des Moines. We had a fair-sized crowd

WATKINS, 1977, leading a chant at the Twin Cities ERA Walk-athon. WATKINS: *"What do we want?"* AUDIENCE: *"ERA."* WATKINS: *"When do we want it?"* AUDIENCE: *"Now!"*

there and we were trying to prioritize what issues we would work on. One member rose to suggest that we should support lesbian rights at which moment two or three "friends" (I don't think they were members yet) walked out. So there was from the beginning some controversy about issues, although I really was pleased that things with the chapter did go pretty smoothly in the early days. Basically people were enthused about working together and we got along well.

Once we began getting coverage on television and in the news-paper, it became easier to recruit members and we started having a few actions which generated publicity. We had a cocktail party, which was a fund-raiser to help establish a national NOW lobby in Washington, D.C., and at which we raised the largest amount of any local chapter. I remember that we had some pretty important people at this party including Attorney General Richard Turner and his wife, Charlotte. I was really delighted. On the national level we peti-tioned Congress in behalf of the Mondale child-care bill. This com-prehensive child-care bill did pass Congress but, unfortunately, it was subsequently vetoed by President Nixon. We also held a letter-writing campaign for the Equal Rights Amendment, which had not yet passed Congress. On the local and state level we worked with the West Des Moines school district to get maternity leave for teach-ers who had come to us for help. We lobbied the Des Moines City Council in support of extending the city civil rights ordinance to prohibit sex discrimination. We set up a state legislative lobby, and

state representative June Franklin agreed to introduce a preratifica-
tion resolution for the federal Equal Rights Amendment. Representative Charles Uben, whose daughter, Mary, was a member of the
Ames NOW chapter, agreed to introduce a joint resolution to amend
the Iowa constitution to give women equal rights. These efforts,
though unsuccessful, were a beginning. In addition, we did consciousness-raising and some unofficial networking, particularly for
women in women-owned businesses and for women candidates for
public office. We did not have a political action committee at that
time. That wasn't something that national NOW had established
yet, so we couldn't officially endorse candidates, but we did get the
word around about women candidates who were supportive of our
issues.

In September 1971 Des Moines NOW was one of ten women's
organizations which participated in an issues forum called by the
Governor's Commission on the Status of Women. This group called
for the legislature to triple the current annual appropriation of
$90,000 for the Iowa Civil Rights Commission so that the commis-
sion could do more work on sex discrimination cases. The forum
noted that the commission had no female investigator and asked
that one be employed. This meeting generated some good publicity
and raised public consciousness as to what the issues were. I moved
to the Twin Cities shortly after this meeting and Kay Plymat took
over the presidency of the Des Moines NOW chapter.

As soon as I arrived in the Twin Cities I got active in politics
again, particularly the women's movement. The Women's Political
Caucus in Minnesota was being formed and I worked on its formation. Of course I also joined the NOW chapter, which was about a
year old. Immediately, there was a vacancy for secretary, so I became their secretary. A year later I became president of the Twin
Cites NOW and served in that job for three years. Then I was the
Minnesota state president for two years and then I served six years
on the national board of NOW. In that capacity, I was also the Midwest regional director. Iowa was part of the Midwest region I represented, giving me the opportunity and the pleasure of working with
Iowans again.

The Twin Cities NOW worked quite a bit on employment discrimination. We made many joint efforts with minorities and built a
unified alliance to strengthen resources in both our interests, rather
than fighting over a divided and inadequate pie. We succeeded in
having the veterans' preference formula changed so that there was
still a little bit of preference left for veterans but it wasn't quite so
onerous to the rest of the population and women would have a bet-

ter chance of getting civil service jobs. One of the big issues at that time was the Equal Rights Amendment campaign. Even though ultimately we didn't succeed in amending the Constitution, I think we did a lot to draw attention to the fact that women didn't have equality. In the process of working on the ERA, many side issues became resolved. In other words, it was fairly easy to build a lot of other prowomen, pro–civil rights types of legislation and to make headway in a lot of other places, such as in business or the church or whatever. This was because either the ERA was anticipated and so it was felt that in order to comply changes needed to be made, or else it was simply because the public's consciousness was raised to the fact that there was a problem. I spent many hours, many days, weeks, months, and years on the ERA. I don't feel that it was a loss just because of all the other progress that was made in anticipation of the ERA.

Another one of the issues that I have worked on is that of reproductive freedom, especially abortion rights. Iowa is a much more liberal state than Minnesota on that issue. As a matter of fact, when I moved to Minnesota and read the account that the NOW lobbyists had written about the vote count in the Minnesota legislature, I almost fell off my chair. The so-called prolife, or antichoice, majority in the legislature was just shocking. That's still true and I think that as the *Webster* case [1989 U.S. Supreme Court decision giving the states more leeway to restrict abortions] plays out that Iowa will do less than Minnesota to restrict abortion, if it does anything at all.

Most of the time that I have been in Minnesota I have worked outside the home. When we first came here I managed the index department of the Minnesota legislature, and then I was a community organizer for the Greater Minneapolis Day Care Association. For the past ten years I've been the lobbyist for the Minnesota Social Service Association. [Watkins' current position is executive director of the Minnesota Social Services Association.]

Louise Rosenfield Noun

helped organize the Des Moines chapter of NOW, and has fought valiantly for women's issues ever since. Besides this book, she has written a history of woman suffrage in Iowa, *Strong-Minded Women,* and her memoirs, *Journey to Autonomy.*

"We need to keep our vision broad; to remember that as long as any segment of our population is oppressed that women will be oppressed."

I am a Des Moines native and a graduate of the Des Moines public schools and Grinnell College. I also received a master's degree in art history from Radcliffe/Harvard. My mother was a frustrated feminist who would have been very happy with the current feminist movement. My father was in the department store business and let Mother run the show at home, which she did with a very firm hand.

An art collector since my graduate school days, in recent years my concentration has focused on collecting works of art by women, especially women of the early twentieth century avant-garde. I am a founding member of the Des Moines League of Women Voters (1944) and headed this organization during the successful drive for council-manager government in Des Moines. I was president of the Iowa Civil Liberties Union during the Vietnam War years when the union won a landmark freedom of speech Supreme Court decision con-

LOUISE R. NOUN, 1990. *"In recent years I have concentrated my collecting on works of art by women."*

NOUN honored as a founder of the Young Women's Resource Center at its fifth anniversary, 1983. *"The most tangible evidence of my activity as a feminist is the Young Women's Resource Center."* Photo by Karen Johnson

Unveiling the sign at the opening of the Young Women's Resource
Center, January 1978. (*From left*) Billie Ray; Joanne Fine,
director; LOUISE NOUN, president.

firming the right of students to wear black armbands to school in
protest of the war. In 1971 I helped organize the Des Moines chapter
of NOW, which was a very active and radical group in its early days.

I am the author of *Strong-Minded Women: The Emergence of
the Woman-Suffrage Movement in Iowa,* which was published by
Iowa State University Press in 1969. Doing research for that book
was in part frustrating because of the lack of material that had been
preserved about the first wave of feminism in Iowa. It would have
been wonderful to have been able to talk with the women involved
and learn more about their lives and their philosophy but, alas, they
were all dead. So when starting to think about a history of the emergence of the current feminist movement in Iowa I decided to interview women who were involved in this movement in the late 1960s
and the early 1970s while most of us are still alive. Their stories are
varied but they all reflect the general air of change in our society at
that time along with the feeling of hope and excitement that infused
the movement.

This sense of hope and excitement is expressed in my speech to
the Iowa International Women's Year Conference in Des Moines in
1977 when many of us (mistakenly) thought the ERA was about to
become law. Pointing out to the delegates that laws alone would not
change societal attitudes, I advised them, "We need to keep our
vision broad, to remember that as long as any segment of our population is oppressed that women will be oppressed. Equality means a
society where women—all women, black, white, Chicano, Native
American—can live up to their full potential as human beings; it
means an economic system which doesn't prosper by keeping

women and third-world people on the lowest rung of the employment ladder; it means an educational system administered by
women as well as men, and teachers sensitive to the needs of
women and minorities; it means a nonsexist judicial system in
which women are an integral part; and it means an end to milita-
rism and a new vision of a cooperative world society." This is still a
dream for many of us but achieving our goal looks ever more dis-
tant.

Former award winners at the Iowa Women's Hall of Fame
ceremony, 1987. (*From left*) Minnette Doderer, Alice Van Wert
Murray, LOUISE ROSENFIELD NOUN, Louise Rosenfeld, Mary
Garst, Willie Glanton, Edna Griffen. *"When women earn $1 for
every $1 men earn instead of 59 cents; when women occupy 50
percent of the seats in the Iowa Legislature instead of 11
percent; when the governor who so graciously hands out these
awards is as likely to be a woman as a man, then the time will
have come when we can do away with a women's hall of fame
and we can compete on even terms with all Iowans for the
honors of the state."*—Noun, acceptance speech, 1981. Photo
courtesy of Iowa Commission on the Status of Women

Ginny Benware headed

an effort by Des Moines NOW to interest clerical workers in unionizing. She also spearheaded the founding of the feminist bookstore, A Mind of Your Own. She is currently a personal financial planner in Portland, Oregon.

"The bookstore was a real labor of love for everyone involved."

My father was in the air force and I grew up all over the United States. I never lived anyplace more than three years until I moved to Iowa in 1975. In many ways I consider Iowa home because I lived here thirteen years. Having to adjust to new situations and the influence of my father are the major contributing factors to my independent attitude, i.e., that of a change seeker. One of the important events in our family was dinnertime discussions. They always involved current affairs and political events. We had lots of discussions about civil rights. I come from an Italian background and my parents grew up in a time when Italians were not well thought of. My father's stories of the discrimination that he faced in college and as a young practicing attorney in upstate New York impressed me. Probably those kinds of things led to my becoming a civil rights advocate and eventually an active feminist.

I started out my activist career working for minority and low-income rights with a couple of run-ins in college working on issues affecting blacks. After finishing a bachelor's degree at the University of Nevada in Reno I felt as though I needed to move away from the civil rights movement and find my own place, which became the feminist movement. I was a charter member of a NOW chapter in Pullman, Washington, in 1972, which is where I lived until I moved to Des Moines. In Pullman I started at the consciousness-raising level and got involved with other women who were going through the same kinds of things.

When I moved to Iowa I was seeking identity with people that I would have something in common with and naturally looked for feminist allies. It was ironic that in a master's social work program of the University of Iowa in 1975 my practicum placement was at the United Way of Greater Des Moines. This was at the time of United Way's first fund-raising campaign after they had agreed to change their giving guidelines and approach to soliciting money because of the criticism of their coercive methods by the Des Moines chapter of NOW. I'll never forget a board meeting where United Way president Don Rowen stood up and said that the United Way wasn't meeting its goal because of Louise Noun and those NOW women and all their talk criticizing how United Way raised its funds. I just kind of looked around the room in amazement at all those community leaders on the United Way board and felt as though I was with the enemy.

After I left my practicum at United Way in 1975, some of us in NOW got very involved in trying to organize clerical workers. It seemed to be the right place at the right time. As a matter of fact, I did the equivalent of a master's thesis on the similarities between organizing in the 1930s in industrial sectors, especially with auto workers, and the current effort to organize clerical workers. I did a comparative analysis of the kinds of benefits that the auto workers were bargaining for relative to that population—which was 98 or 99 percent male—and what was important to the clerical population in the mid-seventies. I made the case that one of the reasons it was hard to organize clerical workers was because the unions weren't bargaining for what was important to women. The unions were bargaining for the same kinds of things that the auto workers were asking for, and they weren't willing to look at child-care issues, flexible hours, and job sharing, which were some issues that would have been more helpful to a primarily female population. Clearly wages were an issue, too, but the unions were using the same stuff they had always used and were not speaking to the population they wanted to organize.

I led the NOW task force on a project to organize clerical workers in Des Moines. There had been an attempt sometime earlier that had not worked out. I think it was led by a very small union in Des

GINNY BENWARE in A Mind of Your Own bookstore, 1976. *"You could just drop in and have some good conversations with kindred spirits."* Photo by David M. Lewis

Moines, which was primarily composed of women who worked for unions as secretaries in administrative-clerical types of positions. There was a core group of about seven of us in our NOW task force who thought organizing clerical workers was a real need. We did a series of four leafletings in an effort to educate office workers. We would stand on the street corners in Des Moines when clerical workers were getting out in the afternoon, or even when they were going to work in the morning, and hand out our leaflets and invite them to a meeting. Our aim was to spark some interest in the clerical community and to talk about the issues they were interested in.

On a few occasions we got some women to attend a meeting but we never got them to attend more than once or twice and really work on the issues. When we talked to the younger women whom we were trying to organize they seemed to look at their positions as a short stop on the way to somewhere else so they didn't have any vested interest in becoming organized or in forming a union. The older women, who were more secure in their positions and were farther up the ladder, weren't willing to take the risk. They knew that some of the younger women would be doing clerical work forever but they had sort of made it—at least within their profession. There was a woman who was president of a local secretarial organization who worked with us a lot. But on the whole, it was very discouraging. We thought we were trying to help people help themselves and there wasn't a lot of response. It seemed clear to us what needed to be done. At that time there were numerous articles in the *Des Moines Register* about clerical wages and how low they were. But it was hard getting off the ground.

In 1976 Des Moines feminists started a bookstore we called A Mind of Your Own. The idea came to me because I had attended a number of national NOW conferences and saw that there were women's and feminist bookstores in other communities and it seemed that Des Moines could have one if anyone else could. I remember this pretty distinctly because it was a project that I was instrumental in starting. A group of about fifteen or twenty of us got together in my living room. I had drawn up a two- or three-page proposal about the way I thought we could start a bookstore and handed it out. We talked about whether it would be a nonprofit or a for-profit project, how we would get the seed money, and how it would be structured. We also discussed whether it would be a women's bookstore or a feminist bookstore and what segments of the community we could attract with certain labels. We didn't want to be too offensive but we certainly wanted to stand by our principles. We decided to call the project a nonsexist book store as opposed to a feminist book store because even in 1976 too many people were threatened by the feminist label. Nonsexism seemed the less threatening term.

We made a very conscious decision that we would only carry nonsexist, feminist materials. We decided to locate in the Drake University area. There was considerable discussion and we hemmed and hawed from a business perspective about trying to compete with the Drake book store and carry textbooks, but most people felt that they wanted this to be a comfortable gathering place for feminists and not a place dependent on mass-market appeal. It was clear at that point that we would have to be a nonprofit organization. Everyone at this meeting took their checkbooks out and wrote out a check to get the project off the ground. We raised a couple of thousand dollars at the initial meeting. After that we started making grant applications. Incorporating the store as a nonprofit, educational organization enabled us to apply for grant funding. We were successful for two or three years in a row in getting CETA [Comprehensive Employment and Training Act] funding to hire an employee for the bookstore. The people we hired took exhibits of feminist and nonsexist literature to libraries and colleges around the state.

The bookstore was a real labor of love for everyone involved. I can remember days over at that storefront on 25th Street, sandblasting interior walls so that we could have a natural brick effect. We got some old bleachers and sawed them up and varnished them and made bookshelves. We just kind of scrounged things wherever we could. The bookstore sponsored reading groups which would meet on a weekly basis. It was a comfortable place for feminists to be, and I think that was part of the goal—that you could just drop in and have some good conversations with kindred spirits.

The bookstore stayed open for five years, which was long-lived for feminist bookstores in a market our size. There were bookstores in communities much larger than Des Moines that were failing before ours did. Someone recently told me that New York City finally has another women's bookstore which replaces Women's Books, a store which had been a women's institution in the city and closed several years ago. I figure that if New York City can't support a women's bookstore our effort by comparison was pretty successful.

NOW was very important to me as a woman and as a feminist. It also exemplified what I had done at that point in my life, which was a lot of issue politics. Both my professional life and my community activities were centered around issue politics. It became clear to me that I needed to work inside the political system to advance issues of importance. In 1979 I took a position managing Elaine Szymoniak's first mayoral campaign in Des Moines. Although we were the top vote-getter in the primary we didn't win the general election. We were out-organized by the winner, Pete Crivaro, a man with a more extensive community history than Elaine. After that I went to work for Tom Harkin in his 1980 Congressional reelection campaign. I used this as an avenue to affect social policy. After the 1980 election I worked in Harkin's Washington office for a year as a legislative assistant. Subsequently, I returned to Iowa in an administrative position for him. Between 1982 and 1987, I continued to manage Harkin's political and congressional affairs through his election to the Senate in 1984 and the first half of his first U.S. Senate term.

In 1987 I went to the Kennedy School of Government at Harvard and completed a degree in public administration. I have just finished managing John Chrystal's primary campaign for the Democratic nomination for governor of Iowa, which we lost yesterday [6-5-90]. The money that it takes to run for office and the control that television advertising has over the outcome of races is not serving our country well. With each election cycle I become more interested in focusing on policy at a grass-roots level and the educational process. I probably will have come full cycle in my activism. I'll get back into issue politics again because I've become somewhat discouraged with the political process. I've learned a lot about partisan

BENWARE, 1990. *"Younger women have a sense that they've made it and they have no idea how recent the struggles were."*

politics. I've learned more about different kinds of organizing. I don't like what I see in the lack of education of the electorate and how easily they can be swayed.

I think the feminist movement today is fragmented. The movement appears to be focusing strictly on elective politics. The grass-roots organizing, putting pressure on different points in the system on various issues that NOW was so great at seems to have been abandoned. I'm not active in NOW anymore and maybe they're doing some of that but it's not what is apparent. It seems younger women have a sense that they've made it and they have no idea how recent the struggles were that got them the opportunities they currently have.

Sally Hacker, a professor

of sociology at Drake University in the early 1970s, was a leader in the women's movement in Des Moines during this period. She was a soft-spoken, radical woman who wore boots and rode a motorcycle to school.

Sally died of lung cancer in August 1988 at the age of fifty-one. During her last illness, Sally's friend Dorothy Smith of the Ontario Institute for Studies in Education conducted an extensive interview with her. The following material is extracted from the transcription of this interview; from Sally's book, *Pleasure, Power and Technology,* which was published posthumously; and from the editor's 1990 interview with Sally's husband, Bart Hacker.

"It seems to me that what you can do best is to really keep listening to working people—working women particularly—whose voices have been so stifled."

I came, not quite off the farm, but out of the "boonies" in downstate Illinois. Small-town southern Illinois Republican was the background I came from. We lived in a typical Southern, lower-middle-class, working-class community. Mom and Dad were working-class Republican. Republican meant independence and unions meant bullies and people who told you what to do. That's about the level of my awareness. I didn't know shit! Mom was the first of a farm family—a family with many children but few acres—to move into town and take a job in the Kodak shop. Dad's mother died when he was an infant, his father died when he was only twelve, so he was earning his own living at a watch factory by the time he was a teenager. While I was growing up Dad worked as a clerk in the post office starting at 4 P.M. and napped afternoons.

When I talk about technology and pleasure, I'm thinking about the backyard. My older sister Sue and I helped some, but mostly squatted and watched, as Dad dug the foot-deep hole, filled it with cement, and eased the six-foot piece of plumbing pipe upright in the mix. When it set, he fastened an elbow joint to the pipe's top. It held the horizontal bar whose other end lodged firmly into the maple. He made two trapezes and a swing from lengths of chain, small pipes, and a slab of wood, and hung them from the bar. The dozen or so kids in the backyard tribe gathered to see what he would do next. A lower horizontal bar off to the right supported the teeter-totter, a long, flat board nailed to iron circles the bar ran through. Then came the Tarzan rope, which swung from the maple's largest limb.

My favorite was the trolley. Dad wrapped a cable high up around the old maple, above a platform, and winched it tightly around the other tree next to the house. He bolted the trolley to a pulley that ran along the cable. The trolley itself was an upside-down T. We drew it up to the platform with a length of twine, held onto the upright, climbed on, lifted off, and flew down the cable, angled so you could back into the tree at the other end of the yard with just the right amount of force. Maximal excitement, minimal damage, although over the years, the maple near the house showed a shiny barkless circle from the battering of small feet.

Mom, solid, strong, and fun-loving, managed the backyard with a firm hand but usually let us solve our own problems. She fixed lemonade or cocoa depending on the season, cleaned and labeled a small drinking can for each of us, and lined the tins up on the sill outside the kitchen window. Now homemaker, wife, and mother, yet she encouraged an exuberant equality among the children, discouraged gender differentiation with a cold look or a sharp word. She admonished, "Be fair!" "Take turns!" and "No running that trolley between 2 and 4 P.M." while Dad napped. She enjoyed the backyard most, I think.

Beyond the third grade, physics and astronomy were my first loves in school. I was fascinated. I then got into Freud because I found what people did to each other was most peculiar and fascinating. So I decided I would be a psychiatrist.

In Chicago there was a tool-and-die plant and there were Italian workers. They were promised the world by the company if they would move to southern Illinois and help set up a tool-and-die shop. They would have free housing, transportation, etc. They did that but then got fired one by one as the nonunion men in southern Illinois learned the skills. But they were there long enough to impregnate half the county because we had never seen the like of "duck tails" and leather jackets.

Sally was expelled in the eleventh grade because she was pregnant. She finished high school by mail. Sally and the father, Richard Teresi, married and had a son, Mark, born in 1954. Later Mark was adopted by Sally's third husband, Bart Hacker.

Meantime all the workers had to be urged back to Chicago. Richard, who was the son of one of these workers, was a printer and there was simply more work in Chicago. We went back and I started school by television because it was nonintrusive. This was a family which did not believe in college even for its men. Anyway, the television set blew out and I went back to the community college [Amundsen Junior College] to get my $5 refunded. They encouraged me to take night classes. That was the beginning of trouble in the first marriage.

Most of the teachers at the community college were from the University of Chicago, a school I had never heard of. They were people getting their Ph.D.'s, so there was some good mentoring. One of the women put me in her car and drove me through Hyde Park to show me the university and to say, "See, you'll feel at home, they wear blue jeans here."

I got to the university [she won a scholarship] and I was in sociology. I ignored the guys who would suggest that I was not really professional material. I ignored the people who said, "What you really want is a terminal master's." I ignored the counseling which said, "Well, you do have a child, don't you think you shouldn't . . ." It sounded stupid. What I learned in Chicago were methods—high-powered, sophisticated, numerical. I was delighted with methods because I had always loved math and physics. I did my graduate work at the National Opinion Research Center (NORC) where I worked under Alice and Pete Rossi. I loved approaching a problem from many different ways and using many different methods and getting the same answer. I loved feeling good about the skills. All these methods turned out to be useful later.

SALLY HACKER at Oregon State University, 1986. *"I don't know how some people live one way and write another, how they separate words from daily life. For me, it was always a kind of struggle."*

There were some civil rights actions even on the campus at the University of Chicago. There was a sit-in against Walgreens in sympathy for the action in the South. [Blacks in the South were sitting in at Walgreens' lunch counters in protest of Walgreens' refusal to serve them.] I remember that you got a choice of either going across the line and actually getting arrested or simply picketing on the other side of the street. With a husband at home who was upset at my even going to college, I was fearful that going home, having been arrested or ending up in jail, there would be more hell to pay than if I were simply going to school. Richard was a nice, good, fun-loving man but as far as college and politics went, it was, "Don't bring it home, don't get involved." I remember feeling I was betraying the cause by not stepping over that line, not going the whole distance, because my feelings were there. So there was a little bit of civil rights education, learning what things were about. Studying under Alice Rossi I was looking at sex discrimination in the same way and getting those two general feelings of fairness, equality, equal opportunity going together.

Sally and her first husband, Richard were divorced around 1960 while she was a student at the university. Her second marriage to Bruce Frisbie, a University of Chicago student, lasted about six years. When that marriage was breaking up Sally met Bart Hacker, a graduate student in history at the university. They married in June 1966.

That year Sally and Bart moved to Houston, Texas, where Bart had a job as a historian of Project Gemini for the Manned Spacecraft Center. Sally found a job as an evaluator with a mental health research team, where she worked while completing her dissertation.

Houston was a whole new experience of political action. The young people in *Space City News* [an alternative newspaper] were quite an education. A black guy, Lee Otis Johnson, who was a SNCC [Student Nonviolent Coordinating Committee] organizer, got busted for allegedly handing two marijuana cigarettes to this undercover agent. He didn't smoke to begin with and he knew the guy was an agent, but he got thirty years. So it took two years standing on the street corners and gathering signatures and visiting these fish-eyed prison officials to get any action on that case. At the same time, in Houston daily life was changing. We were getting our house fire-bombed and our windows broken and our tires slashed. We were writing leaflets. We were working with many different people, sand-bagging at an elderly couple's house (the guy was a railway worker and a "socialist") because the rednecks would come and shoot his house up periodically.

I don't know how some people live one way and write another—how they separate words from daily life. For me, it was always a kind of struggle. I wanted both to be of a piece. Perhaps women don't like those sharp separations between home and work and leisure so you are forever trying to pull them together.

Alice Rossi was one of the founders of NOW [in 1966] and she dropped a note to Bart and me a year after it was founded and said, "It's an organization you might want to join." We decided to start a chapter in Houston and when we announced a meeting, much to our surprise, dozens of people showed up. Our house was so crowded there was no place for people to sit. The chapter soon became very large, very powerful, and it started out very left compared to others. It was concerned with economic issues.

AT&T people in Houston suggested that AT&T be a major project for NOW. There was a man and his wife, both of whom worked at the top levels of the corporation, but not executive officers. They were active in NOW and wanted us to protest. They gave me a little book on AT&T called *Monopoly*. It showed how bad the company was on women, minorities, defense, and just stratification. It tied it all together and was beautifully efficient. This couple wanted a straight-forward affirmative action position, moving women into nontraditional jobs. They had some data laid out. But when we began to look at the data we could see that the affirmative action plans projected a decline in jobs for women after three years. Their data showed that more women were moving up, but we were looking at the marginals. Women were becoming an increasing proportion of certain levels of management, but they were becoming a smaller proportion of the work force because of automation. So we showed our research to this pair who were being so helpful, but they were not interested in tackling the organization of technology, or what the implications of the shift from an electrical mechanical system to an electronic switching system were, or in questions of the degradation of work at the craft level, and whether the women who were going to work their asses off getting into those jobs would have any future in them because the jobs were already on their way out.

When we tried to talk to the workers about the capitalist system, the farther away we got from their real concerns, at least what they wanted to talk about, such as trouble with their husband, trouble with their boss, trouble with their kids. Who is going to take off work when the kid is sick? A woman at the telephone company having to explain, "It is better for me to take time off because my husband earns twice what I do."[1] A forty-five-year-old woman who was a teller at AT&T told what happened to her on the night shift. She would sit there and open the mail all night (this was before automatic opening), and at the end of the night her supervisor would show her this tally sheet showing how many times she had yawned, how many times she had scratched, etc. She thought they were trying to get rid of her so they wouldn't have to give her early retirement. It was stuff like that that had the women terrified and furious.

It seems to me that what you can do best is to really keep listening to working people—working women particularly—whose voices have been so stifled. This is not looking at the working class. You feel a part of them and, given my roots, much more similarity. My

---

1. This interview took place in Des Moines. Sally is confused about the time but not the substance.

HACKER, 1986. *"Sally learned roofing and tried communal living, and a motorcycle became her preferred mode of transport."*—Bart Hacker

drinking companions, for example, are not likely to be academics, so it's not all for the sake of sociology or all for the sake of the movement. There's a lot of it that's fun. I think that it makes for better sociology.

So I worked by listening to the people and going in the direction they wanted and then figuring out how it was all put together. Sometimes your own analysis is better, more comprehensive, more progressive. I could see that we shouldn't just be working to get women into management jobs. I didn't want to work to have just a few token women get something. I could see that another kind of explanation was needed which would make sense—a Marxist interpretation—but that would set the women's teeth on edge, both women in NOW and telephone workers.

The research we did went into a national NOW campaign. I had to be a national NOW board member to be its director. In NOW you could work on one project and so that's what I did. AT&T stopped giving us any kind of support, but that didn't stop us. We ferreted out old unpublished dissertations in Harvard's Widener Library with the help of a friend who had a card; we got data from peace groups such as the American Friends Service Committee, which was interested in AT&T as a defense contractor. We helped form networks and a newsletter among groups of women across the country who worked at AT&T. We learned from their experiences at work, at home, and in unions.

Our research showed that planned technological change would eliminate more jobs for women than affirmative action would provide. When we discussed this with management they were slick, but they were not all that conscious. The middle management in a

company like AT&T would be the head of the state telephone company, which is a big business in itself. Sometimes they just wouldn't
know. They would say, "Automation creates jobs." It was a litany.
We would say, "Do you have data?" Of course we knew they
wouldn't give it even if they had it, but it was a gentle way of "calling" them on it. They would splutter, and so we would show them
the data for their very own company. Some people, faced with that
would just say, "Oh, space it." You just cannot keep them focused in
on data that shakes their view of reality. Other people would look at
it and really feel bad. They would say, "You know we were *really*
beginning to try." They would just shake their heads and would say,
"Well, you see we are moving some women up. We're moving some
black women up." It was true. And we would say, "But the overall
. . ." Jesus, I get pissed just thinking about it.

While we were involved in our AT&T study, the EEOC [Equal
Employment Opportunity Commission] was trying to pick a city in
which to hold its hearing on that corporation and Houston was the
only one that sent a lobby to Washington to prevent the hearing
being held there, so EEOC knew Houston would be a great city to
investigate. So they went down there. At first EEOC tended to hold
meetings on women on one day and minorities on the other. There
was a lot of divisiveness there. Anyway, we had a really good day at
the hearings getting people to testify.[2]

In Houston Mark was acting up in school. We had moved him
from the University of Chicago Lab School to the Houston school
system at the age of twelve, so obviously he was in trouble. I was
talking to this therapist and he thought that Bart and I were not
playing our proper sex roles. I said, "We like different things, like I
like hammering the shingles back on the house and I like trying to
deal with the plumbing." He said, "If you do that, I am sure you are
doing it in a feminine way." I should have punched him in a feminine way!

Bart's cousin from Chicago had talked with me at length and
suggested I would probably be interested in some left-wing or social
anarchist literature. He and the literature had a great amount to
say. In Iowa the anarcho-communist collectives fit well with how I
was beginning to see things. Decentralized and radically political,
sex and other stuff were legitimate issues, at least enough for open-
ers, along with class.

---

2. Sally's research of sex and race discrimination in the American Telephone and
Telegraph system, which she began in Houston and continued in Des Moines, strongly
shaped NOW's key role in the landmark $54-million AT&T settlement of 1973.

In 1970 Sally and Bart moved to Iowa, where Bart
had a teaching position at Iowa State University in
Ames. Sally found a job at Drake University in Des
Moines soon after her arrival in the state. At first Sally
and Bart lived in a rural area about halfway between
Ames and Des Moines.

About a year and a half after we moved to Iowa I left Bart [in
September 1971] and moved to a women's collective called Motley
because it was on Motley Street. Also, about twenty of us formed the
very serious Feminist/Socialist Group [in December 1972]. We read
an awful lot of stuff—different forms of socialist/communist literature, Marx and Mao and so on—we read a lot of anarchist material.
We didn't read enough feminist material, but that was early seventies. There wasn't that much about. Firestone, *The Dialectic of Sex*,
was the only thing we formally read. We got *Red Stockings* newsletters. Somebody would Xerox one and fire it in. So this group of
people living in various collective arrangements settled on a kind of
a blend of feminism and anarchism—social anarchism. And that's
been my political orientation ever since, which makes me marginal
whichever political group that I'm working with.
    In the collectives, many of us had to learn as children do, slowly
and clumsily, how to use tools.[3] We learned related habits, too, such
as cleaning and replacing tools when we finished with them. We
learned to buy tools, a particularly difficult lesson for some of us. It
was even harder to keep them in hand. At a regional meeting a
college professor took a hammer from the hand of a young woman
at work. He wanted to help finish the job more quickly and effi-
ciently, he explained at the meeting called to discuss the issue. We
talked about the differences between long- and short-term efficiency.
    Trying to work things out, we talked a strange and sometimes
awkward language about "deprivatizing our possessive relationships." Eroticism does get constructed with a very heavy element of
dominance/submission. Trying to figure out, how do you have
"community" and eroticism at the same time? In the cooperatives,
whenever eroticism emerged, you know how threatening that is. We
were forever worried about a couple who was privatizing their rela-

---

3. Throughout this section Sally uses the term *collective* when she is referring to
the Feminist/Socialist Group, which was composed of people living in various collectives as well as people like herself who were living independently. The Motley House
Collective broke up in the fall of 1972.

HACKER, 1989. *"For anyone who knew her—kin, colleague, student, friend—she epitomized integrity and courage."*
—Bart Hacker

tionships. Then the rest of us would sneak out and make up fictions. If you start lying in your collectives, you are in a lot of trouble.

But "secret" was the only way that you had "private." Things may be shifting so that we can do a better balance, or have a wider variety of erotic kinds of choices. That's going to take "degendering."

When Jacob was born to one of us (who pointed out to the many that she was the only person doing child care, while the rest of us did revolution), we talked about deprivatizing our possessive biological relations. After many discussions, Jacob became a child of the collectives, moving every week or so among the four- or five-member households. The men encountered more opposition to taking Jacob to work with them than did the women, and for some—the construction worker, the bank teller, the kitchen worker at the hospital—it was impossible at that time.

I was now a college professor, one of the grannies of the group. My research and action centered around women and work; I shared salary and tasks within the group. Mom and Dad, by now old, still rural and of modest means, still small-town Republican, came to visit once. Dad walked in with two sleeping bags under his arm, looked around, cleared his throat, and said, "Ah, this is a nice pad you all have here." They took the politics, posters, and unfamiliar sexual orientation of some in stride. They were pleased but surprised at a healthy, expressive, and self-disciplined Jacob, but they couldn't go along with deprivatized possessive biological relationships. *That* was family.

Like many social anarchists, we were very disciplined and often overdid organization. Once, when Dan was to create some kind of entertainment at a party, he got stoned instead with his buddy and was criticized at the next meeting for failing to create spontaneous joy at 8:30 P.M. So we learned as we went.

The collectives would decide where energy should go and then we would help each other individually, decide if we were overextended. That's a fine line. A number were working in hospitals. One guy was a cook at the hospital and there were a couple of aides who published a hospital workers' newspaper and tried organizing the workers there. There was a grape and lettuce boycott, and there was the anti-ROTC action to protest a move to put an ROTC program in the schools.The Des Moines board of education had put it into the junior highs, so we had an action, which meant demonstrations, and literature review and leaflets and all that sort of thing. There was also a food co-op.

These anarchists are more compulsively organization-oriented than *any* group I have ever seen. I tried putting forth AT&T as a group action but they voted it down. In this case they thought it was too academic. It was an exciting time. There were a number of us who had a meek and mild-mannered, sort of PTA style. Butter would melt in our mouths, but we were saying the most outrageous things. It was exciting. There's no doubt about it.

Organizing the women in one of the banks was also one of the actions within the group. Des Moines is full of banks and insurance companies, and when the banks started to organize we tried to get people in from Nine to Five [a Boston-based working women's group], but they were scattered too thin. They had just started and they couldn't send anybody out. Then there was the United Electrical Union (UE). They got thrown out for being commies in the fifties. We were trying to get in touch with them for help and it seemed like nobody would come. Finally, the Office and Employees Union, I think, sent some turkey. He didn't know how to talk to women and there was some fiasco. He gave somebody cards to be signed and management started coming around and picking up the cards, so they knew everybody. The women didn't expect it. Nobody was ready for that. They didn't know *not* to give them the cards. So it was back to scratch. I don't think anybody lost their job, but we heard that people who tried to get hired after that were illegally questioned closely about whether their father had been a union member. So we shifted a little bit because people were complaining. We listened to what was bothering people.

The clerical women started complaining about the United Way. You sign up and they take you in a room and twist your arm in a little way: "You want this job, you're going to sign up." They don't put it like that, but they ask them if they will sign up to have a certain proportion of their income donated to the United Way. We had been having some general, liberal complaints about how much more the Boy Scouts got than the Girl Scouts. I thought, "Jesus, I'm not too interested in either one." But we took it up as an issue and then we started looking again where the money came from and where it went. This town (Des Moines) runs to clerical labor, many of whom were earning under the poverty level. They were still encouraged to give 1.9 percent or some such figure, which was more than the company was giving. We did that kind of analysis. We had some public meetings with the media. I remember one woman saying, "I'm a mother of four." And I said, "I'm a grandmother." So there we were playing "family status" with each other, which is not to be proud of.

The United Way action became an extremely well-publicized effort because most of the money was coming from clerical workers, many of whom were girls right off the farm, and it was going back—disproportionately—to racquetball courts used by middle-class males or to organizations for poor boys and not for poor girls. It was taking from the poor and giving to the rich. Then we got into telling the Defense Department to bake their own cookies with volunteer money and we should take tax money for child care and stuff like that. It seemed very easy to broaden those issues. But if you mentioned capitalism or socialism, you would just lose 75 percent of your backing. We also wrote a musical lampooning the United Way and got it produced.

At AT&T we had the government on our side, prying information loose that is not loose in private industry and there are a number of ways in which private industry can try to mess up the works. For example, the United Way refused to give us any data about what the corporations were giving. They said they didn't have it. One time my friend Louise Noun and other NOW representatives were having a meeting with United Way officials and Louise got up to go to the bathroom and came back and . . . psst! And so I went out and went to the bathroom, didn't know why, and here are these books lying open on the table in the outer office and there was the data they *would not* give us, the amount the corporations had donated to the United Way as compared to the amount the clerical workers had been "encouraged" to give. We each took a turn going to the bathroom, copying down as much as we could and leaving a little marker on how far we'd got. That is getting data that we weren't supposed to have one way or another. That's the gray area and I don't care because to me that's not private property. Lying is something else, or dissembling or being deceitful. I'm not good at that.

Although Sally and Bart did not live together after

her move to Des Moines, they continued on friendly
terms and were mutually supportive as long as Sally
lived.

The Des Moines experience was crucial in the development of Sally's political philosophy, which Bart says
was essentially a pragmatism of the left. "If you think of
the left as that part of the political spectrum that's concerned with individual human lives and their better-
ment," he explains, "then that was where Sally was
from the beginning. Finding out what the formal philosophies were, learning about Marxism, learning about
radical feminism, learning about all of the other ways
that people were trying to develop during the late sixties and into the seventies, and devising techniques to
deal with them, was something that primarily happened
for Sally in Des Moines. Basically, what Sally was concerned with was making the world a better place for
ordinary folks. For people living in the United States at
that time Marxism made the most sense if that was
what you were concerned with. It seemed to offer not
only an explanation of why things were the way they
were, but also a program of action. But for Sally, in
time, it became quite clear that Marxism didn't entirely
fit."

Bart goes on to say that "Sally was never very comfortable with authority so anarchism appealed to her,
especially when she started reading in the classic anarchist writings. She found out that what she had always
heard about anarchists was essentially conservative or
establishment propaganda and that it had very little to
do with the kind of stereotypes she had been exposed to
in college. It seemed to Sally that economic motives
didn't explain everything in a capitalist economy." Bart
describes Sally as a pragmatist. "She would use whatever was suitable in dealing with the problems that she
was currently addressing. Eclecticsm comes closest to
describing her."

All of us in the collectives had notions of how industry and work
might be organized. Then in the mid-seventies came word of the

Mondragon producer cooperatives in the Basque country of northern Spain. This system of 19,000 worker-owners in over a hundred
firms embodies the structural principles of organization we had
come to believe were most productive of good workplaces and community. They not only worked, they thrived. It was ten years before
I could go to see for myself and to explore the status of women in the
Mondragon cooperatives and in Basque society. (Now, after years of
collaboration with Bart, my work centers on gender, technology,
and cooperation, and I have recently [1987] returned from sabbati-
cal in the Basque country of northern Spain.)

In the summer of 1973 I started investigating agribusiness. A
boyfriend who was a Vietnam vet couldn't do heavy work so he was
going back to get an electronics degree and drove up and back on
his motorcycle the fifteen miles to the community college. I figured
out that sharing a ride and sharing gas with him would only cost
about a quarter a week; it was so efficient. Soon after that I got my
own motorcycle. That was as bad as being a teenager again. That
summer I sat in on courses in agribusiness at the area college for
five, six, seven hours a day.

By that time I had decided that I wasn't going to write for professional literature; I wasn't going to take the time to write for professional grant money. I had heard all this analysis that it's all dishonest money. Well, along came the Ford Foundation and said that
they were going to do something about women and technology. Bart
encouraged me to apply because it was $11,000 for one year. I said,
"Naw, Ford money, nobody wants to take it." He said they had
never before funded something the way I wanted to do it. Give it a
try. The practice in writing to get access helped. Write it in such a
way that you don't lose your integrity, which you are not willing to
do, but you are also not lying about what you want to do. So that
came through.

Eleven thousand dollars was too much for me to live on; it was
excess. Irene Talbott (Tally), one of my friends in the collective, had
resigned from her job at the Iowa Commission for the Blind. She
was an economist. So we decided we'd split and she would take
insurance and printing and I would take agribusiness. My thought
was to make a study of automation in these industries comparable
to the AT&T study and see how much variation there was by industry. Tally had a master's degree in economics but when she would
try to bring her academic skills to bear on the data it just didn't
work. She felt bad. She wrote up a few things with a combination of
some stories, which are good; also an analysis of wages. Maybe it

was my problem in interpreting the stuff, but she was not satisfied
with it, either. In agribusiness you couldn't get the damn numbers,
and the numbers you did get wouldn't agree with each other, so
there was no way to do what we wanted to do.

About this time [1975] there was an opportunity to apply for a
fellowship at MIT [Massachusetts Institute of Technology] funded by
the Mellon Foundation. Again, I said, "I'm not going to take that
kind of money." Bart encouraged me to apply. Again, like the Ford
grant, he cast it in terms of "do what you want to do and they can
take it or leave it." So I did. It would be just a delight to get inside
MIT after talking to telephone engineers and agricultural systems
analysts and managers, to find someplace where business and industry were so tightly fused. I wanted to learn how technological
decisions were made that shaped industrial technology. Having an
MIT postdoctoral—12,000 bucks, which is big money—made it a lot
easier to begin. I wasn't quite sure what I wanted to do or how I was
going to do it. I just wanted to be there and kind of soak it up, just
sort of get the sense of the place. But it was also true that my lover
at the time in the collectives was messing around with somebody
else and so it made the decision whether to stay politically active in
Des Moines or move out of town a little easier. The reason I bring
that up is that in honesty, it's those kinds of experiences for women,
those personal things, which affect our decisions in important ways.

In 1977 Sally accepted a position at Oregon State
University in Corvallis, where she continued to teach
until forced to retire because of her health. During these
years Sally continued her research into how engineering
practices mold societal practices and ideology. While
still teaching she enrolled as an engineering student
and at one point she took a leave of absence to study
industries in Los Angeles where she worked as a secretary for an engineering firm. In 1984 Sally made the
first of several trips to the Basque area of Spain where
she studied gender and technology in the Mondragon
Cooperative. The results of her research are included in
Power, Gender and Technology, published in 1989.

In February 1987 Sally, a heavy smoker, learned
that she had cancer of the lining of the lung, an untreat-
able condition. Facing the prospect of death with the
same intensity and interest with which she faced life,

Sally made plans for her final days. She researched the Hemlock Society and found out how to end her life when it became too unbearable, but despite intense pain, her will to live overcame her desire for a quick end to her misery. Meanwhile, Sally consulted a hospice service, which agreed to train friends who wished to share in her care. During the last seven months of her life fifty-five friends and acquaintances rotated around-the-clock shifts, looking after her in her own home. She was hospitalized only for the last three days of her life, after she had slipped into a coma. She died in Corvallis in August 1988. According to her wishes, Sally's release from suffering was celebrated by mourning friends with a "going away" party.

"Although she organized and directed and lectured and discussed, mostly she led by example," Bart Hacker says. "For anyone who knew her—kin, colleague, student, friend—she epitomized integrity and courage. Throughout her life she did what needed doing without ever counting the cost."

REFERENCE

Sally Hacker, *Pleasure, Power and Technology* (Boston: Unwin, Hyman, 1989).

Karen Johnson and

two of her Coe College classmates formed the New World Collective in Des Moines in 1972. This collective was instrumental in organizing the Feminist/Socialist Group which consisted of about thirty idealistic young women and men searching for ways to make the world a place where all people are truly equal. She currently is an artist who works primarily in the photographic media and teaches photography at the Horace Mann School in New York.

"Since we considered ourselves revolutionaries, we wanted to try to be revolutionaries on all levels of our lives. We would live as a collective and share all of our income and energies to meet our needs collectively."

I grew up in Kansas and then later in Missouri. I have one brother, Hal, who is six years younger. My father's parents were tenant farmers, and for a while my parents farmed. After World War II, Dad became an auto mechanic. As time passed he drank more and more and would break into drunken rages. Mom divorced him when I was thirteen, but we always kept in touch to some degree. After she divorced Dad, Mom immediately became involved with another alcoholic. Our economic class slipped from lower, semirural working class to urban poor. I always knew how hard Mom worked to provide for us. At the same time I felt the inconsistency caused by her attempts to keep peace in an alcoholic family. There were times when she would call home to say that she and my stepfather (he didn't actually marry Mom until years later when he could afford a divorce from his first wife) would be home soon for dinner; they had just stopped for one beer; they had just started talking to someone they hadn't seen in a long time. Eventually they would arrive, but I would feel angry and betrayed. In many ways Hal and I had to provide for our own emotional well-being.

My maternal grandparents, especially my grandmother, were a source of great stability and strength for me when I was growing up. Their home was situated on several acres on the edge of a small town in north-central Kansas and I spent most of every summer with them. My early memories are framed by the comfort and security of their home. I had a playhouse in a former chicken coop, complete with adult furniture, a swing, and a croquet court where the neighbors would join us for games. The days seemed long and pleasant but sometimes lonely. As I grew older I felt the social isolation, and the summer after my junior year in high school I stayed home to work and take a special summer course in creative writing.

My stepdad had difficulty keeping a job and we couldn't keep up on rent. The result was that we moved so many times during my first two years of high school that I was ashamed to go to the office to change my address. But there was always a value placed on education. Mom had quit high school when she was needed at home and she wanted us to get an education and to do well. We knew that she was proud of us for "being smart." In March of my senior year the high school guidance counselor called me in and said that I should go to college. At his suggestion, I sent out my transcript and a letter which basically said, "Here I am. I don't have any money. Are you interested?" Coe College in Cedar Rapids, Iowa, offered me a lot of scholarship and grant support, so I decided to go there. This was in 1967.

I remember driving up to Coe in our old car—it looked sort of like the Batmobile. The parking lot was full of Cadillacs. My stepdad was wearing a suit he had bought at the Salvation Army. My roommate's father was a leading chemist for Standard Oil. The father of a student next door, Mary Grant Purdy, was vice president of a big aerospace corporation. It took me a while to figure out how I could fit in at Coe, but it was a great time for me to be there. The period 1967 to 1971 was when student activism was a part of our culture. I started to become aware of feminism and I became active in the antiwar movement. I was the first woman to be elected student body president at Coe. I was so scared that I cried myself to sleep the night after the election. I survived and with other progressive student leaders worked hard to democratize student government and to establish more student influence on the college administration. I learned a lot about institutions, power, public speaking, and diplomacy.

At Coe I formed two of the most influential relationships of my life. One was with Grant Purdy. Grant and I developed a deep sense of trust, understanding, and shared vision that continues even now. The other was with Bob Davis. I became lovers with Bob Davis during the early fall of my senior year. His father was a sheet-metal worker and his mother worked in a pencil factory while he was growing up so he was very working-class identified. He studied political science and history and was more ideologically aware than I. Bob was the first person to encourage me to look at my past with a sense of pride in our survival skills and rural background.

After I graduated from Coe in May 1971, Bob and I started living together in a small apartment in Cedar Rapids. Later in the summer Grant came to visit and never left. She was unsure of what she wanted to do but felt she could figure it out more easily hanging around with us than with her family. The three of us began to study various political philosophies. We read Kropoktin, Bakunin, Alexander Berkman, and Emma Goldman on the anarchist side. On the Marxist-Leninist side we read some of Lenin and Chairman Mao. Then we read some of the feminist classics including Shulamith Firestone's *Dialectic of Sex* (1971).

When I was offered a job in Des Moines in January 1972 we decided that all three of us would move there. Since we considered ourselves revolutionaries, we wanted to try to be revolutionaries on all levels of our lives. We would live as a collective and share all of our income and energies to meet our needs collectively. When Grant's parents were about to visit we felt that our collective needed a name and we decided on the spur of the moment to call ourselves the New World Collective. We lived in a couple of places in Des Moines but the main house was on the corner of Eighth and Franklin. It is a very large house, which made it a useful resource for the progressive community in Des Moines. We held meetings and celebrations there and housed a library and office. Grant, Bob, and I remained the core group of the collective, but there were other members at different times. For a while my brother, Hal, was part of the collective.

We saw ourselves as a feminist alternative to the nuclear family, which we felt was oppressive. To overcome traditional sex roles, we rotated all of the maintenance tasks. For example, we had one task that was called finances, which meant that you paid the bills. Another was car maintenance. We divided the cleaning tasks and the

KAREN JOHNSON, 1975. *"Student activism was part of our culture."*

yard work and rotated who cooked dinner and who did the dishes. We didn't want to fall into typical sexist roles and we wanted everyone to have the opportunity to learn various skills. We made decisions by consensus and spent a lot of time and energy on internal personal and collective processes. We practiced criticism-self-criticism—a style of constructive but frank criticism and praise. We were very holistic, eclectic, hopeful, but practical.

We also wanted to reflect our belief in communist-anarchism. By communism we meant "from each according to ability, to each according to need." In anarchism we were identifying with the non-hierarchical and libertarian tradition. We believed that authority and organization had to rest on the most local level with power remaining in the control of the people most involved. Federations could be built to coordinate activities on a larger geographical basis.

When we first moved to Des Moines we had difficulty locating other progressives and finally visited other cities as possible places to move. One group we met in Kansas City volunteered to come to Des Moines and do an educational on revolutionary thought if we could organize a group of people. We finally found some prospects through a connection we made with other Des Moines progressives at the Draft and Peace Center. We held the educational in December 1972. Fifteen people attended including people from a cooperative living group called Rufus Jones House. The following weekend eleven of us formed the Feminist/Socialist Group (FSG). Although the name and structure changed some, this group continued as a political organization throughout most of the 1970s.

People in FSG tended to see our living situations as a political arena, even for those few who lived alone. There were four living

The New World Collective, 1975. (*From left*) Grant Purdy, Hal Johnson, Bob Davis, Jacob Price-Noah, KAREN JOHNSON. "*We saw ourselves as a feminist alternative to the nuclear family, which we felt was oppressive.*"

groups in Des Moines during this time: New World Collective, Rufus Jones House, Motley House Collective, and a group which was just called House. We tended to refer to all of them as collectives but the actual political commitment and structure of the houses varied a lot. New World Collective was the most self-consciously political in our organization and commitment to each other. Rufus Jones House, organized in 1971, went through a variety of cooperative structures. Midge Slater, Bill Lamme, Carol Hayse, and Craig Kaldenberg are the people that I think of as the core group. House, established in 1969, also went through a lot of changes. Tom Leffler was the consistent person at House, but Lynn Price and Dan Noah lived there at one time, also Mark Hacker, Sally's son. Motley collective was a women's house that was organized in 1972 by several feminists including Sally Hacker, Irene (Tally) Talbott, and Kay Plymat. Rufus Jones, House, and New World had big houses where we held parties and potlucks with a lot of singing and dancing. We would use the IWW (Wobblies) songbook and we would write our own revolutionary songs. This celebratory quality was part of our feminist, anarchist, and counterculture tradition.

Everyone in the FSG community worked. Several people worked in health care as orderlies, housekeepers, nurse's aides, cooks, or central supply workers. Several people worked at Pittsburgh-Des Moines Steel. Sally Hacker was a professor of sociology at Drake University. Others were clerical workers. A few had jobs with socially conscious groups like the American Friends Service Committee. A couple of us worked for the state government. I was youth services coordinator for a while and administered programs for high school dropouts or potential dropouts. Then I worked as an offset printer, a legal assistant, and finally, as a photographer. Many of our members had middle-class backgrounds. Though people of color participated in our actions, none ever joined FSG. At the largest, there were probably about thirty people in the group. When we got too large we broke into two groups and referred to ourselves as primary revolutionary groups, or PRGs.

Each meeting of the FSG was divided between study, action, group maintenance discussions, and criticism-self-criticism. Several people would select readings and then write discussion questions. Some of our studies included readings from *Women in the Chinese Revolution; The Political Economy of Women's Liberation;* excerpts from *Sisterhood is Powerful;* and *The Bell Jar.* We also had in-depth studies on the history and structures of racism and on various political movements and revolutionary organizational structures. Some of our members were involved in the food co-op. Sally Hacker and Tally were active in NOW. Some members were active in a health care workers' caucus, and others participated in an organizing attempt at Central National Bank. I was active in the Des Moines Anti-Imperialist Caucus. We worked against the Vietnam War early on and later fought an unsuccessful battle to keep the JROTC [Junior Reserve Officer Training Corps] program out of the high schools. In order to support our political activities we would collect money from ourselves, according to our ability to contribute.

We also tried to nurture personal growth by sharing skills, rotating tasks, and making space for people to be heard. We would talk about the need to lead balanced, creative, and committed lives. You might be very active in all this political work, but were you playing? And if you weren't playing at all, that could easily become a topic of discussion. I often heard that I needed to learn to relax. I felt that this was a very feminist influence in this group. Nurturing is played down in our culture and we were saying that this traditional gift of women is just as important as being on a picket line. That set us apart from a lot of the political groups I encountered during those years.

One of our activities was organizing an anarchist conference, which was held at the Black Theology Center in Des Moines. It drew a national attendance. This conference inspired the founding of a small newsletter called *The Anarchist-Feminist Notes.* I served as the coordinator. It was a loose communications network of women who shared a belief in anti-authoritarianism—that there shouldn't be a hierarchy of control and power—as well as a belief in feminism. We received mail from Japan, New Zealand, Greece, and other places around the world in addition to places all over the United States. We printed any article or letter that was submitted. We asked for donations to help pay expenses, but we would mail the paper to anyone who wanted it. FSG paid for anything that donations didn't cover.

Soon after FSG started we began to identify sexist dynamics on the part of some of the male members. We decided to form men's and women's caucuses as one way to deal with sexism. Part of the understanding was that women needed to meet together to support each other; to raise our own consciousness, and to enable us to deal with the effects of sexism in our lives. We felt that the male members had the responsibility for dealing with the ways in which they were sexist and oppressive. A policy evolved that at any time a woman felt there was something sexist in the dynamics of a meeting and didn't feel she wanted to confront it individually, she could say that she wanted a women's caucus right then. No matter what business was going on, the women would just walk out. We felt that it was always more important that we deal with the issues of sexism in our midst. This was particularly important in the early stages of the group.

As a political community we understood that one of the ways women are oppressed is through the isolation of the nuclear family. There is an expectation that issues should be kept within the family, thus, "privatized." To counteract this we developed a practice we called "deprivatization sessions." Usually the individuals involved would ask members of the community to meet with them. They would share what had been happening from their perspectives. We would try to analyze the situation and make positive, supportive, and at times, critical suggestions. Sometimes these sessions involved people who were lovers and sometimes they involved people with personal and/or political conflicts.

The anarchist analysis of property and the feminist analysis of sexual repression also influenced our understanding of our personal relationships. Bob and I decided early on that legal marriage was an oppressive institution. We decided to have a celebration of relationship that would involve Grant and my brother Hal as our collective members, along with our biological families, comrades, and friends. We held the celebration on Bastille Day [July 14] 1973 at a union hall in Des Moines. We continued to refuse to take advantage of

JOHNSON with Jake, 1975. *"We decided to form a child-care collective. Jake would live a couple of days during the week at each of the collective houses. . . . I cherish memories of this experience."*

"heterosexual privileges" such as tax and health insurance advantages, and although we felt very committed to each other we never represented ourselves as married. We also felt that sexual freedom had to be part of a revolutionary relationship and considered ourselves free to be nonmonogamous. Bob was supportive in 1976 when I became lovers with a woman. By that time other lesbians were part of our community and solidarity among women was valued. Being "woman-identified" was seen as a revolutionary stance for all women. Many of us felt that people are naturally bisexual but become heterosexual or gay for largely historical and cultural reasons.

Jacob, who was born in April 1973, was the son of Lynn Price and Dan Noah, who were both involved with the political community by that time. Lynn had heard us talk about community responsibility for child care and called a meeting of interested people to discuss alternative ways to rear Jacob. She wanted Jake to have the advantage of relating to more people than her and Dan and to have the security of community commitment. We decided to form a child-care collective. Jake would live a couple of days during the

week at each of the collective houses and each house would take
turns caring for him every third weekend. Some people who lived
alone would come to our houses to help with Jake's care. We kept a
notebook with details about his food, his health, his activities, and
met regularly to discuss his developmental needs and our attitudes.
We tried to be very consistent. When Jake started school we
thought it would be best for him to live in one location during the
week, but he would stay at the various houses on weekends. We
continued this until Jake was about ten. I didn't spend as much
time with Jake as some others, but I cherish the memories of this
experience. Jake knew who his biological parents were and knew
his relationship with them was unique, but when he was small he
knew that there was a group of people he could call upon for help
and love. I saw him when he was about thirteen and asked how he
felt at that time about collective child care. He thought it was
"pretty good."[1]

There were so many different things that we were involved in
during those years. We organized women's awareness and support
groups. We taught each other to find our cervixes and how to monitor our health. Some of us played softball on the Slammin' Sisters
team. Every fall for several years women went camping at the 4-H
camp. Many were not members of FSG but were still considered
part of the community. We tried to bring our political values into our
daily lives.

From the beginning, a topic of discussion in FSG was how we
should incorporate new members. The New World Collective saw it
as a real tension between building a strong and cohesive organization and trying to bring new people into our community. In the
winter of 1974 we decided to organize an educational on revolutionary thought, which would provide a background to new members
on the issues which we had studied. Then after the educational
those people who were interested in us and who we felt would be
positive additions to the group would be invited to join FSG. After
much discussion we decided to do a two-day in-depth educational
which included discussion of Marxist economics, oppressed group
analysis, and communist-anarchism on the first day. The second
day focused on methodology and was divided into two parts. In the
morning we discussed what we called "the revolution against our
selves"—the feminist struggle and the dialectical method of criticism-self-criticism. In the afternoon we discussed revolution in soci-

---

1. Jacob moved to Missoula, Mont., with his mother after the breakup of Rufus
Jones House.

ety—organization and strategy. Participants were asked to read three hundred and ninety pages of material before coming to the educational. Tom Leffler and I were the facilitators. About fifteen people attended (including you, Louise). About ten of the participants decided to join FSG.

Big changes started to happen in the late 1970s and early 1980s. The New World Collective had always said that we existed to meet our needs as individuals and if the group started to get in the way of individual growth, we would change. So in 1980 we decided to end the collective. It was difficult. We grieved. But people needed to go off and do different things. That's what happened to the radical community as a whole.[2] I went to New York University to study photography and I now teach photography in a private school in New York. Bob went to London to attend a cooking school. Some people, including Grant, stayed on in Des Moines. The Women's Cultural Collective is a legacy of that period.

I am both fearful and encouraged by the possibilities that present themselves in 1990. I hope we can make them the "Gay Nineties" in a truly celebrative and liberatory sense.

REFERENCES

Shulamith Firestone, *Dialectic of Sex* (N.Y.: Bantam, 1971).
L. Landy, *Women in the Chinese Revolution*, pamphlet (International Socialism, n.d.).
Robin Morgan, ed., *Sisterhood is Powerful* (N.Y.: Vintage Books, 1970).
Sylvia Plath, *The Bell Jar* (N.Y.: Harper and Row, 1971).
The Political Economy of Women's Liberation (United Front Press, 1969).

---

2. Rufus Jones and House both disbanded in 1979. Motley House operated from September 1972 to September 1973.

Bev Mitchell

was one of the organizers of the Cedar Rapids Women's Caucus, an independent organization that later affiliated with NOW. She is editor of *Lilith Speaks,* the lively newsletter of this group.

"You don't care what history says if the important thing is to get the girls a place to play tennis off the street before they get hit."

I am an insurance agent who grew up in Fremont, Nebraska. I was an only child. My mother was a waitress and struggled really hard. My stepfather was a gas station attendant, that's not a very high-status job. They both worked at Al's Cafe, a steak house–gas station combination. My grandmother with whom we lived before my mother remarried had a tough time of it, even though she didn't work outside the home. She came from some money, but I don't know what happened to it. I always heard that my great-grandmother on my mother's side of the family was an odd woman, but no one ever said why. I came to find out gradually that she was prominent in the DAR (Daughters of the American Revolution) in Stevens Point, Wisconsin. She was also prominent in the Socialist party and she was a suffragist. The DAR must have changed. It was the suffragist thing that my family was so embarrassed about. All along I thought my great-grandmother must have had illegitimate children or run off to Europe with someone, but instead she was very strong in the suffrage movement. Inadvertently my family made me identify with her. I was a good reader and they would say, "She takes after her great-grandmother."

I became a feminist in 1971 when I went to Chicago for a weekend with my someday-to-become-ex-husband. We were just two Nebraskans gawking at the big buildings. There was a women's liberation rally in Grant Park. It was just about the most exciting thing I had ever been to. It was also scary. I remember one woman dressed in nothing but the American flag. Her fingernails were three inches long and she had a sparkly top hat. It was fabulous. It was the first time I had ever been to a speech or a political rally where I agreed with every single point, or it was something I had never thought of before and in the next twenty minutes I mulled it over, and said, "Yes, that is true."

I came to Iowa City in 1971 to get a master's degree in English education. I had been a high school English teacher and I thought I wanted to get a master's in that. But these were the years when you couldn't even assign homework and everyone was "free to be you and me." I thought, "I can't teach English with no rules. There's got to be some, and how do you teach English well if you can't assign homework?" So I decided not to go back into English and I never finished the master's. I went to work at Frank Magid Associates, a market research company in Cedar Rapids.

In 1971 the teachers that I had gotten to know in grad school were thinking of forming a teachers' version of a women's liberation group in Cedar Rapids. Then we thought, "Why should it be only for teachers?" So we expanded the idea. In those days everyone was trying to be non-elitist. We held one meeting just to see who was interested. Without our knowing it, the very same week a woman named Sally Madden [now Professor Sarah Hanley] called a meeting at her home to organize a women's group. At the time Sally was married to Henry Madden, who ran Harneschfeger, a very big factory in Cedar Rapids. Since the first meeting would likely be friends and neighbors, in Sally's case her group included upper income people, women with positions of power, or they were married to men with positions of power. When the two groups found out about each other, we joined forces because in those days women's liberation was an unpopular cause and the going was rough. Sally was a tremendous driving force in our combined group. She was getting her doctorate in history at that time, and I can't say enough about how much she did and how much of her influence she used to just stomp in and fix things. We called this group the Cedar Rapids Women's Caucus.

Cedar Rapids had gotten its civil rights code not too long before we organized and, of course, women were not included. So the first order of business was to get that fixed. Reverend William Cotton, a liberal minister, was the first head of the Human Rights Commission, as it was called then. Sally Madden and the other important women went on a rampage. They just said, "You will do this." They were supported by the scary, hippie women whom they'd just met and formed a bond of sisterhood with, women dripping with beads. Remember that the eleventh commandment of waspdom is, "Thou shalt not make a scene." We used this as a tool. The men on the commission were not used to seeing blue-collar women. They were scared to death that between their wives, who were capable of incredible fury, and these hippies, God knows what would happen. So protection for women was put in the code.

Then there was the "make them enforce it" bit. Putting nondiscrimination in the code was one thing, teaching the commission what's discrimination was another. I'll tell you how accepted it was here in Cedar Rapids. There were two family-owned department stores, Killian's and Armstrong's, that had been here forever; the twin pillars of the Cedar Rapids retail community. Downtown was thriving in those days, and both stores had segregated lunch rooms for men only. So one of the first things we did was to desegregate these lunchrooms by sitting in until the stores changed their policy. The whole thing was terribly embarrassing. With black people, when they integrated a lunch counter, at least they were flattered enough to create hostility. Our job was tougher. Rarely did they do us the compliment of hostility. It was usually just ridicule, which, for an American, is harder to face. Americans like to be liked.

Someone—to this day we don't know who—sent us a copy of the disaster evacuation plan for Merchants National Bank. The plan was simple and very clear—men go first. Needless to say, the bank backed off very fast when we filed a charge with the local Human Rights Commission.

At this time the daily papers, the *Cedar Rapids Gazette* and the *Des Moines Register*, hired only boys as carriers. They alleged that this was for safety's sake but that claim was ludicrous when one compared an eight-year-old-boy to a sixteen- or seventeen-year-old girl. We filed a discrimination complaint with a peach of a candidate, a sixteen-year-old straight-A daughter of an Episcopal priest, and she had karate training, too. We won. Every time I see a female carrier now, I smile. To me, this and other youth jobs are much more important than is currently credited by feminism. Money from them gives lower-class girls the ability to dress well enough to stay in school, the ability to have free choice in their social life, and the opportunity to go to college. It is a devastating early discrimination to have girls relegated to pay-nothing baby-sitting while boys reap

BEV MITCHELL with her father, Richard Bales, 1969. *"I always heard that my great-grandmother was an odd woman but no one ever said why. I came to find out . . . that she was a suffragist."*

the benefits of most of the commercial employment.

We also had child care and self-defense and women's medical self-help classes. I wasn't on any of these committees but they were well attended. In addition, we offered a course on women in religion, a two-week program with professional materials, that we did for local churches and adult education classes.

We made honest men of the media by having a summer Camp Bra-Burn, two weeks of tent/trailer lakeside encampment for women and children. Women would stay for a few hours, a few days, or the whole time. Every morning we raised a bra on an improvised flagpole while a member, usually Rosie Rimrodt, played "God Bless America" on her kazoo.

Often, as I was running errands to Washington High School, I would interrupt the girls' tennis team practice. It was as unavoidable as it was annoying because the girls had to play tennis in the school driveway, sans net. The tennis courts were for the boys. When we complained, the school allowed the girls to use the courts, but like the gyms and other playing areas, only when the boys didn't "need" them. This was justified, the school system claimed, because the boys had a larger sports enrollment. Of course, that is a circular reason. The boys had a larger enrollment because they had uniforms, prime practice times, new equipment, travel budgets, well-paid and good coaching.

Then Title IX was passed and we had a tool with which to change it all. Like almost all school systems, ours did *nothing* different after Title IX was passed, except perhaps to make their public budget materials so voluminous and confusing, no one could tell exactly how much was spent on what athletic category. But then the solution to our problem dropped in our lap one day when a copy of the current Cedar Rapids schools' budget, which was prepared for school board members only, was found in our mailbox. This budget was arranged differently and clearly. Circled was the category, *Girl Athletics, 9%* with the hand-printed notation, "Thought this would interest you." (Years later, we learned that this information came from Barbara Bjornson, a school board member, who did not support us openly.)

So with this information in hand we filed under Title IX to have all the federal aid to the Cedar Rapids public schools withheld until the situation was corrected. That got some action. There was a coach by the name of Tom Ecker, whose claim to fame was that he'd written an article for a national magazine on Russian women athletes, saying they were all just men, or women pumped up with men's hormones. That is the reason they had done so well. Since nobody publishes much in Cedar Rapids, Iowa, this article made Ecker a celebrity. He was the coach sent to negotiate with us. He was so upset at the possibility of equality for women that the veins on his face would pop and he would scream epithets down four flights of stairs as we were leaving negotiation meetings. Eventually we were able to meet with a committee of other coaches who had some modicum of maturity. We hammered out a deal for equitable athletics. The deal was written so that the schools could take full credit for the plan that we came up with. That was a common tactic then as now. We got a lot more done than we'll ever get credit for, but credit is something you can trade. You don't care what history says if the important thing is to get the girls a place to play tennis off the street before they get hit.

Then, as now, there was the battle with the textbooks. We had every mother or everyone with an access to one of these books go through the books. This was really great because it involved blue-collar women in a white-collar project. They were pleased about that and it made them grow in confidence. I don't mean to be patronizing, but they came with a new eye to those textbooks and could find things that the rest of us had skipped right over. Then we would raise heck with the schools about that. In the lower grades it was mostly a matter of sex-role stereotyping. In secondary schools, it related to sins of omissions. My God, you would think men were born by spontaneous generation and carried on all of human history by themselves. There just weren't any women there.

What good did all this do? Who knows how much a child is influenced by the pictures of stay-home mothers in the textbooks?

MITCHELL, 1990. *"This movement never stops. It rises and subsides, just like waves and, like waves, it erodes what it cannot smash."*

There were absolutely no working mothers in any school materials, when half of the mothers worked outside the home. That situation has now changed. Unfortunately we weren't being watched in how we got things done by the ecology people or other good folks. We were being watched by people who I feel have to be called neo-Nazis. So now we have this business with "creation-science" and all that, and textbooks have become so sterile. I feel bad about that. I never thought our example would be copied by such awful people. There is a vital difference between our demands and those of the right wing. All we wanted, then and now, is for textbooks to reflect reality, such as the actual number of working mothers, women in history, and nontraditional families. Textbooks were distorting reality—a form of lying—to keep the patriarchy in place.

We were more successful in the media. Just by a fluke, we had some influence over television that was way out of proportion to our numbers. Through Kathy Gurvey, one of our members, I got a job at Frank Magid Associates, the leading opinion and attitude research firm in the United States specializing in the media. My job was doing quality control in market research. Carol Dillard, another caucus member, was an analyst in the same department. Over time we recruited more friends and at one time there were twelve of us working there. We did a lot of market research testing for evening prime-time programs, so we were able to influence a lot of the images of women portrayed in the media. For instance, it was upon our suggestion that the Bionic Woman was tested as a viable program of its own. On every market the company went into we would ask, "Why don't you test a woman in that market?" Our very presence made them more sensitive—sensitive is a complimentary word—more anxious to exploit this new dimension of society.

Our influence would permeate every study but we were not always successful. The Mormon Church hired us to do a study on how to take over the world. I am not kidding. It was one of our few studies that was international. It was done in fourteen countries including the United States. I remember working on that study and feeling like a Jew or socialist or homosexual working on the Nazi party *Times*. We came up with fourteen recommendations including drop the tithing, and drop all talk of polygamy. I hadn't taken into account that there were people in the church who really believed this stuff. Spencer Kimball, the head of the church, read these fourteen recommendation and just flipped. They did exactly the opposite of our recommendations. I believe the tithe now is increased and polygamy started to be emphasized again. We used to kid that we should have put our recommendation on gold plates and buried them in Kimball's back yard. Then he would have found them believable.

Membership in our group reached to about one hundred fifty. We met in members' homes, which was a fabulous system. You got to know people, formed a bond, and no one cared what your home was like. We tried to make every meeting self-contained so that you could go to a meeting, get involved in a project, and you could come back when you and the other people who had said, "Yes, we'd like to take care of that, too," had finished taking care of it. Each meeting was its own little episode and you didn't feel like you were getting in the middle of a soap opera. For example, someone might have a personal problem, like her ex-husband is harrassing her. Someone else might say, "I think male managers in my place are being paid more than I am." On every local issue we would ask, "Who wants to help her?" Then there would be people who would bring their material from Women's Equity Action League (WEAL), NOW petitions, or other national things to be a part of. We actually had enough enthusiasm to sustain all this.

We had a very active speakers bureau and we got a lot of members from that. That was a wild and wooly time of life. Sally Madden was a diminutive woman who hated public speaking although she was excellent at it. She is one of the few people I've seen who hate something and be so good. One night she was speaking to some men's group, it may have been the Shriners, and she was shaking like a leaf. The men had been drinking and they almost rushed the stage. I don't know what they were going to do with her. After that experience we developed a policy that we didn't speak to men's groups when alcohol was served.

I'll never forget the panel on a variety of feminist concerns that we had for Washington High School Issues Day. It included a minister's wife who was becoming a minister herself, and several other professional women including a woman named Charlene who was a printer's apprentice or something like that. The students were up on the bleachers and these women on the panel were buried in a barrage of vegetables thrown from the bleachers. It was like the Roman arena, but nothing that dignified. The savior of that day was Charlene who had the good sense to just reach over and grab a carrot and start nibbling. That kind of diffused the situation.

Why were the students so hostile? First of all, the physical arrangements were horrid for such volatile issues. Because so many students signed up for our presentation it was held amphitheater-style in the gym. The panel was seated in the "pit" with packed raised bleachers of students all around. This setup brought out the worst in the Romans and still works its magic at soccer matches and show trials worldwide. Second, a number of male faculty and administration were themselves very threatened by the women's movement. During the weeks preceding our appearance they were publicly insulting to female teachers and students who were caucus members and thus tacit approval was given for what was to come. Contrary to school policy, the ringleaders never were punished. If I remember correctly they were just quietly lectured in private. Though we never again had an experience like Issues Day—we made sure of that—we did continue high school speaking engagements.

The worst groups to talk to were men and sororities made up of women who never got to go to college and who apparently felt that what they had missed most was belonging to a real sorority, so they formed these little business sororities. They treated our people awfully. Two of our prettier members from very wealthy backgrounds, just the type of women the small "s" sororities sought to emulate, were forced to sit on the floor on one speaking engagement. They were not offered a chair, and here they were in short skirts, high heels and hose, and they had to sit cross-legged on the floor. When everyone else was served dessert, they weren't served anything. People who invited us to speak often looked at us as freaks who were there to be looked at and have their prejudices confirmed. So we developed a thing called the "token lovelies," two squads of women that were outstandingly good-looking. Those were the ones that we sent to all men's groups and those ersatz sororities. This was awfully sexist of us, but sometimes it was whatever works. They were always the first troops to hit the beach. At least the audience came away with, "My God, you know, these women are not as freaky as I thought." Hopefully, that allowed the message to be heard. I don't know that I would do the same thing today. It's an awfully tawdry thing to do, but we were desperately pushing for the Equal Rights Amendment.

We also started *Lilith Speaks,* a newsletter which is still going. I edited it for six years, then I left, and now I've been back since 1989. Early on we decided on a policy that we would print the truth, name names, whatever. The only difference between *Lilith* now and then is that once in a while now I will have an attorney look at it before I send it out. You don't realize how much the press is not the press until you sit down and write a newsletter that's full of the truth.

We were probably the first mainstream feminists to organize in Iowa but I think Iowa City had some groups before we got going. There were twelve women there who lived collectively in a house, one of whom worked. They called themselves the Amazon Women's Collective, or something of the kind. They were Marxist-Leninists and their newsletter was called *Ain't I a Woman.* They scared the devil out of most of our members. To this day, the two groups have had a hard time interacting. When it came to things like picketing a factory which was about to lay off all its women employees, we thought, "Hey, here are those Marxist-Leninists. They would be just wonderful to help." Nope! We couldn't even get help from them because they said we were helping perpetuate an evil system by being reformist. So it was funny. We couldn't get help from the lower class because they were afraid of losing their jobs, or the middle class because they feared embarrassment, and the communists wouldn't help us either.

In about 1973 national NOW wanted to prevent an anti-ERA woman from forming a chapter in Cedar Rapids so they asked us if we wouldn't consider becoming an affiliate. As a favor, we agreed to do so. That is how we became the Cedar Rapids Women's Caucus NOW. We were the only chapter in the country that was allowed to keep its name. I think that becoming an affiliate of NOW may have been a bad thing for our productivity. In our productive period there were no officers. Each meeting was self-contained. We didn't raise money unless we needed it. NOW insists that you have to have officers, so we just drew straws and put names on the forms. In the last ten years, however, there has been a gradual change of attitude. We now have people who seriously campaign for office and somewhere along the line, NOW brought us into line on our name. We had to be just Cedar Rapids NOW. This was a name we resisted because the local acronym was CROW.

We used to have a lot of Catholic members, some of whom were against abortion. Even after becoming a NOW chapter we were able to do that because we kept a two-tiered membership. You could belong to the local and not the national and be assured that no part of your dues was going toward abortion. Abortion was about fifteenth on our list of priorities. We didn't think there was a chance in hell of getting that in the near future. This was before *Roe v. Wade* was decided. Our number one priority was economic equity, and it still is. As a matter of fact, economic equality is prochoice in the purest form. Most women who give up babies for adoption do so because they lack the money to bear and keep a child in at least middle-class standards. Well, gradually, national NOW got so domineering that according to them, there is just no room in the feminist movement for women who do not believe in abortion. I think this is a tragedy. Our priorities have been set for us and we are divided.

Right now our chapter is involved in a brouhaha which has gotten a lot of press over Gary Fisher, the optometrist in Monticello who also has an office in Marion [a suburb of Cedar Rapids]. Until 1977 Fisher was doing eye exams with the patient nude from the waist up, checking for scoliosis. These exams were confined almost exclusively to women and were usually done with no one else in the room. Eventually, in 1987, six of Fisher's female patients, ages seventeen to mid-twenties, filed a complaint with the state optometry board. This board voted unanimously that Fisher had done nothing wrong. At his request the testimony was sealed. One of our NOW members who had been on another state board said, "Our board once voted unanimously to censure someone affecting their license. What turned us around was that the person we voted to censure threatened to sue each of us individually for millions of dollars. There is no insurance protection for board members. We met again within a week and voted unanimously the other way." That gave us an idea. One of our members was assigned to put a letter in the *Cedar Rapids Gazette* encouraging all women who might have this nude eye examination in the future to be sure to sue the individual members of the Board of Optometrists if they felt they had been violated. The board met within two weeks and made the strangest ruling I have ever seen. Without reopening the case, they altered their verdict and sort of issued the equivalent of a cease-and-desist order: "Don't do it any more." Fisher is appealing this ruling. [The appeal was denied in 1991.]

Our position deals with more than this quirky "holistic" optometrist, who also owned a tanning parlor. It addresses the long-standing professional sexual abuse of women. We believe nude exams should be the province of MDs, where malpractice insurance provides a deep pocket for abuses and the AMA mandates nurses in attendance. The exception, of course, would be chiropractic and massage therapy where the patient logically expects to be disrobed. But women should not be subjected to requests for gratuitous nude or seminude exams within what their members call the "independent" health professions where malpractice insurance does not cover procedures outside the scope of their professions.

As far as the future of the women's movement is concerned, I think it has to hold steady at the moment. I'm especially anxious to get back to enforcing the employment laws that we have and putting some of them back that have been gutted in the last ten years. I think the movement will definitely rise again in the sense of fervor because we're going through a period of materialism and ultimately materialism is a dead end. My generation were children of materialism and I look forward to working with the kind of women that these little yuppie high school girls raise. They will be angry with their fathers for being such shallow sexists in a subtle way and so furious with them and their mothers for being vapid and materialistic, and so starved for meaning in their lives that they will come in and help finish another big segment of our work. This movement never stops. It rises and subsides, just like waves and, like waves, it erodes what it cannot smash.

Ruth Cotter Scharnau

is a Dubuque resident who teaches in the
Galena, Illinois, school system. She is a charter
member of the Dubuque chapter of NOW. She
and her husband, Ralph, took part in the first
gay rights demonstration in Dubuque, where a
hostile crowd pelted them with eggs.

*"As we walked to the rally I was so
scared I was shaking. There were
hecklers and crowds of people
laughing among the onlookers. But a
strange thing came over me. It
empowered me. I thought, 'You jerks,
you stupid, ignorant people.'"*

I was born in Waukesha, Wisconsin, in the worst year of
the Depression. I was the third child of a seven-child family. My dad
was a police officer and my mother was a homemaker. I went to
Catholic schools. Even though people make disparaging remarks
about nuns, I think they were very strong women in lots of ways.
After I got out of high school I started doing stenographic work,
which I found to be very boring. I didn't have very high self-esteem
but I thought I was brighter than just to be sitting at a typewriter all
day. I decided that I would try the University of Wisconsin. I was
twenty years old, a unique age for a college freshman at that time.
My folks didn't have much money but my brother said, "Go for a
semester and see how you like it." I liked it. I worked part-time and I
was able to make it for the first semester so I decided to go for a year.
Then I thought, "That wasn't bad at all. I might as well go for two
years." I ended up going all four years. During my college years I
was kind of rebellious in a way that other women were not. At least
the ones I knew were not questioning things. I began to question

Catholicism in a big way and decided to leave the church.

In the fifties, you were destined to be a nurse or a teacher if you were a college-educated woman. I knew no women who were going into anything else. So I thought, "I like children. I'll go into teaching." Then I took education courses for one semester and decided, "I will dig ditches before I'll continue in these courses. They are insulting to my intelligence. They are so stupid." For instance, one course, entitled Education in a Democratic Society, which could be very exciting and meaningful, was garbage. I wanted to be an elementary schoolteacher but I thought, "I won't put up with those courses for four years." At the end of my sophomore year I decided to go into speech therapy. This field permitted me to be a teacher and relieved me of the requirement of taking a lot of education courses. That is a back-door way of choosing a major.

I graduated when I was twenty-four. Then I led some bicycle trips for American Youth Hostels for a few years during the summer, one in Vermont and Massachusetts and one in Europe. This was in the fifties and people thought I was absolutely out of my mind. Why would a woman alone do something like this? Well, it was wonderful. I was doing things that were nontraditional but there was no label. I had no role models. I was just doing it. I wanted to do what I was interested in.

As far back as I can remember I thought, "I don't know why young girls and women want to get married so soon." I know now that I felt that way because my parents had such a struggle in their marriage. I didn't marry until I was almost twenty-eight and, miraculously, I am still married almost thirty years later.

I think I was a feminist before I knew it. I'm sure that happens to most women. I wasn't active in any organization other than the League of Women Voters but I had a sense that things just weren't fair. I knew that my mother had a rough time. She used to say, "It's a man's world." She would say, "Married you can always get," and, "Marriage is not all peaches and cream. Remember the wedding day is only one day and the honeymoon is soon over." But she would never explain why she thought it was a man's world or why she felt the way she did. So I had some of these feelings.

The Feminine Mystique was published in 1963 when my daughter was very little. At the time we were living in graduate student housing at Northern Illinois University in DeKalb where my husband was working for his Ph.D. A woman in our dorm kept urging me to read the book and I just wouldn't. I knew that it would open a Pandora's box and I was afraid I would never be able to close it. Of course you heard things on television and read about events in

Iowa NOW group at ERA march in Washington, D.C., 1978. (*From left*) Keith and RUTH SCHARNAU, Liz Starleaf in hat. *"There was a huge national ERA march and rally in Washington, D.C. My husband and I went with our three children."*

newspapers and periodicals, things that were happening in the cities, but I always thought, "They are so radical." I bought the line of the media, as I am sure many women do. It wasn't until we moved to Dubuque in 1970, when Andrea was eight years old, that I became involved in the women's movement.

One day in the fall of 1972 my husband, who teaches history at Dubuque University, came home and said, "There's going to be a panel tonight at the university on women's liberation. A couple of professors and a couple of women from town will speak." I decided to go and find out what "those girls" were up to. I don't remember specifically what they said, but they piqued my interest. There were about twenty-five people there and some of us started talking afterwards. Then we went out for coffee and talked some more. One of the women, Susan Gorrell, said, "Why don't we meet again next week? I'm tired and it's late and I need to go to work in the morning." So for months we would meet each week at the university. Nobody would bring food. We would have cokes from a pop machine in the building. We would start at seven o'clock and continue our meeting until midnight or even one in the morning. There were maybe eight of us. At first we did not have a set program. As far as I knew we were just getting together and talking. Susan was careful not to call it a CR [consciousness-raising] group although that was what it really was. I think this was a way of keeping people who might have been afraid of the term. It prevented us from marching away too soon.

Susan eventually said, "We are such a cohesive group and we've got some good thoughts, why don't we call ourselves an organization?" So we called ourselves the Feminine Equality Movement of Dubuque. I laugh when I think about that now. I don't know how long it took, but Susan's next step was to say, "Why don't we affiliate with a national organization?" She brought literature about the National Organization for Women and we said, "Sure, why not?" So we began to meet as a NOW chapter in early 1973 and we received a charter in early 1974. From then on we became very active.

There was a flurry of activity and new enthusiasm. We were a cohesive group of women mainly in our late twenties and thirties. At that time I was about thirty-nine and the oldest person in the group. We were considered really radical in Dubuque. One action that was radical in 1974 was to call the various elementary schools and ask them why they didn't have girls on the school patrol. I remember when Pat Bennett, the president of our chapter, called William Watters, the principal of one school, about using girls on the patrol. He said, "That's not a job for girls." Pat said, "Why not?" Watters replied, "It's too cold out there. Girls have got their jobs; they wipe the tables after lunch and take care of the kindergarten children once in a while." Very stereotypical jobs, of course. Pat replied, "But Mr. Watters, I've seen children out waiting for the school bus. I'm going to have to call their parents and warn them that it's too cold for their children. I've also seen girls walking to school and that is not good for them. You are probably right, girls should not be on the patrol." She was being very sarcastic and, of course, Mr. Watters didn't like that at all. Our survey showed that there were very few schools that were allowing girls to be on the school patrol. We thought, "That's not fair. That is a very visible, responsible job." Somehow the press learned of our interest in the school patrols and that turned it around. They printed the fact that we were taking a survey and it didn't take long before school policies changed. By that time there were equal opportunity laws. These helped.

When Roxanne Conlin came to speak about the ERA in April 1974, she gave examples of the way children were treated in schools and how bad that was. I remember going up to her afterwards and saying, "You know, Ms. Conlin, the junior highs in our town require boys to take industrial arts and girls to take home economics." Without batting an eyelash, she said, "That is clearly illegal." There was a reporter standing nearby and he then began to ask her more about this situation. He also interviewed me and the president of our NOW chapter and contacted the equal education enforcement agency in Kansas City. Because of our actions the school board was forced to change its policy. Then, also in junior highs, they were having a boys' and a girls' entrance and we said, "Why separate them? They've got to learn to get along together in the world." Those were exciting days.

We had a women's health fair in 1974 as part of Women's Awareness Week, which was funded in part by the University of Dubuque. Several of the women in our group were students there and we were considered a student group. We had speakers come from Des Moines. That is when I met Irene Talbott (Tally). Rita Huber came from Cedar Rapids. Now I realize how very progressive this program was. The speakers talked about doing your own vaginal exam so that you could detect changes in the cervix. They also talked about menstrual extraction. At that time I didn't realize that this could mean an early abortion. Some of this was taking place before the Supreme Court ruled that abortion was legal or it might have been soon after the decision and abortions were still difficult to get. It was really exciting for those things to have happened.

In February 1977 we called a meeting on establishing a rape crisis line in Dubuque. Sixty to seventy-five people came. Kathy Stuart and Corinne Whitlatch from the Polk County Rape and Sexual Assault Care Center in Des Moines presented a slide show describing the operation of their center. Shortly after this we established a rape crisis line in Dubuque which was operated by volunteers for the next seven years. Meanwhile, in 1981 there was a really awful sexual assault here, where a young woman was raped and murdered by four men. A shocking thing like that will get people out of their lethargy in any community. We started meeting with people in social service agencies to see what could be done to strengthen our program. We also involved the police as advisors. It took a lot of pressure from lots of people—some men but mostly women—who pressed for a paid staff that could coordinate the rape crisis and sexual assault program. Finally, in 1984 a woman was hired, at first half time and later full time. The center still operates, thanks to the organizing of NOW and other women in the community.

Then there was Sandra Kirkbride who in 1986 put up a billboard that named the three co-chairs of NOW, Virginia Lins [later Lynns], Tamara Prenosil, and Linda Osterkamp, as "baby killers" because of NOW's prochoice stand on the abortion issue. This woman was very right-wing. She was on the fringes of the so-called right-to-life movement, but she must have had funding because she did not have money and billboards are very expensive. The day the billboard was put up the NOW women went there and held a press conference. They were upset but as time went on they decided just to ignore the affair, feeling sure that eventually the woman behind it would hang herself. There were lots of letters to the editor saying how awful it was that she did that, and the widespread response in the community against this action indicated how many people were truly prochoice but were afraid to say so. [Dubuque has a predominantly Catholic population.]

We worked very hard on the ERA. Jean Fagen (who now lives in New Orleans) and I organized a bus to Springfield, Illinois, in May of 1976 to help lobby the Illinois legislature for ratification of the national ERA. We had one full busload of mainly women, some of them from as far away as Mason City and Fort Dodge, but there were some men, too. We went to Peoria first where we stayed overnight. While we were there we campaigned in the malls and other shopping places, passing out information on the ERA and asking people to sign petitions and to influence their legislators. From Peoria we went on to Springfield where people from all over the Midwest were assembling. It was a very well organized affair. Our fourteen-year-old daughter, Andrea, reluctantly went along with us. At first she was excited but when she realized that there would be very few kids her age around, she thought, "This is for the birds." But it had an effect on her as a young adult. In 1980 we organized a bus trip to Chicago to campaign for the ERA. This time we were mainly women from the Dubuque area. It was a school bus because we couldn't afford anything more. These actions certainly gave one the feeling of being part of something bigger. Now these efforts seem futile [Illinois did not ratify the national ERA].

In 1978 there was a huge national ERA march and rally in Washington, D.C. My husband and I went with our three children. I was president of our NOW chapter at the time. We stayed at the William Penn House, a Quaker facility. When we got up on Sunday morning, the day of the march, I felt personally responsible for this event. Everyone was urged to wear white and as we went out for breakfast I saw lots of people in white. As we walked around the streets more and more people showed up with white on. It took us a long time to find the Iowa contingent because there was such a huge crowd. Andrea would have been sixteen, Keith fifteen, and Gregg twelve. I wish I had a picture of the three children marching at the front of the Iowa delegation, helping to hold the Iowa banner. Andrea was right up in front, raising her fist, just like other people. I thought, "She's going to be all right."

At that time I was very naive about people who are gay. I re-

Dubuque members of NOW march to meet the Galena chapter on Mississippi bridge for ERA rally, 1979. RUTH SCHARNAU and Keith on railing; behind banner (*from left*) Andrea Scharnau, Linda Knutson, Virginia Lins, Nancy Challed, Tricia Bowen, Ann Gindorff; Gregg Scharnau in front. *"We were considered really radical in Dubuque."*

member going to a regional NOW conference in Milwaukee sometime in the mid or late seventies with Irene Talbott from Des Moines and a woman from Cedar Rapids. I was state coordinator of NOW. One of the workshops was conducted by a woman whose name was Shepard Holderby. She was about thirty-five, a natural beauty, and very articulate. The workshop was titled Distributive Leadership and the thrust of Holderby's argument was that we need not be hierarchical like men's organizations or as patriarchy functions. She talked about having used this nonpatriarchal system in the lesbian task force in the NOW chapter in Denver. My first thought was, "They sound like they are really sharp." Then Holderby would say, "We did this," and "I did this," and I thought, "Isn't that nice of that straight woman to help those lesbian women." I had the stereotyped image of lesbians which, of course, is totally false. It was not until Holderby kept on using the first person in her talk that I realized that she was lesbian. Up until then I probably had not known that about half the women I was meeting throughout Iowa who were active in NOW were lesbians. Gradually, as I became more active and more enlightened, people would trust me with this information or in some way they would let me know they were lesbian.

The upshot of all that is, I just thank goodness for my involvement in NOW because our daughter, Andrea, is lesbian and she has had no difficulty in our immediate family. When Andrea was in high school she wasn't interested in boys at all. At first I attributed this to her extreme shyness. As she became more composed, she still didn't want to be around boys. They would ask her out, but she just didn't want to spend much time with them. Then she went to college (Earlham College in Indiana) and she would write about the difficulty she had with guys. I had the feeling that she was working up to telling me she was lesbian and wasn't sure how she could do it. I wrote to her and said, "Andrea, just remember it doesn't matter who you love. It's that you love someone." I was trying to give her an opening. Now we laugh, because she says that went right over her head. She thought I was still referring to men.

When Andrea was about twenty she told me that she is lesbian. She was real nervous about it but I just hugged her. It was a little harder for my husband but he, too, has been very accepting. Andrea lives in the D.C. area and when we go to Washington we stay with her and her housemates. Many of them are amazed because they say, "Andrea's parents come from Podunk Hollow, Iowa, and they are so accepting." Many of Andrea's friends are from so-called sophisticated East Coast cities and they are either told, "Don't come home with anybody," or, "Don't come home at all." I'm just so grateful for my involvement with the women's movement because when I was growing up I had a lot of homophobia.

There were two or three gay rights rallies in Dubuque, the first in the fall of 1988. Before the first one, Ralph and I had gone to see Andrea in connection with a conference Ralph attended. He said, "You know, Andrea, I don't think your mother and I are going to go to that demonstation in Dubuque. That's just asking for trouble." "But, Dad," Andrea replied, "you and Mom have gone to every other civil rights demonstration. Why wouldn't you go to this one?" After his return to Dubuque, Ralph said, "I'm going. Andrea convinced me." I replied, "I hate to think about it. It's going to be awful." But I went. The demonstration was held on a chilly, gray Saturday morning in September. Downtown Dubuque is usually dead on a Saturday, but as we drove nearer to where the rally was going to be held there was so much traffic, my heart just sank. I knew the crowd was not going to be supportive. We had to park blocks away and as we walked to the rally I was so scared I was shaking. There were hecklers and crowds of people laughing among the onlookers. But a strange thing came over me. It empowered me. I thought, "You jerks. You stupid, ignorant people." So we just walked together and went to the rally site. There were twenty or thirty of us. People came from Iowa City and Des Moines and I think a few from Madison. If it hadn't been for them there would have been only ten supporters from Dubuque. There were at least five or six hundred onlookers. During the speeches my husband felt as though someone had tapped him on the back. He turned around and found that someone had thrown an egg at him. He was the first one to receive anything. Then people began throwing eggs and even a few rocks. We all got hit. I felt emotionally like we were being stoned, but I also was empowered by it for some reason. There were some real mean-looking people around us, just real scary. So I just started taking pictures of them. They would give us the finger and I would say, "Do that again," and feign more picture taking. Then we marched around a few blocks but they shortened the demonstration because there was almost no police protection and people were yelling terrible things at us.

The next rally was held the following May. It was a beautiful day and people came in buses from Minneapolis, St. Paul, Chicago, Madison, Des Moines, and Iowa City. There were even a few people from New York City and Washington, D.C. There were more people from Dubuque. Six hundred people demonstrated and I was so excited about how wonderful it was I didn't have time to count. We received good media coverage. This time there was good police protection. The third rally had fewer people, maybe a hundred, but they didn't organize as heavily for that one.

Currently I'm teaching second grade special education classes in Galena. These are not retarded children. They are learning disabled, so I'm able to influence them by choosing things to read to them that present the sexes in a multicultural, nonsexist kind of way. I'm glad I can do that. Next week I'll go to the [1988] state Democratic convention, not because I like those things so much, but because the prochoice issue needs support and we need to be there. People know that I'm a feminist but I now feel accepted. Often, I can influence people because I don't come on too strong. I just do it quietly. I'll continue doing that kind of thing.

Deborah Nye is one of

the founders of the Emma Goldman Clinic, a feminist health center run by women in Iowa City. She worked at the clinic from its inception in January 1973 through June 1986. Deb is currently practicing law in Phoenix, Arizona.

"I always left the clinic feeling I had helped to empower some woman or many women, no matter what service I participated in. This feeling comes from doing what you believe in."

I grew up in a dynamic middle-class household in Cedar Rapids. My father, Frank Nye, was the associate editor of the *Cedar Rapids Gazette.* He was very active in public service organizations and as a public speaker. He also excelled in tennis, squash, and handball and was well known and regarded in our community. I was often reminded by people wherever we went that my father was a wonderful man and citizen. During my childhood he was an activist in Iowa's reapportionment campaign, frequently absenting himself from home in order to deliver persuasive speeches all over the state. Or he might be absent covering his main beat, the Iowa legislature and Iowa's state and national politicians. He was the dominant personality in our family.

There were interesting stories told about my father's grandparents. My great-grandfather, who engaged in various entrepreneurial enterprises was at one time mayor of Essex, Iowa. He left an interesting autobiography for his family. In it he described being on a trip to South Dakota in his youth and witnessing the sad and tragic surrender of Crazy Horse and his people. Just as interesting to me was a wonderful story about my great-grandmother, a published poet as well as mother of their twelve children. One day my great-grandfather jokingly remarked to a group of women, including his wife, who were organizing homecoming festivities for the young Essex men who had served in the "front line trenches" in World War I that the real trenches for men were on the domestic front. He said that he had been in one since he was twenty years old. My great-grandmother, obviously angry and hurt by the unnecessary verbal barb directed at her in front of their friends, composed a poem which she subsequently read from the speaker's podium at the homecoming celebration. I share a part of it because it expresses thoughts many women wish they have the courage to utter, although the poem may not stand as poetry today.

> We've played and worked together, 'neath the matrimonial tree,
> An' there's always been the places where we never could agree.
> It sometimes gave your tender and loving heart a wrench—
> But you've never been, my honey, in the first-line trench!
> You've never washed the dishes, nor given the kids a bath,
> In the time we've been a comin' down the well-worn path!
> You've never wiped the tears away when they got licked at school—
> You laughed and said,—"Well, then, be good! I never broke the rule!"

Of course the beauty of the story was that it was incorporated in my great-grandfather's autobiography as one of the points of education in his life. That's sort of the way my dad was, too. My father had been reared to believe men and women each had their respective places in the world. Nonetheless, he wasn't averse to listening and thinking about women's problems once they were pointed out to him, especially when these problems affected families, not just women.

My maternal grandfather ran away at age eleven from forced child labor in the coal mines of New York State and apprenticed himself to a jeweler in New York City. He eventually settled in Red Oak, Iowa, owning his own jewelry establishment on the town square. He met and fell in love with my grandmother, Lena Pilkington, when he hired her to work in the shop. Lena's mother was a midwife who had raised eight children by herself. Lena raised five children, including my mother.

My paternal grandfather, Franke Nye Sr., was an insurance salesman and an excellent tennis player. I don't know how he met his wife, Clara Swan, but I do know he died young leaving my grandmother a widow who needed to earn her own living. She took jobs here and there, working for many years as a housemother at

Grinnell College. I remember she liked to write poetry and eat Bavarian mints. After her death, among her papers, were writings longing for a better life for women like herself, who were widowed young, without a male protector, and with no real job opportunities even though they were educated.

My mother, Georgia Nye, was a witty, warm, and a strongly intelligent woman. When she was born prematurely, at seven months in 1912, she was kept alive by being incubated in a shoebox with hot bricks by her midwife grandmother. When I was growing up, Mother was a member of the Cedar Rapids school board. (She was the only woman on the board at the time she served.) She eventually served on Iowa's Higher Education Facilities Committee and the National School Board Association and was active in many civic service organizations such as the League of Women Voters. My mom battled feudal minds on issues such as letting pregnant high schoolers go to school and participate in extracurricular activities—in short, treating women like human beings in all contexts.

After she died I was going through old clippings and found a brief newspaper article which was very condescendingly written about her attempt at a school board meeting to break down the sexual barriers in certain sex-stereotyped classes. In that instance she was protesting against the policy that allowed only boys to take computer programming, while only girls could take data entry. The reporter noted the laughter that ensued among the men when she brought up the topic. Reading that clipping reminded me of how I was channeled by the same school system when I was in junior high into home economics, while my male contemporaries took industrial arts. When I walked by and saw the boys building furniture out of wood, I felt angry and left out because the one time in school I had worked with wood in an art class, I loved it.

My parents were a very loving couple and led their lives together as a team. Dad had very traditional notions of his role as male head of household, but we all realized that my mom had tremendous, if quiet, influence. My parents always encouraged their three daughters to finish college and to become employable, preferably by earning a teaching certificate (a traditional field for educated middle-class women).

It was well known in our family that as the third child I was to be the boy Father always wanted, and I tried to be the boy Dad wanted. Lord knows, I was a tomboy. My father always bemoaned, especially at the dinner table or sometimes outside the one full bathroom we had, that he was surrounded by a bunch of females. It always sounded pejorative to me. I was pretty certain my father felt outnumbered and uncomfortable for he said so repeatedly. He was, after all, a man's man. Locker rooms and smoked-filled political and newsrooms were his beat. That was probably the beginning of my feminism; it was a reaction to a well-meaning man's repeated joking about being surrounded by women. Nonetheless, I enjoyed the female atmosphere at our home, idolizing my near-perfect mother and creative oldest sister, and I could never understand what Dad was fussing about.

Since my father's news beat was Iowa politics, we were constantly being exposed in our home to state politicians. Some hung around to curry favor, others became my parents' good friends. These contacts led to my first ambition: I wanted to be the first woman president. Later I just wanted to be J. D. Salinger and write well.

As a result of speeches at home on participatory democracy, it was natural for me to want to exercise what I thought were my First Amendment rights at the first opportunity. That came in 1964 when I was fourteen and in my last year at McKinley Junior High School. At that time girls could only attend school in skirts and dresses. Culottes had become the rage in girls' fashion but were forbidden at school. I found them eminently practical, particularly for biking. At my parents' suggestions, I circulated several petitions, which only girls were allowed to sign and quickly got signatures from over 50 percent of the female student body, but to no avail. The principal was furious but refused to speak to me directly. We may have had the power to petition, but the petition had no power. It was ignored by the school administration. Instead, the principal sent the male student body president with his threat to kick me out of school. When I later witnessed the trouble the Tinker kids had in Des Moines when they tried to wear black armbands to school to protest the Vietnam War, I didn't feel so bad. Maybe culottes were just as threatening a symbol as black armbands. Black armbands protested war in another land; perhaps culottes were just a symbol of a quieter war about to begin at home—the war between the sexes.

Another major influence in my becoming a feminist must be attributed to my experience at Camp Hitaga, the Camp Fire Girls camp near Ely, Iowa, where I went every summer from 1957 to 1965 or 1966. I remember being profoundly influenced by the philosophy of my camp counselor, Lynda Jones. I spent two full summers at Hitaga under her influence, feeling as though I was playing Plato to her Socrates. She taught me many lessons about getting along, thinking of others, and taking life in stride in our artificial,

all-female society. During one of those summers, I talked to two girls
who had come to Hitaga by way of some social service program. I
listened intently to their rather matter-of-fact rendition of their father's sexual abuse (it was called incest then). Later, as an adult
working in the women's reproductive health movement, I came
across many such women who had similar tales, but this was the
first incest story I had ever heard. I was impressed that this was
such a deep secret in our society and I wondered how many other
girls it affected.

When I was in high school I dated a boy who didn't have his
driver's license. I used to drive when we went out on dates and my
father just couldn't stomach the arrangement; it was foreign to his
notion of how men and women behaved. My dad was steeped in the
differences of male/female culture and was very particular that everyone play their biologically assigned role. In this instance, it was
boys drive and they pick girls up, not the other way around. Boys
telephone girls, but girls do not telephone boys. This sort of thing. I
had a hard time catching on and accepting my dad's (to me phony)
barriers between boys and me. It put me off balance.

At age seventeen, in 1966, I became pregnant. This was before
there were any Planned Parenthoods or Emma Goldman abortion
clinics. At that time middle class girls who became pregnant were
whisked away to unwed mothers' homes to live in isolation and
shame (or so I perceived it) to await the birth of their illegitimate
child and then give it up for adoption. I had seen this happen to girls
in my high school who had become pregnant. My mortification over
being in such a predicament stemmed from a sense of disappointing
my parents, somehow humiliating them in their social circle. This
is what I surmised their reaction would be. In reality, I would never
know, because I never shared my predicament with them.

All I knew was that I didn't want to be pregnant. I didn't want to
be shipped off to some unknown destination away from family and
friends to be left alone to deal with the birth of a baby. I didn't want
to have a baby at all. Abortion was not really an option in my mind.
It was illegal in 1966, for one thing. For another thing, I had no idea
how to seek even an illegal one. Yet by some miracle and twist of
fate, I spoke to a local minister who was part of the clergy consulta-
tion network in Iowa and an abortion was arranged for me with my
consent. I didn't have the money or time to absent myself to Japan
or Sweden where abortion was legal, so only an illegal abortion was
available to me.

I was probably between six and seven weeks pregnant when I
drove with some adult friends to a small town in northern Missouri,

Emma Goldman Clinic at Iowa City, 1973, DEBORAH NYE
behind sign. *"A small group of women, ever changing in
identity, met . . . for the purpose of putting a clinic together . . .
which would encourage each woman's sense of empowerment
over her own life. . . . Our average age was twenty-four."*

the name of which I long ago forgot. There was a nice brown clap-
board house in a nice neighborhood with a D.O.'s shingle hanging
from it. The floors were polished oak and it had a nice Midwestern
feel. There were office staff (women) behind an old-fashioned
wooden reception bar. They expected me and ushered me into the
doctor's office. It was a large room with a bathroom off of it and
contained an old rolltop desk, various medical apparatuses, and an
exam table. I handed the doctor $300 in cash, which he didn't stop
to count. I was given what I now believe was valium intravenously
and I have no memory of the actual surgical procedure. I was
dressed when I woke up and was quickly ushered out while still
drowsy. I have very little impression of the doctor's personality but I
don't believe that I was put off by anything. I felt trust. I definitely
saw the doctor as a savior of sorts. It occurred to me and my companions that the whole town must have known about this doctor
from the various out-of-state license plates parked outside his office.
My guess is that he was receiving some kind of protection from the
town powers. When my parents found out that I had played hooky
(the one and only time), I got in trouble. I took the punishment
administered in good stride because I had achieved my goal and I
was alive.

This incident left an indelible impression on me about the way
men make laws concerning the most intimate decisions a woman
may ever have to make. I was aware that the overwhelming major-

ity, if not all, of the lawmakers in Iowa at that time were men. I resented the fact that the customs of the time prevented my access to birth control, and once pregnant, my choices were further limited to birthing and raising a child too early, or birthing and going through the heartbreak of giving up a child for adoption. I began to see that our culture did not adequately attend to women's needs. I suppose this was my first experiential perception of the male-dominant culture and how it deeply affected my life.

After high school I attended Grinnell College, and this is where I was when the new wave of feminism hit the nation in 1968. I enrolled in Grinnell's first feminist literature class and was exposed to Betty Friedan, Kate Millet, Germaine Greer, and Simone de Beauvoir among others. The class was small and experimental. Although I was reading these works for the first time (many of them were newly published), the basic ideas had been inside me like a gray fog. Reading these works gave form to this fog.

As a project for my feminist literature class I took an informal anonymous poll of the student body to determine how many women had had abortions. This was my first attempt to see the issue in its broader context. The replies were small and out of these there were only a handful who reported they had had an abortion. But when I multiplied the number of girls who reported having an abortion (a small percent of the actual number who had actually had one I suspect) times the approximate number of high schools and colleges in the country I projected that the number of women who had been forced to use illegal and underground methods of dealing with an unwanted pregnancy was *at least* in the tens or hundreds of thousands. In biology I wrote a term paper on the conception and implantation of the human embryo because I wanted a well-rounded picture of the issue.

One vivid memory of my college experience is the day that a group of students—the same people who previously had planned and executed the famous *Playboy* demonstration in the spring of 1969[1]—placed the Montreal Health Press's *Birth Control Handbook* under the door of every dorm room. It was, and still is, the best literature available on birth control methods. This was a radical move because the college did not offer birth control services nor were there any formal presentations given on the topic in the

---

1. A group of men and women removed their clothes at a meeting at the college addressed by a representative of *Playboy* magazine. This action was in protest of *Playboy*'s treatment of women as "lapdog female playthings with idealized proportions and their junior executive-on-the-way-up possessors."

dorms. Yet such information was desperately needed by the student population.

I had one memorable experience in obtaining birth control while in college. This was when I consulted a private physician in Grinnell. I had to listen to a prerequisite lecture before the doctor handed me my birth control pill prescription. He told me that I was ruining my chance to marry a doctor or a lawyer! Of course it never occurred to him that (1) I might not ever want to marry; (2) I might not want to marry a doctor or a lawyer; (3) I might become a doctor or a lawyer; (4) a man might want to marry me because I was the doctor or the lawyer; and mostly that (5) sex might be the means to sincere, healthy, shared intimacy rather than a means to a husband.

While I was in college I began to see strength in numbers. Until then I thought my experience was an isolated one. At graduation in 1971 I was chosen to be baccalaureate speaker largely because I had started private speech-making among my friends on feminist topics, and they thought it would add some flavor to the affair. I talked about the inequities between male and female students, yet it did not occur to me to speak of the failure of our system to address women's reproductive needs. As a result, I failed to speak honestly of the one real life experience I knew. For me, the topic was still taboo in a public setting.

After college I attended the University of Iowa College of Law. Law school in 1971 proved to be my second-most-radicalizing experience. Our class of one hundred eighty students had approximately twenty-five women. The second-year class had approximately fifteen women and the third year class had about five. It was my first total existential experience of being the "other." It didn't feel like anyone really wanted me there. The halls were lined with male portraits. The faculty and administration were 100 percent male. The textbooks had gratuitous examples with women's breast jokes thrown in as attention-getters. One professor's hypotheticals involved Mr. Smith and Miss Willing, along with Mr. Jones and Miss Shapen. Professors were constantly asking us what a "reasonable and prudent man" might do. We women students were assured, when one of us had the courage to ask, that these were generic terms, but in truth they arose at a time when only male landholders could sit on juries. Besides, any reasonable person knows that if you contemplate what a reasonable woman would do versus what a reasonable man might do in any given situation you might get a different answer. That is why the term *reasonable person* needed to be substituted.

I estimate that half of the women in my class identified with the feminist movement. It was enough to start making a difference. The core feminist group started meeting and formed what later became OWLS (Organization of Women Law Students and Staff). Prior to that, ad hoc groups met with professors in often stormy sessions to demand changes in attitudes and rhetoric. The group also perceived that if the system was to become humanized more women needed to be recruited. None of us were at law school through any recruitment programs. So our ad hoc group set up a recruitment program, which is today run in conjunction with the school's admissions office. Back in 1971–72 our representative was ridiculed by the then Dean of Admissions when she requested funds to help defray the group's expenses in visiting Iowa's various colleges in order to recruit more women students.

I left law school at the end of the first semester in January 1972 and didn't return until the following fall. (After completing the 1973–74 school year I again left school and did not return until 1986.) Meanwhile, along with several other women law students I found an outlet for my energy at the university's Women's Resource and Action Center (WRAC). A couple of these students became active in the ad hoc group which dealt with rape crisis issues; this group later became the Rape Victims' Advocacy Program (RVAP). In the fall of 1972 I was persuaded by Barb Yates to help her set up the legal self-help pleadings file at WRAC. The first day I accompanied her to WRAC I kept overhearing a group of women in an adjoining room who were discussing abortion, which was still illegal in Iowa.

Eventually I drifted into this group and began to work with them. They visited abortion facilities in states where abortion was legal and were now acting as a referral group for women who wanted abortions. They set up appointments primarily through a facility in New York City. Women could fly into New York City in the morning and return by late evening. Each of us would be on call for a specific period of time and whenever a call came in we would meet the people involved and discuss options. Since many came to us knowing what we did, we often referred them to New York. We referred five to eight women a week in this manner.

Also in the fall of 1972, another highly influential event occurred. Carol Downer, founder of the Los Angeles Feminist Women's Health Center, came to town and presented a reproductive self-help lecture. She spoke of her own experiences as a woman, a medical consumer, and a mother. She felt that control of her reproductivity resided solely in the hands of male doctors and legislators.

DEBORAH NYE, at the tenth anniversary of the clinic, 1983. *"I currently work as a lawyer in a large defense firm in Phoenix, but I am never able to reproduce the feeling I used to have when I left after a hard day's work at the Emma Goldman Clinic."*

She wanted women to reclaim their bodies and control of their reproductivity.

Ms. Downer promulgated a very revolutionary idea. She advocated women forming small cells (four to six women) termed "self-help groups." These women would meet regularly for group self-examinations in order to become familiar with one another's bodies. Once this familiarity was achieved, women would have an all-female group from which to seek support whenever confronted with unwanted pregnancy or any other obstetrical-gynecological issue. Included in this kit was a vaginal speculum and a menstrual extraction (ME) kit. The ME kit was simple. It was made out of a mason jar with a rubber stopper from which two tubes emerged. The tubing was approximately 4 mm in size. One tube was attached to a 50-cc syringe and had a device on it which allowed the tubing to be clamped off. When assembled, the syringe could be drawn back and the tubing clamped off to create suction in the jar. The other tube leading from the jar could then be placed into a woman's os (cervical opening) at the time when menstruation should occur, and the suction in the jar would extract the menses in a matter of a few minutes.

Two things could be accomplished by the kit. For women with painful menses, their bleeding could be reduced to a matter of minutes instead of days. Additionally, for women who had become pregnant, this could be a means to terminate pregnancy. This was before the days of the extremely sensitive home pregnancy tests. By extracting the menses a woman would never know for sure whether she was, in fact, pregnant.

I'm sure this sounds rather drastic, but it should be remembered that this was the beginning of the new feminism and it was at a time when abortion was strictly illegal in most states. Without a means to effectively control our reproductivity, most of us would always be in fear of an unwanted pregnancy. Ms. Downer wasn't just worried about the young single woman. She was just as concerned about married women, older women, victims of incest, and victims of rape, all of whom might someday be confronted with an unwanted pregnancy. She advocated the ME kit for every woman's bathroom as a woman-empowered answer to male legislators, rule makers, moralists, and the like. For those of us who wanted to control our reproductive destinies, this was a fantastic answer! (These kits, by the way, were readily adapted for use by the medical industry when abortion became legal. With refinements, they are still in use today.)

Within four or five months of joining the Abortion Referral Group and seeing the self-help presentation, the *Roe v. Wade* decision was handed down by the U.S. Supreme Court. By this time I had re-enrolled in law school and was continuing my activism at WRAC. I had gone back to school with a fervent idealistic notion that I would battle for women's rights, specifically the right to choose. Suddenly the decision I most wanted to see happen was decided once and for all (or so it seemed then).

When I heard the news about *Roe* on January 23, 1973, I literally danced with joy through the lounge at law school. I remember saying to my male friends, "Isn't this wonderful? Isn't this incredible?" No one thought much of it. One professor made an asinine comment about it not being a very important case because it dealt with such a narrow, relatively unimportant issue. So I headed across the river to WRAC. There, by some spontaneous magnetic pull, were many of the women I worked with in the Abortion Referral Group. We all gathered together, celebrating the moment, giggling and making toasts. We were naive and promptly telephoned local gynecologists to find out when they would be starting to offer abortion services so that we might stop referring Iowa women to New York and refer them to local doctors instead. That's when we got our first inkling of the terrible resistance there would be in the medical community to embracing this new option for women. The doctors we called were going to have none of it. They intended to exercise their half of the control granted by the Supreme Court's decision and continue to deny their skills to women in need.

Some of us formed a new group in order to explore ways to provide Iowa women with abortion services. We talked to gynecologists at the University Hospital and while it appeared that they might eventually provide these services, it was also clear they were going to be delayed while administrative and political details were being settled. Iowa's Planned Parenthood organizations wouldn't even consider offering abortion services in 1973. (This is a rather ironic twist in light of the fact that Planned Parenthood of Mid-Iowa has opened a clinic in Iowa City in competition with Emma Goldman despite numerous community requests that they not do so.) As a result, a small group of women, ever-changing in identity, met consistently between January 1973 and September 1973, for the purpose of putting a clinic together, which would not only provide abortion services, but also provide them in a distinctly feminist manner that would encourage each woman's sense of empowerment over her own life. This was to be done through woman-to-woman support and validation of choices and decisions each woman might make for herself.

Of course we had no real money to put into our venture and were driven by pure idealism. Our average age was twenty-four. Some of us were in college, some were not. Some had graduate degrees, and some were AFDC moms. Some women identified as lesbians, some were celibate, and some were with men. The banks laughed at us when we approached them for capital. Sometime in the spring of 1973 our plan jelled when one very brave committed woman, Roxie Tullis, purchased a furnished house for us at 715 Dodge Street with $5,000 down payment. This was money she had received from insurance proceeds after becoming a military widow. Four others of us (myself, Melissa Farley, Ginny Blair, and someone I can no longer remember) managed to cajole, coerce, or beg four older and more financially sound individuals into cosigning personal loans in the amount of approximately $1,000 each. One friend, Charlie Eastham, gave us some money he received at a speaking engagement. We also received a $500 grant, written by Barb Yates, from a socialist organization whose name I no longer remember. The clinic was capitalized for under $10,000 (all borrowed) and with lots of volunteer labor.

The house was purchased in May or June 1973. That same month Richard Winter, M.D., agreed to go to California to be trained in early pregnancy termination and then to return and work with us. One of our members, Robin Christenson, who had spent some time working in the Los Angeles Feminist Women's Health Center, passed along her knowledge and experience to the rest of us.

I spent the summer of 1973 doing things like painting, laying linoleum, cleaning, and scrubbing the house, all the while listening to the Watergate testimony which was going on before the Senate investigating committee. The clinic opened its doors on September 1, 1973.[2] It was the first clinic offering abortions in Iowa and one of the first clinics offering legal abortion in the Midwest. We were the fourth feminist clinic to open anywhere in the United States. The other three were all related to the Los Angeles Feminist Women's Health Center and were in California. Throughout the following decade many feminist clinics opened across the nation. In Iowa there were clinics at Cedar Rapids, Cedar Falls, and Ames. The Emma Goldman Clinic initiated and staffed for one year the Cedar Rapids clinic, which is the only other one of these clinics still in existence in Iowa.

Amazingly, the Emma Goldman Clinic remains one of the healthiest and strongest feminist clinics still active today. I attribute this largely to the staff's original commitment to remain financially independent of any government funding and to depend upon their own earnings. I also attribute it largely to excellent community sup-

---

2. The clinic was named after Emma Goldman (1869–1940), a Russian-born anarchist and supporter of women's rights. She was jailed in 1916 for violating laws that prohibited the distribution of birth control information.

port. In the beginning relations were rocky with physicians in town, but gradually relationships developed between the ob-gyn physician staff at the University Hospital which have cemented strong regard between the two institutions. The clinic owes a lot to those doctors who, over the years, have sacrificed their time and money in order to work with us. Most of the doctors who have worked with us have found our staff to be incredibly committed to their work and basically fun to work with because of our team approach.

The clinic is known primarily as an abortion service but it has also offered and continues to offer many more services. For one thing, the clinic involves itself heavily in community education on topics concerning women's health care. We often appear on radio and television public service shows and in public debates, not only on the abortion issue but also on issues having to do with pertinent health topics like toxic shock syndrome and AIDS. The clinic staff gives birth control education talks in the schools. For the last five years or so the clinic has donated "birth control kits" to local schools. These kits offer hands-on information about the various methods, their effectiveness, advantages and disadvantages, and techniques for use. There is no advocacy involved; it is simply informational for those students who need to know. I suspect it fills gaps left by many parents in the education of their children.

One of the clinic's more interesting services involved the prenatal care for women choosing to have home births. This service evolved out of the prenatal classes which were offered and lasted until about 1986. In this way the clinic was involved with helping to bring into life many babies—including my own daughter, Sophie, in 1984. Gynecology services were routinely offered over the years, including screening for sexually transmitted diseases, routine examinations, pregnancy testing and counseling, as well as AIDS testing and counseling.

The clinic prints informational brochures on numerous topics and our literature has been shipped to all fifty states and overseas. Probably the most popular booklet is the one on cervical caps. We were pioneers in bringing the cervical cap to the United States and successfully planned and participated in a FDA-approved study which ultimately led to its approval as a birth control method in this country.[3]

The clinic expanded in 1977 by purchasing the house next to our original building but it quickly outgrew the two buildings. My proudest accomplishment at the clinic was achieved in 1986 when

3. The FDA approved the cervical cap on May 23, 1988.

we were able to purchase a lovely office building near downtown Iowa City which was perfect for our needs. It used to be a pediatrics office and is large enough to house many exam rooms and offices for the staff.

Something that many people do not know, other than the women who have worked at "Emma's" (as the clinic became affectionately known among its workers and fondest supporters), is the way in which the clinic's organizational structure, maddening though it might be at times, served to empower the numerous women who served on Emma's staff. Most women left their work at the clinic affected in a most positive and strengthening way. At first the clinic operated on a consensus basis—everyone had to agree to a policy before it could go forward. Needless to say, one's political and compromising skills were tested to the limit! After the first four years, a more streamlined decision-making structure was superimposed, forming service committees and an executive committee. Subsequent changes have occurred as well, but there has always been a mutual respect between the co-workers allowing for a free flow of information and criticism, which primarily serves to strengthen the group's identity and purpose. This is not to say there has never been divisiveness and rancor, for this most certainly occurred. Mainly, though, working and making decisions together despite outside pressures to quit, including the 1978 fire-bombing of our building and the innumerable and inevitable picketers, only served to increase each woman's individual resolve and strengthen her individual political skills. Our constant group analysis of the personal, societal, and political forces which serve to oppress women had to sharpen each woman's awareness of her own private journey through life and the choices each of us is given. I saw many lives change in positive ways. Some women became aware, for the first time, of a new sexual identity, a new spirituality, or some other personal powers.

In my thirteen years at the clinic I worked with many different groups of women. Each group's identity remains solidly a part of me. Some were filled with angst and fervent political striving for justice. Some were spiritual, and others loving and fun. Our winter solstice holiday parties were often a reflection of the group's identity. I remember one where we all formed a human chain and danced the night away. Each group's efforts and policies left its imprint on the clinic's herstory. Of course, each individual woman left her imprint on those women using the clinic's services.

I left the clinic in 1986 to return to law school and finish my studies. I currently work as a lawyer in a large defense firm in Phoenix, but I am never able to reproduce the feeling I used to have when I left a hard day's work at the Emma Goldman Clinic. I always left the clinic feeling I had helped to empower some woman or many women, no matter what service I participated in, or whether I had only gone to staff meetings that day. This feeling comes from doing what you believe in.

Naomi Christensen,

a farm woman, came to her social activism through her association with the United Methodist Church. She is currently chair of the Iowa Commission on the Status of Women.

"The men at that meeting were saying, 'She wouldn't be a good candidate. She's so outspoken and she's very assertive and comes off strong.' I said, 'These are exactly the qualities that you look for in a man.' "

I live on a farm near Hastings in Mills County in southwest Iowa. I have two children, a son and a daughter. I grew up on a farm near Malvern, a town of about 1,500 (probably 1,200 now) in Mills County. To me that was a pretty big town. There were five girls in my family. I was kind of the tomboy of the family and worked out with my father all the time. My mother's parents had come over from Sweden and when Mother started to school she could only speak Swedish although she was born in this country. The other children ridiculed her and she had a hard time adjusting. By the time her sister started school they were speaking English at home instead of Swedish. Mother had only an eighth-grade education but she instilled in us the necessity of an education and being concerned about issues that were going on in the world.

I went to a one-room country school for eight years. There was one teacher and about thirty pupils. Although we went to the small Baptist church in Malvern, my first real association with people from town was when I went there to high school. Then I went to a church-related college in Sioux Falls, South Dakota, where I majored in speech and English. As soon as I graduated in 1956 I married Bob Christensen. We had both been active in 4-H as youngsters and I had first met him at the Iowa State Fair.

When we were married we went to live down at College Springs in Page County where Bob's family farmed. It was hard for Bob's mom to accept the fact that I would willingly drive a tractor and help with haying. She kind of resented it if she had to go out and drive the pickup when somebody was unloading hay. After we'd been married about eight years we moved to our present farm in Mills County, which we eventually bought. We have never had any hired help. I drive the tractor, disk and plow, and plant and harvest. I help take care of the cattle and the hogs. We have a herd of 150 Simmental cows, and we farrow-finish 2,000 head of hogs a year. We have 1,800 acres of row crop, half corn and half soybeans. I always walk through the fields and help clean up the beans—I mean cut the weeds out.

Do all this in addition to the housework? Yes, indeed. That is one of the things that's hard to understand. Sometimes I have been out in the field since five in the morning. We've eaten breakfast and taken a lunch to the field so that we could just keep rolling. Then you come in in the evening and you chore and sometimes you hit the house at 10:00 or 10:30 at night and then you have got to cook a meal. Bob can shower and pick up the paper and sit and read a little bit while I've got to get that meal on and and then I've got to do up the dishes. In addition, my father lived in our home for nine years. None of my sisters wanted to care for him. I hated to see him go into a rest home but finally we had to put Dad in a home for the last year before he died. He had Alzheimer's and we couldn't leave him alone.

When we were living in College Springs I don't remember that I did too much other than serving as the 4-H leader and going to church. But when we moved to Mills County it wasn't long before I was asked to be a district officer in the United Methodist women's organization. Right from the beginning they stressed social issues a lot at meetings on both the district and conference level. Then I began to go to state meetings and to the national assembly. The first assembly I attended for the United Methodist Women was in Houston. There were ten thousand women there. This was in the late sixties when the Vietnam War was an issue. They had some prominent speakers and issues of the day were discussed. I had been exposed to some of these issues at other conferences but this conference really got me caught with women's issues and concerns.

I moved from a district officer to a conference officer. Now I am serving as the director of the General Board of Global Ministries. There are forty-two women elected and twenty-three appointed from throughout the United States and the world. I've sat in on peace hearings and apartheid issues and also have gone to the UN. I went to a meeting of Methodist women in Zimbabwe in 1987 and spent two weeks there. There were women from nineteen different African countries. I found that the concerns of these women were the same as those of women the world around. Of course, we are a lot better off.

The church also gives you extensive training on women's issues such as the ERA, equal pay for equal work, and comparable worth. I've attended workshops on how to run for political office. The general board has a weekly bulletin on issues which gives action alerts. You can check whatever issues you are concerned with. I do calling on a state level and write to my legislators very often. Most of the general board meetings are out of state and I am gone from home about one hundred sixty-five days a year just for this work.

I worked hard about four years ago to get a woman elected bishop in the United Methodist Church. The men at that meeting were saying, "She wouldn't be a good candidate, she's so outspoken and she's very assertive and comes off strong." I said, "Those are exactly the qualities that you look for in a man." Some people said, "She's young. She will have time later." I replied, "No. If you don't take a firm stand for women now we are never going to get a toehold." The woman was elected after sixty-some ballots. It is terrible the toll that it takes on the woman who's running.

In 1977 I was picked as a farm woman to serve on the planning committee for the Iowa International Women's Year Conference in Des Moines. Beverly Everett was aware that I was doing family farm projects and that I was beginning to be interested in the ERA and other issues. She was a national commissioner of the International Women's Year celebration and I'm sure that's how my name got picked. I was very intimidated the first few meetings I went to. Jean Lloyd-Jones chaired the committee. She was very gracious and came over and talked to me but everyone seemed so knowledgeable I felt a little like a country hick. I was kind of overwhelmed by women such as Roxanne Conlin, Pat Geadelmann, Sue Follon, Jean Lloyd-Jones, Peg Anderson, and Beverly Everett. At first I was too scared to hardly say anything. It took me two or three meetings to begin to feel comfortable, although the women were always very open and made me feel good. I really felt a little bad when we had our farm workshop at the conference. We were supposed to make recommendations that would go into legislation. At the workshop we just put down ideas but didn't really write it in legislative form. When we got out to the big committee to begin to sell issues that

NAOMI CHRISTENSEN, 1991.
"Whatever happens now is not going to make a difference in my life, but I hope it is going to make a difference in the lives of my granddaughters some day."

would be in the platform I realized that we hadn't been very politically astute. I felt I was really a novice. It was not that the women treated you disrespectfully. I just had a lot to learn.

I remember the Iowa International Women's Year meeting as very exciting. I was excited about the ERA. I was excited about the whole prochoice issue and just everything that was moving at that time. I remember going to a workshop on comparable worth. I ran as a candidate to go to the national International Women's Year meeting in Houston, but I was not elected. I was not surprised. I did not have enough background. But in October I had a call from Bella Abzug saying that they felt that they needed representation of farm women and would I be willing to be a delegate at large. I was thrilled. I think Beverly Everett was responsible for this invitation.

The hotel where the Iowa delegation was staying in Houston was fully booked so I reserved a room at another hotel. But this hotel didn't honor my reservation and I went to at least five hotels trying to find a place to sleep. There were lots of other women in the same trap. We would group in cabs together and go from place to place. At the fifth hotel there was a room for me. There was a black woman in line behind me who was about to give up her search for a room and go home. I told her she was welcome to share my room, and so she decided to stay.

I served on a committee that talked on different issues and I spoke about the farm issues. One of the women who spoke was lesbian. We talked and questions were asked. It was my first opportunity to know a lesbian. I corresponded with her for several years after I got home and I began to reevaluate my whole judgmental attitude about people. I learned to accept people for their own worth and not to judge them by their lifestyles. It made me a much more loving and understanding person.

The Houston conference was very exciting, especially the leadership—Bella Abzug, Betty Ford, Rosalynn Carter, and Gloria Steinem. It was exciting seeing people of prominence and hearing the discussion and knowing there was an awareness and concern about women's issues. I thought we were going to conquer the world, that women were really making rapid advancement, and that things were going to go our way. The hard part was to come home and find that the news media had covered this as a meeting of wild-eyed radicals and bra burners.

From this conference on, it was always forward with women's issues for me. I got our church involved working on women's issues and I served as chairperson for Mills County in the Iowa ERA campaign in 1979–80. Kappie Spencer came from Des Moines and spent two days with us. She went from group to group which I had lined up. I can't believe how many she addressed. Then to think we didn't even carry the ERA in our county. That was a very big disappointment to me. I was disappointed in the whole process.

There is one very painful experience in my life that I am not proud of. This is when Bob and I agreed to head Jim Ross Lightfoot's campaign for Congress in 1984. Jim was a farm broadcaster down at KMA in Shenandoah and we had known him through 4-H and other activities. I thought that with Jim being a farm broadcaster it would be great to have somebody in Congress with knowledge about farm affairs. Suddenly, in the middle of his campaign, I realized that I hadn't talked to him about issues at all. I can't believe that I ever did this. But I found out he was ultra-ultraconservative, antichoice, and not any place where I am in the peace movement. I wanted to quit but my husband didn't think that was fair so I finished out [Lightfoot won]. It was a painful experience to realize that in politics you can't think about a single issue; you have to look at the broad spectrum.

In 1981 I was appointed to fill a vacancy on the Iowa Commission on the Status of Women. I credit my appointment to the commission's executive director, Sue Follon, whom I had known through United Methodist work, and also to the commission chair, Pat Geadelmann, whom I had met at the International Women's Year conference. The first commission meeting that I went to was a hearing on legislative priorities. People testified for several hours, issue after issue, and then we had to decide how we were going to prioritize our recommendations. It just kind of blew my mind. I felt like I would never be knowledgeable enough to serve on something

CHRISTENSEN presiding at the Iowa Women's Hall of Fame ceremonies, 1990. Photo courtesy of Iowa Commission on the Status of Women

like this. But other commissioners told me that the hardest thing they ever went through was the first public hearing. I am now serving my third term on the commission and have been chair the past three years.

I firmly believe that in time women will achieve equality but I hate to think that it is probably thirty or forty years down the road. Who is it that said, "Life ain't for me no crystal stairs"?[1] You just keep climbing. You just work at issues one step at a time. We have to encourage women to be mentors for each other and to talk about issues and help people to find out what the issues are where they are willing to serve in making changes. It is a slow process. I thought it was all going to happen in ten years and now I realize that it is not even happening in my lifetime. Whatever happens now is not going to make much difference in my life but I hope it is going to make a difference in the lives of my granddaughters some day.

---

1. "Life for me ain't been no crystal stair."—Langston Hughes

II Political Activists

Roxanne Conlin

Peg Anderson

Mary Louise Smith

Minnette Doderer

W HILE COMMUNITY ACTIVISTS were primarily interested in changing sexist societal attitudes and in establishing institutions to meet women's needs in the early 1970s, other feminists were more interested in the political arena, encouraging women to run for public office and working for legal equity for women. These women, for the most part, worked through the Iowa Women's Political Caucus.

Political activists Roxanne Conlin, Peg Anderson, and Mary Louise Smith were all associated with the caucus. Conlin organized the caucus in 1973 and served as its first president. Under her leadership the caucus became the largest and strongest in the United States. In 1982 Conlin ran for governor on the Democratic ticket. Although she was defeated, her candidacy marks the first time that a woman was nominated for this office by a major party in Iowa.

Peg Anderson, a Republican, was first active in the caucus in Cedar Falls and in 1975 she succeeded Conlin as president. In 1977 Anderson ran for mayor of Cedar Falls. She lost the election because of her association with the International Women's Year meeting, which supported a gay rights law. In 1980 Anderson headed the campaign for an Iowa ERA.

Mary Louise Smith, a leading Republican in Iowa and the nation, was a founding member of the caucus, thus giving support and encouragement to other Republicans who wanted to work for the political advancement of women. Smith, who has been active in Republican politics since 1948, served as chair of the National Republican Committee from 1974 to 1977. She is the only woman ever to hold this office.

Minnette Doderer has served in the Iowa legislature longer than any other woman and twice has been the Democratic candidate for lieutenant governor. Doderer's feminist consciousness grew with her increasing realization of how unfair the law often is as it affects women. She continues to be a leading feminist in the legislature.

117

Roxanne Conlin is the

name that immediately comes to the fore when you mention feminism in Iowa. A lawyer by profession, she likes being a leader rather than a follower and is not afraid to set her sights high, even to becoming the governor of Iowa. Conlin was instrumental in organizing the Iowa Women's Political Caucus in 1973 and served as its first president. She was the Democratic party's candidate for governor of Iowa in 1982. Conlin is currently president of the Association of Trial Lawyers of America. She practices law under the name of Roxanne Barton Conlin Law Firm, P.C.

"I love to win and I particularly love to win in areas where no person has gone before."

I grew up the oldest of six children in an Irish-Catholic family. I was born in South Dakota, lived in Nebraska for a time, then moved to Sioux City, then to Clinton, and then to Des Moines when I was fourteen. I think I was born a feminist. I can recall as a toddler exploring the idea of being a "cowboygirl" and also saying I was going to be a pilot. In fact, I had a number of careers that I felt qualified for when I was a person under the age of five. I'm sure my parents had a very great deal to do with my rejection of limitations.

I'm not sure how they did it. I wish that all parents could do for their children what my parents did for me.

I am sure that a part of that came from the fact that when my dad was in college he had a psychology course and one of the things that he was required to do was give somebody an IQ test. He gave the test to me. It came out that I had an enormous IQ but the teacher didn't believe him, so he brought me to class. I must have been two years old. I have some hazy recollection of this. He asked me the questions that he had asked me at home and he had me fit the pegs in the holes and the like. He got a good grade, I'm sure. From that point on they always treated me, as I try to treat my children, as though I was something very special and as though whatever limitations might apply to the rest of the world, they certainly could not possibly apply to me. I believed all that. Thank the Lord. I never accepted that there was any slot that I had to fill. I always expected that I would do what I wished to do.

I went to St. Joseph's Academy beginning with my freshman year in high school and didn't ever graduate from high school. At that time there was a program at Drake University where you could, by taking tests and having the permission of your high school principal, enter college at the conclusion of your junior year. I took the test and did very well. My mother persuaded Sister Mary Dennis, the principal of St. Joseph's Academy, to sign a piece of paper that permitted me to go to Drake, despite the fact that Sister Mary Dennis had very heavy objections to my leaving high school. When Sister Mary Dennis handed me the signed form she told me that there was no way in the world that I would be able to succeed at Drake at the age of sixteen and that she was not sure that she would accept me back at St. Joseph's Academy when I was required to return. The fact that she doubted me was at least partially responsible for my intensifying my efforts. I did, in fact, do very well at Drake and never had to come back on my hands and knees and seek readmittance to St. Joseph's. I wasted a lot of my life not liking Sister Mary Dennis.

The first time I ever thought about being a lawyer was when I was a sophomore in high school. A nun named Sister Katrine Johnston was appalled that I wanted to be a movie star. She was afraid that I might get on a bus—which I really intended to do—and go to Hollywood. She knew me well enough to think that I might actually do it and persuaded me that I ought to first go to law school and see whether I liked that. Law would give me an opportunity to use my flair for the dramatic and my brain at the same time. Sister Katrine, of course, never suggested that it might be hard for me to go to law school. I had been in an all-girl school and felt that merit alone would carry the day, and I was sorely disappointed. When I got to law school there were times when I really doubted the wisdom of having made that choice, but I don't doubt it anymore.

I completed my undergraduate course work in two years and went to Drake law school when I was nineteen. I was one of very few women. When I was admitted to law school the former dean, Dean Tollefson, still maintained enormous control over the school. He thought it was "cute" that I wanted to be a lawyer and he was my protector. Without him I was in the way of the current dean, Maurice B. Kirk, who seriously felt that women had no place in law school and felt that I, of all people, ought not be there. Unfortunately for lots of people, and certainly for me, Dean Tollefson died in the middle of the first semester of my freshman year.

When I was admitted to law school, I was told explicitly by three professors, professors who had power over me, that I was taking a place that could be held by a man and that I would certainly marry and have children and never practice law. The standards to which I was held were very different from the standards to which other students were held. There was a cut rule—you could only have three times the number of cuts as you had hours. I was the only person against whom that rule was ever enforced. It resulted in my having to drop a course and go to summer school while I was pregnant. I did that, which was a great surprise to the school.

In my first year there were huge classes, sixty or seventy people, which is not huge anymore, but it was then. This was in 1963. I soon learned that any case that had the word *sex* in it, I ought to prepare, because I was certain to be called on. I was a nineteen-year-old person in a society in which most people did not use the word sex. You did not say it aloud. Risqué people spelled it but nobody said it. So here I am, standing in front of sixty men talking about sex. It was embarrassing. If I were a blusher, I would certainly have blushed. What I did instead was do what I had to do, which was recite about sex. If it was a damage case, and it had to do with loss of potency and I had to talk about it, I learned to say *penis* and other words that were not in my vocabulary and were not even in the vocabulary of most of the people in the room. It was a different world then than it is now. It was terrifying. What it did for me, though it was not intended, was to make me understand very clearly the position of women in the law.

I married James in March of 1964, after having known him less than two weeks. I met him on a Friday, and we got our license to marry the following Monday. My parents, of course, had a stroke. So we put off our wedding for another week and a half. This didn't help them; they were still annoyed. But it turned out well. Then I got pregnant. So I began the second semester of my junior year pregnant, with morning sickness. Every morning about a quarter to ten I would have to walk out of Criminal Law and be sick. This pregnancy thing hadn't been done before. It made them very nervous.

It gave Maurice B. Kirk, however, some options that he didn't previously have. I was at Drake on full scholarship and all through the summer between my junior and senior year of law school I had not gotten approval of the scholarship. Approval had been virtually automatic up to that point. I kept calling the dean's office and asking why I hadn't gotten the written documentation that I needed to have. Each time the secretary would say to me, "He says it will be coming." When I called the secretary just a couple of days before school was to begin in the fall, she said, "You're not getting it." I said, "What do you mean?" She said, "He has disapproved your scholarship for your senior year of law school." The dean's timing was perfect. I had only two days to get enough money to pay my tuition and to buy my books. I went to Walter Fleuree, financial aid director of Drake, who had helped me in undergraduate school, and he was wonderful. Walter gave me a national student defense loan, on the spot, bless him. I also hocked my wedding ring. I couldn't wear it anyway because I was so pregnant. So when I showed up on the day school began, able to pay, I am sure the dean was very surprised and, no doubt, very distressed.

The first semester of my senior year, nobody called on me because they were afraid they would upset me and I would give birth in class. It was a lovely, relaxing semester. Jackie was due December 19, which was a Saturday, the day we got out for Christmas vacation, and if she had come on time I would have had two full weeks of Christmas vacation to recover. However, she was not born until January 2, and I was due back in class January 3. (Needless to say, this was not a planned pregnancy.) Finals were beginning January 10. During the five days I was in the hospital I would sit in the sitz bath and study property, and when I came back to school I brought that little doughnut-type thing that you sat on. I brought it with me to my finals. It was horrible.

I began working as a law clerk for Davis, Huebner, Johnson and Burt, a well-regarded, silk stocking law firm, in the second semester of my freshman year in law school. I continued to work for them as a law clerk until the second semester of my junior year when they fired me because I was pregnant. When that happened I went to Larry Scalise, a prominent trial lawyer and Democrat, and said,

"I'm pregnant but I have to eat." He gave me a job as a law clerk at which I worked until mid-December 1965, a few weeks before my daughter Jackie was born. I went back to Davis, Huebner, Johnson and Burt in February 1966 and remained there as a clerk until after my graduation in June. I then became a full-time associate with this firm.[1] They did the best they could. They represented railroads and insurance companies, and I was not comfortable there. I stayed for only a year and then became a deputy industrial commissioner for the State of Iowa.

By that time, I had become very active in politics. When I was in law school, I had run for and won the position of president of the Polk County Young Democrats. This was a big fight—lovely fight, actually. It was an enormous organization with a thousand members and we could put four hundred of them on the street. That is raw political power. It gave me the opportunity to assist and talk to candidates for statewide office, among them Harold Hughes, who was running for governor, and Larry Scalise, who was running for the office of attorney general.

When did I become an active feminist? Certainly in law school. I'm not sure I had all the words. I read Betty Friedan's *The Feminine Mystique* sometime after it was written, 1966 maybe, not immediately. I did not see it as relevant to my world and I'm sure that in those early years I was as guilty as any woman of accepting compliments like, "You think like a man," without comment. But I was uncomfortable. So I started looking at the literature and reading lots, everything I could get my hands on. *The Feminine Mystique* certainly had a lot of impact on me as it did on any number of women. It was not because of the way I had ever lived but was the way my mother lived. I was an activist, whatever I was, so obviously being a feminist meant that I would be an activist feminist.

I had my son, J.B., in 1968 and I quit working for a while because he was hard to carry. At that time I belonged to a bridge club and we talked about women's issues at club meetings. Mary Lou King, the spouse of a dentist, asked me if I wanted to come and talk to her adult Sunday school class. I said yes. I'm sure that this was the very first speech that I ever gave about the women's movement. It was a class of thirty or forty people and everything that I said to them was outrageous and offended them deeply. I couldn't quite get into my head why they were so angry with me. Oh, my goodness, they were angry. They ridiculed some of what I said. Mostly they

---

1. The Drake law school wouldn't let me interview for a job when I was pregnant. They also wouldn't send me to interviews because I was female.

ROXANNE CONLIN campaigning, 1982. *"So I talked to a
number of people about running for governor. Most people said,
'Don't run. Don't be silly. . . . It's a crazy idea,' which in my ears
says, 'Let's give this a try.'"* Photo by Chas Geer

were just angry. What I was suggesting was that men and women
are not equal in this society and that's wrong. It was such a surprise
to them.

Congress had passed the Equal Employment Opportunity Act
in 1964 and it went into effect in 1965. The first EEOC chair publicly said that he had no intention of enforcing the law with respect
to women. I had just become a lawyer and in this period I contacted
a woman named Sylvia Roberts, a Louisiana lawyer, who took the
Weeks case, the first employment rights case involving sex discrimination. I didn't help her in any way, just talked to her and knew
what was going on. I knew that built into the law was the option for
women attorneys to circumvent the EEOC and that lots of feminist
attorneys were going to do it. We set up a very informal network of
people who called one another periodically. In 1969 Attorney General Richard Turner, a Republican, hired me as assistant attorney
general for the State of Iowa and the first thing I did was to try the
first civil rights case, a race case, under the 1969 Iowa Civil Rights
Act. Boy, I was a bad lawyer. Fortunately I didn't lose the case.
Obviously no one could have lost it. Then there were lots of wom-

en's cases that came along and I tried them all. Of course, that's an easy way to get a better understanding of sex discrimination and its impact.

I remember going to Virginia Watkins's house in 1971 to talk about forming a chapter of the National Organization for Women. Louise Swartzwalder, a *Des Moines Register* reporter, drove me. There weren't very many people there. I was active in NOW for a few years, though less active after Karen DeCrow became national president in 1974. I was very uncomfortable with her and didn't think she was leading us in the direction that was healthful for us to go. I dropped my membership and didn't reinstitute it until the early eighties.

The National Women's Political Caucus held its first convention in Houston in February 1973. Ione Shadduck, director of women's athletics at Drake University, called and asked if I was going. I didn't know anything about it but I was able to get myself down to Houston. I was the only one from Iowa who could go.[2] I don't remember that it was a huge convention, but there was lots going on because it was a brand-new organization trying to form itself. I remember that's where I met congresswomen Shirley Chisholm, Barbara Jordan, and Bella Abzug; also Jill Ruckelshaus, whose husband headed the EPA under Nixon. I mean it was a heck of a time because there were so many wonderful people in the same room at the same time. But it was tough to write bylaws and to get this organization moving forward.

When I came back I got real busy and I didn't do anything about forming the Iowa Women's Political Caucus for a couple of months and then decided that I had to get on with it. Because I don't type, I sent a handwritten letter to everyone I could think of along with a map to my house. Lots of people came. We adopted some preliminary bylaws and we planned a state convention. This must have been about June. Between then and September, we put together a program. Jill Ruckelshaus was our luncheon speaker. Sissy Farenthold, a prominent Texas Democrat, spoke on Friday night. On Saturday we had concurrent workshops on every possible political subject. Then all day Sunday we tried to kill each other over the bylaws. It was wonderful fun. We planned for two hundred people and we had information packets for two hundred. I don't know how many came for sure; it was nearly a thousand. We got a wonderful article by Louise Swartzwalder right on the front page of the *Des*

---

2. Conlin is apparently unaware that Mary Lou Houston of Dubuque also attended this meeting.

CONLIN in Solon Beef Days parade, 1982. *"I just thought I was the people's candidate."*

Moines Register. That was a helluva thing. It was all so clear that this met a need. There were women who were feminists who wanted to learn how to do politics and there were political women who needed to understand feminism. We got them all together in a big room and they tried to kill each other but we ultimately formed a heck of an organization that was enormously effective. About the time of the convention, seventeen people who were either members of the state caucus or endorsed by their local caucuses—we had a dozen local caucuses by that time—ran for city council and sixteen of them won. Their success almost certainly had nothing to do with the Iowa Women's Political Caucus but, of course we took immediate public credit for it. It really got a lot of attention.

We passed a series of resolutions at the convention, things we wanted to do. A great number of those were passed by the Iowa legislature. They were easy because the the laws we attacked were so outrageous. One was elimination of the corroboration requirement in the crime of rape.[3] That was the first one that we undertook because the criminal code was in the process of being thoroughly revised. The committee had already passed a rape section. It retained a corroboration requirement and we went to the hearing. It wasn't even a public hearing, if I recall correctly—it was in Senate Room 1. Lots and lots of women came. Committee members were so surprised to see us. I had written testimony about the corroboration requirement. The first vote was against us and a reconsidera-

---

3. According to Iowa law there had to be evidence other than the testimony of the victim that she was connected to the crime.

tion vote was for us. This meant that the committee would recommend elimination of the corroboration requirement. One of the things that happened in connection with that was a very public fight with Gene Glenn, a senator from Ottumwa, whose work had been to do a total revision of the criminal code. Glenn said publicly and repeatedly that if we changed the law, he couldn't support his own bill, to which I said, "Well, tough." Ultimately that happened. As a result, Glenn was defeated by us in the next election. This was the first victory for the caucus, but we had a number of others.

When I was on the Iowa Commission on the Status of Women [1972–1977] we had the computer read the Iowa Code and pull out every section that had *man, woman, girl, boy, lady, gentleman* and then I wrote a bill based on eliminating all those sections. Some of them were substantive. There was a big quarrel over whether men could go to beauticians. This was illegal at the time. This was also very significant because we were able to generate so many calls into the senate over that issue. Brice Oakley [member of the Iowa Legislature 1973–1976] called me on the phone and said, "Would you call these people off?" I said, "No, I'm not calling these people off until we're done. Vote and then we'll be done." This was not a burning issue and it passed almost unanimously.

We were not as committed to the beautician/barber issue as to other issues in the code, including some changes in the way women were treated in the criminal justice system. A woman in this state could serve longer than a man for committing the same crime because women had indeterminate sentences. There were some very significant pieces of legislation but focus was on that barber/beautician thing, which was fine because nobody noticed the rest of it such as equalization of pensions. It seems to me the issues we were working on were: child care; sexual discrimination and the authority to deal with it in educational institutions; housing, insurance benefit systems, and retirement plans; in-home labor; welfare; rape and sexual assault; and child support [see Introduction, p.2].

There was one among these which we have not achieved to this day. It was fair treatment of people who are on welfare. A priority of the caucus, which was adopted at its very first convention, was to have welfare benefits be enough to live on. That still isn't so. We had some losses, and that is one that we just don't seem ever to be able to get fixed. I served as president of the caucus for two years and then I ran for national president and lost by three votes at the convention in Boston but I continued to be active in the caucus on the national as well as the state level.

Frank Comito, a former boyfriend, remembers that when I was

A farmer in Hancock County, near Klemme, supports CONLIN for governor, 1982. *"People would say, 'Do you really think that you can be elected governor of the state of Iowa as a woman?' I would say, 'Listen I want to be governor and I'm just going to have to do it as a woman. There aren't any other options.'"*

dating him at age fourteen, I told him I wanted to be governor someday. I don't remember that but it certainly became a part of the folklore. I do remember thinking that it would be nice to live in the Hubbell mansion. This was before it became the governor's home. After Jimmy Carter lost the election for president in 1981 I realized that I'd be out of a job. I was a United States attorney and U.S. attorneys serve at the pleasure of the president. I was quite certain I was not going to be very acceptable to Ronald Reagan. So I talked to a number of people about running for governor. Most people said, "Don't run. Don't be silly, you cannot possibly do this. It's a crazy idea," which in my ear says, "Let's give this a try." This is the way I meet a challenge. At the time I was thinking of this I didn't know that ten or twelve other people were also thinking about running for governor of the state of Iowa. Some, of course, ultimately did that, and I was one of them. At one point there were thirteen people in the race, and out of the thirteen I was ranked thirteenth by everybody I knew. I wasn't discouraged because I thought this would happen.

I knew that if I could go meet people and talk to them about my vision for the state of Iowa, that I could persuade them that I ought to be the governor. So that is what I set out doing. I worked as United States attorney and every day at 5 o'clock I would get in my car and I would drive myself to someplace where I knew somebody. I had long been active in the party and I knew the leadership. I knew somebody in every county. I had friends in Young Democrats who were then active in their county parties. I had feminist friends who were active. I knew law enforcement people. I also knew county sheriffs. I would ask them to get together a group of people and then I would go and I would say, "What do you think, should I run for governor?" And they would say, "No." Actually, they wouldn't say no, some of them would say, "Well, you understand that there will be a little problem." I said, "What will it be?" People would say, "Do you really think that you can be elected governor of the state of Iowa as a woman?" (This response got to be so predictable and so much fun.) I would say, "Listen, I want to be governor and I'm just going to have to do it as a woman. There just aren't any other options." There were also questions about my family and whether or not I had the expertise to conduct a campaign, all of that.

I visited all ninety-nine counties. I did it long before anybody else thought of doing it and I did it because I knew that if I did not go and personally meet people that there was no hope. That's held true for women candidates everywhere. It is necessary to get out and meet people and reassure them we can win. That's how I won the primary. About two hundred thousand people voted in the primary and I personally met fifty or sixty thousand of them. That is certainly a factor in losing the general election because you can't meet five hundred thousand people even if you try real hard, and I did.

This was enormous fun. I had the best time going to those little county meetings and talking directly to small groups of people about the future of this state and what we could do and what we couldn't do and what was good and what was bad. I'd spend two or three hours at those meetings, finish at 10 o'clock, get in my car, and drive myself home. I did that five nights a week and on the weekends I'd do two or three meetings. I never had a better time. I drove myself, too, which Jim Flansburg, political reporter for the *Des Moines Register*, ultimately persuaded me I could not continue to do.

That's how the campaign started. It started on a very direct one-on-one basis and the political pundits put me way down in the pack until the J.J. [Jefferson-Jackson Day] dinner in September of 1981, when they were terrifically surprised that I won the battle of the buttons. I was surprised, too. We had a little reception that turned into a big reception and it was all those people I had talked to in their living rooms. I won the primary.

There were two things that I did before I became a candidate. One was make my peace with losing, say to myself, If you lose, can you go on? Will this destroy you? Will you be able to build an alternate life? I was clear that I felt strong enough to do that, though I had no idea what I was getting into. Good Lord, I had no idea what

CONLIN, as president of the NOW Legal Defense and Education Fund, commenting on the progress of women's rights, 1986. *"We have made great gains, but we have not completed our task. It is still true that a woman college graduate will not earn in her entire lifetime as much as a man with an eighth-grade education."*

this would be like. I was so innocent of information and knowledge. The second thing that I did, which I think every candidate must do, was to look at my background. I said to myself, What have you ever done? Have you ever committed a crime? Have you lied? Have you cheated? Have you stolen? What have you ever done that someone could use against you? The answer to that question was absolutely nothing. I thought I couldn't be attacked in any way on the basis of my background. I truly did. Shows you what I know. No one was more surprised about the tax situation than I was.

I promised in the course of the primary that I would release my tax information but the forms had not been completed. Because of my husband's business interests, it always takes us a really long time to do our taxes. I knew he was rich. I knew how he got rich. We started with nothing and he made sound investments. He worked real hard and he painted those apartment units himself at 10 o'clock at night and took lots of risks. There were times when we were extremely needy but we walked this path together. He was very economically successful. I know that part. I loved it. I still love it. All of his investments were in real estate. He made his living as a real estate agent. Nineteen eighty-one was a really bad year for real estate. James wasn't the only one who lost lots of money that year. I did not release my tax returns because James was involved in a number of limited partnerships, and in a number of corporations, and to release the tax returns would have exposed the private financial affairs of great numbers of people who were not running for governor. So what I released was all the data. The data showed that we had only paid $3,000 or thereabouts in federal taxes and owed no state taxes because of federal deductability. Frankly, I've always opposed federal deductabilty. In the primary I had already produced a plan for tax reform. I'm not sure anybody ever heard about this, though I did talk about it periodically. So I owed no state income tax. When that came to me, I looked at it and I said, Boy, this could be a terrible problem. What shall I do? I could send in money, jiggle those figures and nobody would ever notice. Pretty soon the government would send it back. None of the options seemed appropriate to me because I thought I could explain it. I thought I could say, Look, this is what happened. This was a bad year. We have a net worth of more than $2 million but net worth isn't income. That's bricks and mortar and you can't eat off of it. I don't have a job and eating has been kind of tough this year. I really thought that. I attribute what happened to a scurrilous press and to some particular people, David Yepsen, political reporter for the *Des Moines Register*, chief among them.

From the day on which I released my income report, which was July 1, until the middle of October, no article about me appeared in the *Des Moines Register* that didn't mention my taxes. Not one. I couldn't kill this sucker with a pole. I couldn't beat it to death with a club. There was nothing I could do. I have since looked at a couple of similar situations and I'm sure I handled it poorly. There are lots of things I would now do differently, that out of innocence and a great faith in the people of Iowa, I just didn't think I had to. I just thought I was the people's candidate. I had come out with the plan that would make this not happen anymore. None of that mattered. There are people now who think I cheated on my taxes. There are people who think that I almost went to jail. There's all kinds of strange stuff that makes me awfully uncomfortable but there is nothing I can do about it. Senator Nancy Kassebaum had the same situation in Kansas. It was one day in the media and that was all. Interestingly enough, Joan Growe, in Minnesota, who ran against David Durenberger for the Senate, had the opposite situation. Durenberger paid no taxes. The newspaper in Minneapolis, owned at the time by the same people who owned the *Des Moines Register*, editorialized against Joan Growe for making an issue out of it.

Something happened to me that had less to do with my economic situation than with my sex. One of the things I find significant is that no woman who approaches me on the street ever mentions my taxes. They say, "I love you, I voted for you, I worked for you, you lost because you are a woman." That's what every woman says. Men don't. They don't understand. They say, "Boy, that tax thing, that was terrible." I say, "Yes, it was." It had virtually nothing to do with my loss, but it was terrible. It seems to me as though women understand that what happened was desperately unfair. Men, even men of good faith, don't see it quite the same way.

I had other problems as well. Bill Knapp [prominent Democrat and real estate magnate] never supported me, never gave me a dime. The unions, the good old boys, couldn't turn out their people for me. Chuck Gifford [United Auto Workers activist] finally decided he would support me in August and immediately gave himself a heart attack over it and went to the hospital. There were all kinds of things that happened—the highest highs I've ever had and the lowest lows. There were times when I thought I could not get myself out of bed in the morning because people would say horrid things to me when I walked down the street. Someone tried to attack my daughter, Debbie, in a parade in Iowa City. Nobody told me about this until long after the election. The toll on my family was terrible. I've thought a lot about that. I was willing to take the risk. I was the candidate. I had made the choice. They made no choice. The only choice that was made was the choice my husband made to marry me.

In July 1988 I completed a two-year term as president of the NOW Legal Defense and Education Fund. Before that I was its general counsel and I'm still on the board of governors of that organization. I still serve on the advisory committee of the National Women's Political Caucus. Most of what I'm doing now is within the area of the law. I am the first woman ever to serve in office in the Association of Trial Lawyers of America. I was elected last year [1988] in a very hotly contested election to the office of parliamentarian. The tradition is that you start at the bottom of the offices and work up. This year I was elected secretary without opposition. Next year I will run for vice president and after that I'll run for president-elect. If I am ultimately successful, I will serve as president of the organization in 1992. [Conlin is currently president.]

We've done lots of things to improve the position of women lawyers within that organization. At the last board meeting, finally, we passed a resolution that all committees had to have women and minorities on them. That may not seem like a big deal until you look at this organization which is forty-five years old, and this is the "liberal bar." It has never had a woman officer. Over the last several years, we've been moving on many fronts. Continuing legal education is one of the principal functions of this group. We have passed a rule that says that no program is approved by the education department, which I headed for a couple of years, unless it includes women and minority speakers. We just send it back to them and say, "No, I'm terribly sorry, you'll have to look around and see if you can't find some woman and some minority who has knowledge of this." They go out, and sure enough, you can find them. They're there.

Do I still carry civil rights cases? I always carry about a dozen; women, blacks, and age discrimination cases. I have been doing this for twenty years and I know about the law, in part because some of it I made myself. I perceive that there are few lawyers available to take these cases. We get buried in them every now and then. They are emotionally wearing. They are horrible cases to try sometimes, but they are also very uplifting. I love it. I love to win and I particularly love to win in areas where no person has gone before. I will continue to take those cases as long as I draw a breath because I know that there are few lawyers who will take them or who can handle them.

In our law firm [Gilligan & Conlin, P.C.] we are exclusively plaintiffs' lawyers. We only represent people. We don't represent companies, we don't represent corporations, we don't do tax work, we don't do wills, we just represent people. Almost all of our work is on a contingency basis. If you need a lawyer, you come here and if we believe you have a cause of action, we will handle your lawsuit. You don't have to pay us any money. We'll even advance the costs and we'll expect to win. We mostly do win. Every now and then we don't, but we mostly win. We'll take the costs out of the recovery. There aren't very many law firms like that in Iowa. This is the way we built this law firm, so it would be accessible to anybody who had a good cause of action.

I also have developed another interest. I had a grave concern about the victims of crime and have developed a whole new area of legal specialty bringing civil lawsuits on behalf of crime victims against third parties who have created conditions causing or contributing to crime. I've written a long article about this and I have lots of cases, most of them are rape cases or child sexual abuse cases. Paulee Lipsman, a tiny, dark-haired young woman, is the perfect example. She was raped in September 1984 by an assailant who came through her apartment window, which was defective and about which she had complained—in writing—to her landlord on three separate occasions. The assailant was not caught and Paulee was emotionally devastated. Her damages were extraordinary. I know that the damages of most victims of rape are extraordinary. So we sued the landlord and we were successful. I've done that for many other rape victims. I'm very proud of that. I think that's a very important thing to do.

I go around the country speaking to bar associations on this subject because if women happen to make their way to a lawyer's office, the lawyer says, "Well, we don't want to sue the rapist, he doesn't have any money." They don't even think about what other options might be available to get compensation for the devastating injuries that these women suffer. I'm just an evangelist about that. I give a speech called, "Rape, Robbery and Murder: What Civil Trial Lawyers Can Do to Help the Victims of Crime." I've given it fifteen times in fifteen different states, and then I wrote this long article as well (Conlin 1987).

So those are some of the things I do. Other things I do are the things that you do, too. Young women call me on the phone and I give them interviews for their fifth-grade class on women in history. This makes me feel old. I send them things. Women call me and ask whether or not they ought to be lawyers. I've had friends of mine call and say will you have lunch with so-and-so because she's looking for an avenue to make a contribution. There is a lot of informal stuff like that which I think is just very important but it takes a lot of time. I get hand-printed letters from fourth, fifth, and sixth graders and we always respond no matter how much time it takes. It is important to me to pass the torch.

REFERENCE

Roxanne Barton Conlin, "Landlord Liability for Criminal Attack on Client," 35 *Am. Jur. Trials* (1987).

Peg Anderson, a

Republican, led the 1980 campaign for an Equal Rights Amendment to the Iowa Constitution. For want of a better term, Peg calls herself a "professional volunteer." She now lives in Tucson, Arizona. In 1991 she was elected to the executive council (the national governing board) of the Episcopal Church.

"I had a sense of wanting more freedom for myself, combined with this recognition that for the disadvantaged woman the women's movement was essential."

I now live in Tucson, Arizona, but formerly I lived in Cedar Falls and Bettendorf, Iowa. I was born in Chicago. Then my family moved to Evanston [just north of Chicago] and when I was in fourth grade they moved to Highland Park [another Chicago suburb, farther up the North Shore] where I went through high school. I had two younger sisters. Our father had a very good job but he made a lot of time for his daughters. He taught me to play baseball. I had a grandfather who took me to ball games. My mother and grandmother were real influences also, but unlike many girls I had a lot of attention from my father and grandfather.

I went to Smith College on a scholarship and graduated in the class of 1950. I am a strong supporter of Smith and of the experience of a women's college. One of my daughters also went to Smith. She was in the class of 1973. I followed the traditional pattern and got married right after graduation. Most of my classmates did that. When my prospective husband told me that he had a job with John

Deere in Waterloo, Iowa, I felt I was going to the end of the world. That was not exactly my choice of a place to live. But within a month or two after we settled in Waterloo, Karl was called back into service during the Korean War. So we took off and traveled around the country during those years. We had one child during that time. We got back to Waterloo in 1952, where our second child was born. Then we moved to Cedar Falls, where our other two children were born.

I wasn't active in community activities in the fifties because Karl's job took him away for three months every winter and I went with him. It's pretty hard to get very involved when you've got small children and you are traveling like we were. This was a period when I was just concentrating on raising my family and following my husband from place to place. I joined the AAUW [American Association of University Women] in Cedar Falls and that was my outside activity. I belonged to an education study group and a child study group. Some of the neatest people were in that child study group, Evelyn Wood, for instance, and Sally Pinkhem. However, all during that period I had the feeling that there's a world going on out there and I'm not part of it. I had been a government major in college and I was interested in what was going on, but there just wasn't time. With four children, two years apart, I was just concentrating on that.

In 1963 I read *The Feminine Mystique.* When I read that book I said, "That's me." I could feel it. Then we went to Germany for two years, from 1964 to 1966. That whole period relative to events in the United States is kind of blurred for me because I was out of the country. When I came back to Cedar Falls I started getting more involved. I was appointed to the Recreation Commission in Cedar Falls and I taught swimming in the Red Cross program.

From 1969 to 1977 I worked for the Episcopal Church in the urban ministry. Father Dahm, who hired me, said, "We would like to have a full-time black ordained man, but we can't afford that. We can afford a housewife as a half-time worker." I had an office in Christ Church in Waterloo, which was right on the edge of the black community, and I became very involved. I pretty much worked full time. My job was to look at the disadvantaged community and see what the needs were and what we could do to respond to them. We got involved in child care, in housing, in emergency counseling. People would come to my office for help in finding housing and food and that kind of thing. It was an eye-opening experience. I took the lead in putting together a nonprofit corporation made up of five churches and three community organizations to sponsor the Logandale Low Income Housing Project. When I say "I," I mean with some others, but I was really the only person who could work at it full time because the others all had their own jobs and careers. The church, by sponsoring me, gave me time to do that. It took us about two or three years to get the whole thing set up and to get the HUD [Federal Department of Housing and Urban Development] money to build it. Then I did the initial rent-up and hired the manager. It was mostly women with children who needed this kind of housing.

It was while working on the low-income housing project that I recognized that the women's movement was necessary to help poor women; that society really had dumped on them and that they were terribly at risk. That's when the women's movement kind of jelled for me. I had a sense of wanting more freedom for myself, combined with this recognition that for the disadvantaged woman, the women's movement was absolutely essential. That's when I really started getting involved in the women's movement. I also found myself caught up in the issue of ordination of women in the Episcopal Church. That was finally approved at the national church convention in 1976. I was elected as one of the four lay delegates from Iowa to that convention.

In 1971 I ran for the school board in Cedar Falls and won. I beat an incumbent man and went on as the only woman on the school board. It was feminist consciousness that made me do that because I didn't feel real adequate. I had not worked. I wasn't a professional. I didn't have a career. My name previously had been submitted to be considered for an appointment to a vacancy on the board. What the board did was to appoint a white male and they already had six white males. That enraged me. I remember talking to the mayor and saying, "I don't understand how that school board could have made that kind of appointment." He said, "Well, they're just like the city council; we wouldn't feel comfortable with a woman on the council." That did it. I decided to run against the school board's appointee at the next school election. So I did. I put together a full-fledged campaign and got a lot of support. But it was difficult because there were a couple of male friends on that school board and, basically, what I was doing was running against the whole board because they were protecting their own. They did not want an outsider. To some extent it wasn't just that I was a woman, but I think it was more they didn't want to have an incumbent defeated. I defeated him and that was kind of revolutionary at that time. So I ended up being the only woman on the board among men who hadn't wanted me in the first place. It was not real comfortable. There was one man who was very nice to me, but the others were

Supporter and foe at the senate hearing on an Iowa Equal Rights Amendment, 1978, PEG ANDERSON (*left*) and Mrs. George Paradise of Sioux City. Photo by Larry Neibergall, courtesy of *Des Moines Register*

not so great. They kind of ribbed me, and I found that I had to laugh at things I didn't think were funny. But it was a wonderful experience for me because it made me realize that I was as capable as any of those men. In no time I found that I knew as much as they did and that I could learn quicker. It helped my self-confidence. The men changed, too, and by the end of my second term they were encouraging me to run for mayor. Also, Joy Corning [now lieutenant governor of Iowa] was appointed and then elected to the board and I enjoyed serving with her.

In the late 1960s I met Lynn Cutler [who was prominent in Democratic politics]. Eventually [1975] I became president of the United Way when Lynn was chairman of the Black Hawk County Board of Supervisors. We were able to put some programs together and get people working together who hadn't worked together before. It was also at that time that I and some others started the Black Hawk County Women's Political Caucus. We also started a Women's

Center in cooperation with the University of Northern Iowa. It was a very exciting time.

I remember the first meeting of the Women's Center was at my house. I pulled together a group of women; Barbara Johnson was one of them, also Lynn Cutler, and a woman named Elaine Pfalzgraff, who eventually became the director of the center. Probably most of the caucus people in Cedar Falls were involved. At that time I was on a state advisory committee on federal Title I funds for higher education. I figured that we could write a Title I grant for the Women's Center and that is what we did. The center did a lot of training programs and gave support to women who wanted to go back to college. There were one-shot programs and also seminar-type programs to give women a better sense of self-worth so that they would feel more like going back to school. There was also a lot of counseling. The goal was to empower women in their personal lives. It wasn't political like the caucus. The Women's Center eventually left the university and became part of Family Services.

I wasn't at the first meeting of the state Women's Political Caucus at Ames in 1973. I'm not sure why I wasn't there. It was shortly after that, though, that I really got involved in the caucus. So I suppose that the Black Hawk County caucus came shortly after the state meeting. I remember a trip I took to the National Women's Political Caucus meeting in Wichita, Kansas, in 1974. Mary O'Halloran had asked me if I would be interested in going. Mary and I went from Cedar Falls. Minnette Doderer drove with us. That was a consciousness-raising trip for me if there ever was one! I had previously met Minnette but I hadn't really known her well. I was kind of intimidated by what I knew of her. Of course, I discovered that I shouldn't be. We had a great time. Gloria Steinem was one of the speakers at the meeting, and I was very impressed with her. Roxanne Conlin was there. She didn't ride with us but we were together during the meeting. I remember sitting up late one night, having a cup of coffee in a diner, and Roxanne sitting across from me in a booth being very depressed because it was her thirtieth birthday. She hadn't done all the things she'd planned to do by the time she was thirty. I thought, "Oh man, I can't believe this!" From that time on I was very involved with the caucus at the state level and I followed Roxanne as state chair in 1975.

During my two years as chair of the Iowa caucus our primary purpose was to encourage women to run for public office and to give them support. Among the people brought in to help raise money for a "Win with Women" campaign fund were Gloria Steinem and Billie Jean King. We put on workshops on campaigning and we also en-

PEG ANDERSON with Bob and Billie Ray, 1978. *"The day after the election Governor Ray said, 'I really feel very badly about this. . . . I thought the ERA was going to pass and I'm sorry I didn't give more time to it.'"* Photo by Larry Neibergall, courtesy of *Des Moines Register*

dorsed candidates. Endorsement of candidates was a difficult issue with the caucus because there were those who didn't want to endorse any men, and there were those who wanted to endorse those men who were supportive of women. Then there was the other problem of what do you do about the woman who is not real supportive of all women's issues, such as abortion rights or the ERA. The issue of endorsement continues to be an ongoing problem with the caucus.

Then there was the problem of the ERA. This was the period when other states were rescinding their ratification of the federal ERA, and somebody introduced a bill in the Iowa legislature to rescind our ratification. The anti-ERA people in Iowa brought Phyllis Schlafly to testify at a legislative hearing on this issue and to talk at a rally on the steps of the Capitol. We organized a counter-rally on the Capitol steps. I think this was in 1978. It was the first public rally that I had been involved in. We were appalled at the coverage in the *Des Moines Register* the next day because the pictures in the paper made us look like a bunch of hippies. [The Iowa legislature did not rescind its endorsement of the federal ERA.]

In 1977 I decided to run for mayor of Cedar Falls and this is when my association with the women's movement really hurt me. During this period I attended a statewide women's meeting in Des Moines [June 10–12] at which delegates to the National Women's Conference in Houston were chosen. I was elected an Iowa delegate to the Houston meeting and I was very involved. The Des Moines women's meeting hit the front page of the *Des Moines Register* with the headline, "Women's Meeting Endorses Gay Rights" or "Supports Gay Rights."[1] Whatever it was, we did pass a resolution of support for civil rights for all people. Who wouldn't do that? My name was also in the *Register* story as having been selected as a delegate to the Houston meeting.

It was devastating for me. I got identified in Cedar Falls with the gay rights issue. Homer Larson, who is pastor of a huge Lutheran church in Cedar Falls, and kind of a god to many people, just turned against me even though he had asked me to run in the first place. So did Bill Hansen, who was at that time a state legislator. I went to see them both because they were telling people that I was involved in the gay rights movement. Bill Hansen said, "I know where you stand, but unless you make a public denial of your position on gay rights, I can't support you for mayor." I said, "I'm not going to make a public denial because I believe in civil rights for all people." Then I went to see Homer Larson, whom I had worked with on the school board. He said, "I can't support you because I'm absolutely against the whole idea of gay rights." We had some discussion about the theological underpinnings of his view and about my view of the issue, and I lost that argument. I became totally identified, not with what I had done on the school board, but with all of the issues in the women's movement that people felt negative about.

I campaigned hard, going door to door, but I knew before the election that I was in trouble because I was identified with the women's movement. So I lost. That was kind of uncomfortable in my own hometown. Even my opponent, John Crews, was apologetic. He had nothing to do with the charges against me, but it was a dirty campaign, very underhanded.

Shortly after the election, my husband was asked if he would like to take a position at the corporate headquarters of John Deere in Moline, Illinois. By that time I thought it might be good to move. I said, "Yes, let's do it. It's time to start a new life." But I said, "I do

---

1. Louise Swartzwalder, "Women at Des Moines meeting urge Iowa gay rights law," *Des Moines Register,* June 13, 1977.

ANDERSON with Gloria Steinem at an Iowa Women's Political Caucus fundraiser, 1976. *"The real satisfaction comes in the way you use an expertise to pay something back to society and to employ your energies and efforts for the greater good."*

want to stay in Iowa because this is where my ties and my activities are." So we moved to Bettendorf, across the river from Moline.

It was at that juncture that Jean Lloyd-Jones and several other people who had been active in trying to get an ERA on the Iowa ballot came to me and asked me if I would head up the effort. [An ERA to the Iowa constitution was on the ballot in the fall of 1980.] I said I would. That was an incredible experience. There was the problem of bringing together a diverse group of people into that coalition. We had the state committees of the Republican party and the Democratic party. We had the AAUW and the League of Women Voters. The league was a problem for me because they weren't so sure they wanted to belong to this coalition, but they certainly cooperated. Then there were some really strong Democrats from the labor unions, and there were some very partisan Republicans. Mary Louise Smith and Kappie Spencer were involved. Part of the problem was keeping this group working together with a single focus, because this was a presidential election year. Reagan was running against Carter for president, and Grassley was running against Culver for the U.S. Senate. There were really strong feelings.

I decided right away that I couldn't be worried about what happened in the other campaigns. It just had to be the ERA. It was a struggle but we were unusually successful in doing it. We raised about $250,000 with the help of people like Erma Bombeck, Liz Carpenter, and Rosalynn Carter, who came to do fund-raisers. I spent full time on that campaign for the last nine months. I kept an apartment in Des Moines and we had an office there. I hired Kathy Ella as an office manager. She was very good. Towards the end of the campaign we also hired Monica McFadden. Basically, I was the spokesperson. I went out and talked to every little newspaper and every little radio station all over Iowa. It was a fascinating experience. I got to know the people of Iowa.

That's when I recognized an interesting thing about the ERA, which I believe is part of the reason we haven't been successful. It's a religious issue for a lot of people, which goes to the core of their belief about the relationship of men and women in what they consider their Christian family. There's some gut feeling with a lot of women that the woman is subservient to the male. We finally came to grips with that issue and dealt with it to some extent in our campaign, but in general the ERA suffered because there was no answer to this problem.

During the campaign I debated Phyllis Schlafly at a meeting of the Iowa Manufacturers' Association at Okoboji. This was a real interesting experience. I found her to be the most ungracious, cold-fish person I have ever met. I asked to be introduced to her at a social function the night before the debate and she shook hands and then just turned away. She just didn't want to talk. The next day we met to go over the ground rules for the debate and, again, there was no small talk. She was just totally ungracious. I found her to be a cold, calculating person who knew how to appeal to the emotions of the audience.

The week before the election the polls showed the ERA was going to pass, and we were very confident. What killed us was the advertising that Phyllis Schlafly's group brought into Iowa the last week; the print media advertising and especially the television advertising that dealt with the ERA as being a gay rights issue. The television ad carried a picture of the San Francisco gay rights march, which had occurred the year before, with a lot of compromising shots in it. It said, "Do you want this to happen in Iowa?" Two television markets did not carry that advertising, those in the Quad Cities and the market that covered Council Bluffs/Omaha. The reason I'm so sure that that is what finally did us in was because afterwards we did an analysis of the vote and we carried the counties covered by those stations. You just have to believe that it was that advertising that influenced the rest of the state. We also carried the absentee ballots which had been cast before this last spate of advertising. The day after the election Governor [Robert D.] Ray called me and said, "I really feel very badly about this. I thought you were not in any trouble. I thought the ERA was going to pass and I'm sorry I didn't give more time to it."

It was terribly hard to take that defeat. For two years I had been concentrating on that campaign. But I look back at it as a very positive experience. I met so many wonderful people and I really got a feeling for Iowa, traveling all over and doing all those talks in Methodist basements and Baptist parish halls. I had no idea of the number of different little pockets of ethnicity in Iowa. For example, the Dutch Reformed in northwest Iowa that had split off from the ones in Pella, and the Catholics in Dubuque. These groups affect Iowa politics.

I think we did the women's movement good from the fact that we raised consciousness for a lot of women who hadn't particularly been involved before. We had committees in about eighty counties which did the organizing locally. Letters that I received afterwards indicated that people had been surprised to find that the women's movement was not a radical movement. People were surprised that the women who were campaigning were ordinary people like them. We weren't Bella Abzug or Gloria Steinem or somebody they thought of as being radical. So it had a lot of positive effect.

In March 1981 Governor Ray asked me if I would be interested in serving on the Board of Regents. He said, "If I appoint you you're going to have a tremendous senate fight on your hands for confirmation." I said, "I don't believe that. Why would there be opposition particularly to me?" He said, "Because of your involvement with the ERA." I replied, "I don't want to do anything to embarrass you." He said, "I can stand it if you can." My reply was, "Sure, it wouldn't bother me." I didn't really believe it was going to happen. When my appointment was announced a couple of weeks later, there was, in fact, tremendous opposition. Senator John Jensen from Plainfield put in a request for a special hearing on my appointment, apart from the two other appointees. The Governor was getting all those letters about me concerning such things as the gay rights, abortion rights, and "secular humanism." The secretary that takes phone calls in the senate cloakroom told somebody that they had gotten more calls against my appointment than they had ever gotten on any issue.

Finally, the governor's office called and asked, Would I be willing to meet with Senator Jensen? I said, "Of course." We met alone in one of the governor's conference rooms and Senator Jensen and I sat down across the table from each other. He was very embarrassed. I think he had expected a totally different kind of person. I said, "What is the problem, Senator Jensen?" He said, "Weren't you involved in the gay rights movement?" I said, "No, I haven't identified with that movement at all." Then he pulled out this clipping from 1977 (this was now 1981) that had appeared in the *Des Moines Register* and he said, "The women's movement supports gay rights. There's your name in the first paragraph." (This was the article that listed the delegates to the Houston meeting.) I said, "But you know this was a general kind of resolution in support of civil rights for all people, including gays." Then I said, "By the way, Senator Jensen, my husband's going to meet me here in about an hour. Would you like to meet him?" That poor guy was just embarrassed. He was fumbling all over the place. The following week we had the special hearing about my appointment. Mary Louise Smith and Minnette Doderer came to support me; also Ed Voldseth, who was vice president of UNI. Not one of the anti people showed up. I was subsequently confirmed with only one dissenting vote, that was Senator Jensen. But it was very uncomfortable at the time.

The issue of the toilets at Kinnick Stadium at the University of Iowa may be the women's issue I'm best known for during my term on the Board of Regents. It stems from a perfectly innocent question that I asked when they brought the architects in to make their report about the remodeling of Kinnick Stadium, basically building a new end-zone building that would have seats and house concessions. Since it was a new building and I knew there was a problem with an insufficient number of toilets at Kinnick Stadium, I asked them about the toilets. The architects said, "We've got the same number for men and women." I pursued that a little further and discovered, first of all, that they needed to have more for women than men. It just takes longer. But there was also this crazy business about the fact that the architectural code doesn't count urinals, it only counts stools. So if you give the same number of stools to men that you give to women, plus the urinals, the men get a lot more. Of course, when I raised the question about toilets everybody started snickering except for Doctor Percy Harris, who supported me. The upshot of it was that they put more women's toilets, not only in the new section, but they doubled the facilities for women in the old part of the stadium. Although most of the issues on the Board of Regents weren't specifically women's issues I think I was perceived as the "women's rights" member of the board.

I did use my positions on the Board of Regents and on the Coordinating Council for Post-Secondary Education to help organize and run the Way Up Conference for Women in Administration in Higher Education. This was an idea that Pat Geadelmann, Sue Follon, and I had talked about when I was on the Commission on the Status of Women. As a regent, I was in a position to help them make it a reality. These conferences have continued to this day in Iowa. I have brought the idea to Arizona where we are planning the second such conference this year.

(*From left*) Barbara Brown, Black Hawk County ERA coordinator, ANDERSON, Erma Bombeck, and Liz Carpenter at a Waterloo fundraiser for the ERA campaign, 1980.

S. J. Brownley was president of the Board of Regents for the first four years I was a member and I liked working with him. When his term was up he left. It would have been nice to have been elected president of the board to succeed Brownley and I thought I should have been. By that time Terry Branstad was governor. He called people in whom he had appointed and said, "I don't want Peg Anderson to be president. I want John McDonald to be president." Branstad believed that John would do what he wanted him to do and I was probably too independent. Two years later, when my six-year term was up in 1987, we were thinking of moving to Tucson. I decided to tell Branstad that I didn't want to be reappointed to the Board of Regents before he had a chance to not reappoint me. So that is what I did. That about ended my career in Iowa.

Mary Louise Smith

is a quintessential Republican who opposes her party's conservative stand on issues relating to women. From 1974 to 1977 she served as chair of the Republican National Committee, the only woman ever to hold this position. She was vice chair of the United States Commission on Civil Rights from 1981 until 1983 when she was, in effect, ousted by President Ronald Reagan because of her liberal civil rights views. She has been named by President George Bush to the board of directors of the United States Institute of Peace.

"A woman, if she is to succeed, must step forward and say, 'I want to be a leader.'"

I was born in Eddyville, Iowa, and now I live in Des Moines. When I was growing up I don't ever remember discussing women's rights or equal rights with my parents. That was before the day that we focused on it at all. I can only tell you that I came from a family where neither my mother nor my father ever suggested that my sister and I couldn't do anything we wanted to do. There was never any suggestion either that you shouldn't do this because you are little girls. There never was a suggestion that we wouldn't go to college, which in that time might not have been necessarily taken for granted. There was absolutely no bigotry in our family. I never recall any hint of discrimination, either between men and women or as far as minorities were concerned. There never was much opportunity, of course, because I don't suppose there was a black family in Eddyville where I grew up. I had a very good childhood, a very happy childhood, secure.

My father was president of the Manning and Epperson State Bank in Eddyville. The Depression took its toll and our bank closed in 1929. To meet obligations we sold our house and almost everything else of value and moved to Iowa City, where my sister could live at home and enroll at the University of Iowa. In 1934 my parents moved to Omaha, where Dad ultimately became an officer in the Federal Land Bank. After a year of high school in Eddyville, I went to high school in Iowa City but did not graduate because by the fall of 1931 I had enough credits to enter the university without ever actually receiving a high school diploma. I too lived at home until my senior year when I moved to the Kappa Alpha Theta sorority house.

I met Elmer, who was in medical school at Iowa, during my junior year in college and we were married in October of 1934 at the beginning of my senior year. Because my folks thought I was too young, and because we had no visible means of support except our parents, and because, I suppose, we were a little rebellious, Elmer and I were secretly married in Illinois. There were few married couples on campus at that time and we weren't sure how this would be accepted in all quarters, so I continued to live at the Theta house and Elmer remained at his medical fraternity. We announced our marriage in the spring before graduation.

The day after we received our degrees (1935) I went to work as a case aide for the Iowa Emergency Relief Administration in Davenport and Elmer remained in Iowa City for his internship. A job was essential for me then because I had to repay money I had borrowed for college expenses. Early the following year (1936) I was transferred to Iowa City and we finally moved into our first apartment home. Our two oldest children were born during the period from 1937 to 1940 in State Center, Iowa, where Elmer was practicing medicine. Elmer served in the military from 1940 to 1945 (including two years overseas as a flight surgeon) and our third child was born during this period. Those five years were formative ones for me from the standpoint of learning to accept the responsibility for a family, most of the time alone, and developing a sense of personal independence and adequacy. Shortly after Elmer was mustered out of the service in 1945 we moved to Eagle Grove, where he established a solo practice in general medicine. Our children were eight, six, and three-and-a-half years old and we started over as a family again.

I became interested in feminism and women's equality through the political system and first became involved politically there in Eagle Grove. When Governor [Robert D.] Blue was defeated in a primary in 1948, he and his wife came back to Eagle Grove and, of course, they became Mr. and Mrs. Republican in their hometown. They were my mentors politically and sort of led me through the process. I think they recognized a kindred spirit. That was the beginning of partisan politics for me, but as I got into it one of my first observations was that as I was doing things there were no men around. I was going to campaign headquarters and answering the telephones and doing mailings and going door-to-door canvassing and it was almost entirely female. That piqued my curiosity. It seemed to me that surely it was not a party of all women. I knew there were men someplace. The more you began to inquire, what you found was that they were doing the policy-making things. Many of them were down in Des Moines. That was what gave rise to the concept of smoke-filled rooms. When I came to that realization, I suppose that sparked me to do some goal setting. If I was going to spend time doing volunteer work in the area of politics, or anything else as far as that's concerned, then I would want it to be worthwhile. I would not want to be just spinning my wheels some place, but having something to say about the organization and about the programs and about the direction that the party was going. So that really was the beginning of it for me.

I did not think of myself as a feminist at that time. It was pretty much an individual determination. The word *feminist* in the fifties was not in my vocabulary. I would find some kindred souls that would talk about wanting to be on the school board or wanting to be on the library board or whatever, but we never couched it in terms of feminism. The beginning of my feeling about that was when the librarian in Eagle Grove—her name was Frances Thorson—asked me if I would read a book and see if I thought it ought to be on the shelves. It was Betty Friedan's *The Feminine Mystique.* That was in 1963. I read it and, of course, it did go on the shelves. But it did much more than that. It exploded in my consciousness as it did with millions of American women. All of a sudden you realized that this yearning, this not being quite satisfied, happy but not fulfilled, that there was more beyond the kitchen and getting three meals a day. Much as I loved my husband and my children, I needed to reach out beyond that. I wasn't the only one feeling this. This was what the groundswell of that part of the women's movement really

MARY LOUISE SMITH receiving the gavel from George Bush, September 1974. *"I was the first woman to become Republican National Chairman."*

started from. Clearly, I was affected by that. I could time it. I can almost put a date on it. So when you asked me where my association with feminism began, the rumblings began in the field of politics, but the identity with it began with Betty Friedan's book.

In the fall of 1963 Elmer retired and we moved to Des Moines. Of course that gave me an opportunity to move my work. I had come through local-level politics and, as the kids got older, I went to the county level and the district level, but being in Des Moines gave me an opportunity to move to the state and national levels. By that time my children were grown and gone from home. Clearly, that was my opportunity because I not only was able to develop in a leadership way myself, but I became a role model for other women in the party. So the timing was right from the standpoint of my own development and from the standpoint of my work within the party.

I became very much aware that a career in politics was not going to come easily. I believe that yet today. I have a very strong feeling that women have to make their own opportunities. Particularly that was true in the area of politics where I was working. It was a man's world and it still is a man's world. This is not necessarily because of overt discrimination in every case, although there's some of that, but culturally, historically, it's been a man's profession. A woman, if she is to succeed, must step forward and say, "I want to be a leader."

How did I do this within the party? Well, it was very deliberate. For instance, on the national committee, which I was elected to in 1964 after we came to Des Moines, you have to volunteer for positions. You have to put yourself in key roles. You have to become acquainted, and if you have any skill you have to let it be known to party leaders. You have to be able to accept responsibility. You have to be willing to take risks. But most of all it's that whole area of having to promote yourself. It's tough. I almost hate to use those words, but that's the name of the game. Other women can help, and therein develops another very strong philosophy that I have. I believe that any woman who has achieved any degree of success in any field, whether it be politics or homemaking or caregiving or medicine, the legal profession, writing, academics, whatever, has an obligation to help other women.

I went to the 1972 Republican National Convention in Miami. I had some very good friends, much younger than I am. Betsy Griffith, the writer, was one of them. She and some other young women her age were at the convention and they were trying to put together some kind of organization that would affect the platform and that would promote the women's issues that had to do with rules of the convention and rules of the party. It was clearly a women's caucus. Well, even that long ago television was becoming a major part of our political conventions and there were cameras all over the place getting color and background to transmit back home. There were a lot of cameras outside the rooms where the women were having their meetings and I was very reluctant because I was afraid that I would be caught on camera and that would be transmitted back to Iowa and here was this nice, gentle, conservative, Republican national committeewoman walking into a room with a lot of Republican women firebrands. So I said to Betsy, "I am really with you. I believe in what you're trying to do, but I'm really not a women's libber," which was the phrase that was in common usage then. I said, "I really don't feel like this is my battle. I'll support you in everything but I just don't want to be on a soapbox about this because I personally don't need it."

Betsy's answer to me was, "Mary Louise, you will never be free until all women enjoy those same rights." Of course, that's exactly the philosophy that was carried into the formation of the Women's Political Caucus. By the time the Iowa caucus was organized in

1973 I had come far enough that it was actually my desire to say to the public, I want to be part of this. But that was not a revolution for me, it clearly was an evolution. I wasn't born a feminist. I became one. I had tremendous support from my husband. He certainly would have been a man who did not include feminism in his vocabulary, but he felt very strongly that I was doing the right thing. He was very supportive of my entire career and he came to know how important this whole issue was to me. I had all kinds of encouragement there.

How did I happen to attend the organizational meeting of the Iowa Women's Political Caucus? I had gotten acquainted with Roxanne Conlin. She called me about coming to an organizational meeting. I remember Roxanne talking to me personally. It was a big decision for me, whether to go or not. I had every reason to believe that it would be heavily on the side of Democratic women, given the leadership and given what I knew about peoples' impulses, but there was something that made me want to go. I was at that stage in my career where I wanted to express it openly. It wasn't enough to say, "Yes, I'm for it but . . ."

I remember the first caucus convention up at Ames, the outpouring of people and the real emotional high that people experienced from it. If I had ever had any doubts about it, I thought, This is the wave of the future. We've done the right thing. There was that first great wave of enthusiasm after the caucus was organized. We started early with some training sessions for candidates. Then we broadened into some training for campaign managers. The strength of the caucus at that time, and Roxanne deserves much credit for it, is due to the people that put it together. It was truly bipartisan or multipartisan and they made a great effort to have the convenors of the convention balanced politically. There were Democratic and Republican task forces just as there still are on the national level. I think that this bipartisan effort is what catapulted the Iowa Women's Political Caucus into the forefront. Sadly, I cannot say that's true now. I think the decline is not so much the fault of the caucus but the fault of the Republicans who have been reluctant to be identified with it because once you got into the late 1970s and began to get the ultraconservative influences—after you got the Reagan administration in office in 1980—you were seen almost as a dissident if you expressed these views of equality for women. By that time the Equal Rights Amendment was out of our platform. People have their own agenda. I could see where if you had a young woman that wanted to move up to be county chairman or go on the state central committee, that her future might have been jeopardized by a stand.

It was not going to hurt me at that point and still doesn't.

In March of 1974 I went to Washington to become co-chair of the Republican party under the chairmanship of George Bush. On August 9, 1974, President Nixon resigned and Gerald Ford became president of the United States. The following month, September 1974, President Ford named George Bush as our official representative to China and asked me to head the Republican party.

I was the first woman to become Republican National Chairman. I continued then, and still do, in spite of some criticism now and then, to use the term *chairman,* because it was the official designation for signing contracts, legal documents, etc. At one time we tried to change the rules of the party to make the language gender-neutral, but with no success. Generally speaking, the term *party chairman* more clearly defines the position for most people, and I must admit that I came to like the ring of "Madam Chairman." It's interesting to note that this is one of the few exceptions I make in this regard. I speak, for instance, of being "former vice chair of the U.S. Civil Rights Commission." For the most part I understand and appreciate the symbolism and significance of gender-based terminology.

A woman who is a "first" in any field, I think, bears an unmistakable extra responsibility. If she fails to succeed or performs poorly, it affects other women and reinforces the belief that there are some things women just don't do as well as men. There was considerable nervousness and apprehension in my own party about my chairmanship, and many believed it would last only a few months at best. The doubts were almost always expressed in the form of the sexist question, "Is she tough enough?" The fact that I was the first woman to hold this position in our party obviously received a lot of attention but I did not want it to become the entire focus of my chairmanship. I felt confident in my knowledge of grass roots politics. I was not familiar with the Washington scene and the legislative agenda so I made a special effort to learn that part, while concentrating on what I knew—organizational politics. I think this plan paid dividends.

In Washington I had an apartment at the Mayflower Hotel. Elmer stayed in Des Moines and kept the home fires burning. Those years in the nation's capital were exciting, challenging, and heady times for me. There were many highlights, such as coming to know members of Congress and the diplomatic corps, public speaking, TV appearances, and travel to almost every state in the union. At the invitation of President Ford, I attended all cabinet meetings, and in my official capacity as Republican National Chairman I was the

MARY LOUISE SMITH with President Gerald Ford in September 1974. *"President Ford . . . asked me to head the Republican party."* Photo courtesy of Iowa Women's Archives, University of Iowa

first woman to organize and call to order the national convention of a major American political party. That was at the Kemper Arena in Kansas City in 1976.

By far the most important results of my chairmanship, from a personal point of view, are the knowledge and background I gained and the platform it created from which I can speak and act on behalf of issues important to me. The real satisfaction comes in the way you use an experience to pay something back to society in general and to the people who supported you, and to employ your efforts and energies for the greater good.

Why didn't I support Roxanne when she was running for national president of the caucus? That was during my chairmanship of the National Republican Committee, probably 1975. I had told Roxanne early on that I was a party loyalist, as she is. I always thought that both of us would understand that. At that point I was supporting a good candidate, a Republican woman, but the bitterness came because Roxanne was an Iowan. People saw it in the light of what an Iowan should be doing rather than in terms of Republican or Democrat. Roxanne understood that better than most people. It never altered our friendship. When I spoke at the

Iowa convention in Iowa City that year, there were a few who walked out. I think there were some boos. It was Roxanne who cooled that after that election. That would be typical of Roxanne's understanding of the partisan political system. I probably had made a commitment very early on in that race. Nevertheless, it did disturb me because I think highly of Roxanne. She and I frequently talk about this, not that one incident, but we talk about partisanship and when you are a loyal, disciplined party person, you understand the blacks and the whites and the grays a little better than some other people do.

I was chairman of the Republican party from 1974 to early 1977. While I think I had never been seen as a radical, by that time my position on women's rights was pretty well known. Of course, that did give me an opportunity, to the degree that I could, to advance it in the party. It was not until 1980, after I left the chairmanship, that we actually took the support for the Equal Rights Amendment out of the Republican platform. One of the great disappointments of my chairmanship in that 1974 to 1977 period is that we didn't get the Equal Rights Amendment ratified. I was there serving with a president, Gerald Ford, who was in favor of it. Betty Ford was a backer of the Equal Rights Amendment. We missed an opportunity, not that we could have turned the tide, but in retrospect I'm afraid that as a party we didn't do enough about it. Try hard as I might have, we were even then fighting the beginnings of the radical right movement. Whether we could have ever overcome that or whether we really realized the seriousness of it, I don't know. I think support for the Equal Rights Amendment is one of the most conservative issues you could embrace. I never have been able to understand why it gets cast in liberal-conservative terms. As long as I have known anything about the Republican party, one of the principles has been a belief in individual rights, individual freedom, and individual responsibility. It seems to me this is the core of the Equal Rights Amendment.

I don't really know the genesis of my interest in reproductive freedom, only that it fits in with the total concept of individual rights and responsibilities, which I feel are at the heart of equality for women. Flowing out of that emphasis on individual freedom is my belief that women as well as men should be masters of their own destinies. We make choices every day, about whether to get married or not, what church to worship in, and what job to hold, and where and how we live. Basic to individual freedom is the right to make choices. Anything else would just simply go against everything I believe. I am very careful about not indulging in a debate over when

SMITH chairing the Republican National Convention, 1976. "A woman who is first in any field bears an unmistakable responsibility."

life begins or how you might personally feel about the physical act of an abortion. I am obviously no longer of childbearing age and I don't know how I would react if I were faced with a situation where I would consider abortion, because I never had to.

I have been on the board of Planned Parenthood for three years and am now heading the fund-raising committee. My association with Planned Parenthood has been related to my work generally with women's equality. It is also related to my commitment to civil rights, to erasing elements of discrimination. If they were ever to outlaw abortion, certain classes of women would be discriminated against. If you went state by state and you had forty states that barred abortion and the other ten that didn't, abortion would become an industry catering to the wealthy. The women who couldn't take advantage of legal, safe abortions would be poor women, young women with no resources, twelve, thirteen, fourteen years old. They are not going to travel to another state or another country if we ever outlawed abortion completely, so there is an element of discrimination. But I prefer to keep my debate focused pretty much on the element of choice.

Another issue for me in regard to reproductive freedom is the religious issue. I have a feeling that much of the opposition is coming from the religious right and, much as they deny it, if you read their literature and if you read some of the letters that fall into our hands, you can see that it is clearly a religious issue to them. If, indeed, it is that, then it does not belong in the field of politics and government at all.

Let me say a word about my experience on the United States Civil Rights Commission. I served as vice chair of the U.S. Commission on Civil Rights from 1981 to 1983. It was a Reagan appointment. It resulted from the influence of George Bush. At that time my views on women's equality were well known. What they didn't realize was that this is not a separate issue. Women's rights are civil rights. Mary Berry, on the commission, makes this point over and over again—that you just don't separate out women and give them rights, that it's part of the whole picture, the whole fabric of civil rights. Everybody knew that I was for the Equal Rights Amendment and that I would be a staunch supporter of women's equality, but somehow that never got translated into support for a broader concept of civil rights. It goes back to what Betsy Griffith told me, that you are never free until all women are free. You could apply that to all people just as well.

I was not reappointed to the commission. Clarence Pendleton was the chairman. The commission took some positions that were not comfortable for the Reagan administration, putting out a very critical report about the small number of women that had been incorporated into the administration and some other reports about failures in the field of civil rights. Some very strong views were expressed by the U.S. Civil Rights Commission about affirmative action. My own views of affirmative action are that it's perfectly appropriate to indulge in affirmative action when you are trying to compensate for the evils of discrimination that have occurred over the years. I also wish children never had to be bused. I wish they didn't have to be bused in Iowa rural communities when there's no racial involvement at all. But when you are talking about school segregation and desegregation, I don't happen to see anything wrong with busing if it is worked into an effective program and used as a last resort.

President Reagan was unhappy with us because we were pinpointing some failures of his administration. He tried to fire three of the Democratic members but couldn't because they had been appointed by another president. Then they took the route of reorganization and they enlarged the commission. Congress went along in the reorganization but there appeared to be a promise that the administration would name some of their own people in addition to reappointments. I am told that there was a very firm agreement that Jill Ruckelshaus and I would be put back on the commission and that did not happen. They simply ignored the gentlemen's agreement that had been forged with the House and the Senate and the administration. So essentially we were relieved of our duties because in the reorganization others less controversial were appointed.

Mary Louise Smith continues to be active in public affairs. In 1986 she helped found the Iowa Peace Institute. She served on its board of directors until 1990, when President Bush appointed her to the board of directors of the United States Peace Institute. She is a member of the board of directors of Planned Parenthood of Greater Iowa as well as an organizer and advocate of the prochoice position within the Republican party. Other board memberships include the Iowa region of the Conference of Christians and Jews and the University of Iowa Foundation. In 1991 she and Louise Noun worked together to found the Iowa Women's Archives at the University of Iowa.

Minnette Doderer,

tough-minded and outspoken, is the leading feminist in the Iowa legislature. She has served in the Iowa General Assembly longer than any other woman and has twice been the Democratic candidate for lieutenant governor. Doderer's efforts on behalf of women are unflagging. She currently is supporting legislation to achieve insurance equity for women and is responsible for the overwhelming approval of a proposed state ERA constitutional amendment by the 1989 General Assembly.

"I became a real feminist—inch by inch—as Iowa women told me their troubles and how they were treated, and asked for my help."

I was born on a farm near Holland, Iowa. I was the fourth child of six (two girls and four boys) and my dad was a farmer. My dad's father was an ample landowner and businessman in Grundy County who had come here from Germany when he was ten. We went to the Lutheran church where only German was spoken, but I never learned the language.

In 1929 my family lost the farm so we moved two miles away to Grundy Center, where my dad drove a truck and did odd jobs until the sale of beer was legalized in Iowa. He opened the first beer tavern and restaurant in Allison, Iowa. My mother did all the cooking for the restaurant. I was in the fifth grade and I remember walking to school those first few days in this little town, and kids standing on the side yelling "beer mug" at us. I didn't even know why they were yelling. Because of this experience I've always had an empathy for people who are minorities and who get things yelled at them when they can't help it, especially later when I saw the marches in the South and the black kids trying to go to the white schools. It didn't take long, however, before we were accepted into the Allison community.

When I was in the eighth grade we moved to Rockford, Iowa, and a year later we moved to Waterloo. I thought my dad was taking us to the ends of the earth with these moves but actually it was all in a four-county area.

My mother was one of those strong German women who always went along with whatever my dad wanted, yet she ruled the roost. She would get the paycheck, she spent the money, she decided what her kids would do, she ran a boarding house and worked as a restaurant cook, and if somebody asked her if she worked, she would have said no. In her head, women didn't work. She worked the three-to-after-dinner shift so in the morning she'd bake bread at home and do all her housework, and she'd get the night meal ready for us. We just warmed the food. God, what a woman she was! I was too dumb to appreciate her at the time. Her English was mixed with German in my young years and we were poor. Of course my sister and I helped around the house, reluctantly. That's one of my real regrets, that I didn't know how tough it was for my mother. She did complain, but I didn't hear her. It was the old story that you never appreciate people until it's too late. Like many of today's middle-class Iowans, we were poor only from the late twenties until World War II. It just seemed a long time.

Waterloo is really where I grew up. I started working at the John Deere Tractor Company in a clerical position right after I graduated from high school in 1941. I very quickly became the assistant editor of the John Deere house organ that was started during World War II. It was called *The Connecting Link* because it was considered the connecting link between the home front and the fighting front. I worked at John Deere three years before I went to the University of Northern Iowa, which was then called Iowa State Teachers' College, to start my degree. John Deere was forward-thinking because they let me work half-time while I commuted seven miles to the college in Cedar Falls. I was paid $60 a month for half-time work. My starting wage at Deere three years earlier was $55 a month for a forty-eight hour week, so I was really highly paid for half time. Those salaries are just unbelievable now, but I saved money, bought war bonds, paid room and board at home, and paid for all my personal needs. I lived at home most of the time but I stayed at the college two quarters while my mother rented my room in Waterloo and gave me the money so that I could pay my rent in the dormitory.

I quit college at Thanksgiving time of my second year (1944) to join my husband, who was in the service in Texas, because he thought he was going overseas. We had been married the previous August. Fred didn't go overseas so we spent a year plus a few months in Texas and then we came back to Iowa in December 1945. The year I was in Texas I worked for the American Red Cross and the U.S. Army. We both finished college at the University of Iowa after the war. I majored in economics, but it never occurred to me that this was an unusual field for a woman. It took me seven years from high school to get my college degree.

When I graduated from college I was already three months pregnant so I instantly became a housewife. Our son was forty-one on December 1, 1989. I don't know if I was aware of the League of Women Voters when we moved to Iowa City in 1945 but I became very much aware of it because it was an active organization. I could see that all of the women that were involved beyond the university were in this organization. I decided I wanted to be a member, and I think I joined it even while I was finishing my degree. I stayed active in the league for a long time.

Reapportionment [redistricting the state so that each legislator represents an equal number of people] was the first issue that I got heavily involved with in the League of Women Voters and I assumed leadership of the issue locally. I was chair of the local league study group and was later involved on the state level, working with a succession of citizens' committees. I remember going back and forth to Des Moines a lot on reapportionment. The legislature was very malapportioned and the league was early in recognizing this, but there must have been other organizations, too. When we started working on the item in the late 1950s there were one hundred eight members of the Iowa House of Representatives and ninety-nine of them were apportioned, one to each of the state's ninety-nine counties. Then there were nine extra members apportioned to each of the nine largest counties, so Polk County had two representatives. This meant that every vote in Adams County was sixteen times more powerful than every vote in Polk County. Thirty percent of the population controlled the legislature. In 1960 we tried to get reapportionment by means of a constitutional convention, but the voters defeated this effort in a referendum. Then we went to the federal court which in 1964 declared Iowa's apportionment "invidiously discriminatory." Governor [Harold E.] Hughes then called a special session of the legislature to adopt a reapportionment plan. This plan failed to satisfy the courts. The battle didn't end until 1972 when the Iowa Supreme Court released a mandatory reapportionment plan which the legislature had no choice but to accept.

I was unaware of feminism at this time, probably because of my own personal experience. When I wanted to go to college, I went to college, and my folks helped me as much as they could. But there was no one to tell me that women were oppressed and that women were different. When I look back I see that even my mother treated her female children differently. We did all the chores around the house and we were there to help our brothers and my dad. I just assumed that was the way life was. If there were other role models, I was too involved in my own surroundings to notice.

In 1963, a few years after my husband went on the city council in Iowa City, the wife of one of the members of the council that we socialized with after meetings tried her darnedest to get me to read *The Feminine Mystique* and I took it home with me. I read a couple of chapters and I thought, This is terrible, why am I bothering to read this boring stuff? Why don't these women do something instead of just complaining? I never had the patience to change our lives. Also, Fred did help with the children and the household chores. Before I got active in the Democratic party, Joe Crumley, foreman of the campus crew at the university, called Fred and asked him if I would consider being vice chair of the party. Calling Fred instead of me was sexism, and I failed to recognize it. Fred said, "I don't know, you'll have to ask Min." So he asked me and I said, "No, I don't think I ought to start as vice chair of the party. I don't know anything about it. Why do you want me?" He said, "Well, because you're not Catholic and you're a woman." Still a light didn't go on. The reason I was asked is that the chair of the party was Catholic and male. We'd never had a woman as chair, but I didn't know it. Male chairs and female vice chairs were the order of things. I had little kids and we didn't sit around having consciousness-raising sessions in those days.

I remember resenting Clara Oleson at one of our Democratic conventions getting up and trying to get into the Democratic platform that men should equally share in the housework. I thought, Why is she doing this? They're only getting mad at her and they are not going to do it anyway. What did it have to do with the Democratic platform? They did get annoyed. They hooted and howled at her plank. I didn't help them object, but I thought, This isn't the place for it.

I started with the party by being a precinct leader. That was probably in 1952 with Adlai Stevenson. Next I spent a long time being vice chair of the party, probably four or five years. I had at least five male chairs that I served with and I did most of the chair's work. It was frequently clerical and also organizing meetings, getting an agenda together, and filling vacancies. It wasn't hard work but it was really the chair's work. When we'd get to the meetings I'd hand the chair the agenda and he'd lead the meetings. I sort of resented it, but it had to be done. I was unaware that it was because he was male and I was female that we were accepting these roles. At any rate, when the chair resigned (this was about the fourth chair) I said to the Democrats, "I'm going to be chair; I've done all the work." My closest political friend, Merle Full [now Merle Fleming] said, "You can't get elected because you're a woman." I said, "What do you mean? They've let me do all the work." And sure enough, she organized our wing of the central committee against me. My friends supported an assistant Methodist minister. We were the wet Democratic party in Johnson County, and the party was not about to buy this dry Methodist minister. Chuck Klein, a lawyer, also ran and got elected. I got two votes. I resigned that night as vice chair.

Two days later our friends on the committee were at my door asking me to stay on because they had no entré to the party with the new chair who was elected by the other group. Foolishly, I let them talk me into not resigning and I continued to do all Chuck's work. That was about the time that the federal court ruled against our current apportionment. The legislature was called back into special session by Governor Harold Hughes to do a legal reapportionment. Our state representative from Johnson County at that time was Scott Swisher, who had not paid income taxes the ten years he had been in office. He was forced to resign from the legislature as he was in prison. I wasn't aware of my ability to make changes in the political life of women at that time, but I was tired of doing the work of the chair without recognition or hope of being promoted to chair of the local party. I was the expert on reapportionment because I had worked on all of those reapportionment committees statewide and had been the local league chair for this issue. So I decided to run for the seat vacated by Swisher.

Because it was a special election, vacancies were filled by nomination by the central committee for each political party. Bernie Campion, a farmer, ran against me. I was not a confident candidate. I remember being sent out into the hall at the courthouse while the central committee members did their balloting and vote counting. Bernie sat in the hall telling me that he had the committee's votes

MINNETTE DODERER during her first campaign for the Iowa
House in 1964. (*Right*) Andrew Frommelt, Dubuque (*center*),
Raymond Eveland, Boone County. *"In 1965 I started getting
letters from women about rotten treatment by welfare workers,
and rotten treatment by their husbands. . . . That's what made
me aware of lives of women and the laws on women."* Photo by
Tom Mosier, courtesy of *Iowa City Press Citizen*

and that what he was worrying about was who the Republicans
were going to nominate against him. Lo and behold, they called us
in and I had beaten Bernie. I gained a portion of self-confidence from
the vote that night. After the party's nomination, the press de-
scended—"the first woman from Johnson County," the first this and
the first that, which made me more aware of the fact that I had done
something different, and there was something different for me to do.

My Republican opponent in the special election of February
1964 was Dale Erickson. Women ran his campaign. I could see they
were doing it wrong because they ran a sweetheart campaign. They
had valentines, hearts, and a "We Love Dale" slogan. A storefront
campaign office was decorated with hearts. It was strictly a campaign of the women love Dale and therefore the men love Dale, and
Minnette's a woman. All his posters said, "Vote for the man, Dale
Erickson." It wasn't a vote for the man against the woman, it was
just that all campaign literature for every office said, "Vote for the
man," even if there was a male running against a male.

It's really embarrassing for me now when I see an old news
clipping which reports that in a campaign talk I made to a service
club I said, "I will work like a horse and think like a man." I didn't
even know what a concession I was making to sexism. It was terrible. Anyhow, I got elected and got to the legislature. I was the first
female legislator from Johnson County. Now we have three from our
district. It took twenty-two years to become an all-woman delega-

tion from the Iowa City–Johnson County district. In the 1964
seven-week special session we did reapportionment and area
schools. These were not issues which dealt with men and women.
Reapportionment was labeled, "one man, one vote," and still is. The
area schools were male-dominated and still are.

In the special election and also when I ran again in the fall,
many women helped me. In the meantime I was being told by so-
called experts that women won't vote for women. These old cli-
chés—women don't like each other, women will be jealous and
you've got to be careful—were often reported to me. Yet my strongest support came from women. It was very clear to me, on the other
hand, that the women in the Republican party were also working
hard for Dale Erickson. In other words, it was the women doing the
work. Women in the Democratic party as well as the independents
were very strongly supportive of me, partially even then because I
was a woman.

I won the fall election in 1964. This was the year of the Lyndon
Johnson landslide for president and civil rights awareness was
dominant in the campaign. When I arrived in Des Moines for the
regular session in 1965, I started getting letters from women about
rotten settlements in divorces, rotten treatment by welfare workers,
rotten treatment by their husbands, and problems with their kids;
just real women's problems. That's what made me aware of lives of
women and the laws on women. Laws always favored the male.

We had a big fight in 1965 about birth control being made available to welfare women because up until that time the Department of
Social Services could not give information or provide devices to
their welfare clients. It was just forbidden. Gert Cohen, another
member of the house, had a scientific background. She had worked
in some laboratory in Chicago when she was growing up and now
took the lead in the house against Mary Gregerson from Council
Bluffs, who was Catholic and absolutely opposed birth control. I can
still remember Mary saying on the house floor that there are mothers in the state who pop birth control pills into their daughters'
mouths just like candy! Gert took her on in a very calm, scientific
manner, and we won. The welfare issue first made me aware of the
laws against women.

In the 1965 session we had a Democratic majority for the first
time in thirty-some years. It was during this session that the League
of Women Voters had their so-called reform constitutional amend-
ments introduced; the governor and lieutenant governor election
with one check, the shortened ballot, and annual sessions of the
legislature. I don't remember all the reforms but there must have

DODERER at a legislative committee with U.S. Secretary of Agriculture Orville Freeman, 1966. *"Everybody gave me this advice on how to hide the fact that I was a woman."*

been five of them. None of these had a specific effect on women. It was just good government stuff. I was really active in government and legislative reform.

But then in 1967 the Republicans got the house back and Joan Lipsky came in from Cedar Rapids. Joan, during her early career days, was a social worker. She had a different angle on life from most of the other women in the house. Joan and I together—I don't know if she instigated it or I did—became aware that if welfare women got any money at all, from a friend, or the church, or a basket at Christmastime, the amount of these gifts were deducted from their welfare grants. Joan and I decided that wasn't fair. If their kids had a paper route, the state subtracted the child's earnings from their grants. Of course all of those conservatives were yelling about all these welfare people, yet they had them totally trapped in welfare by 100 percent confiscation of their wages. We got welfare recipients $40 exempt from confiscation, which they could use in addition to their grant. That was a real eye-opener for me. Because I took welfare clients' side in this instance, welfare women started writing letters and calling and telling me how tough life was, also how rotten their husbands were, and how the court cheated them.

That's how I became a feminist; just these terrible problems of individuals and awareness of them from the women who were living under great hardships and unequal legal treatment. I had grown up poor, but I wasn't aware of their kind of troubles. We were young and having a good time. God, half the world crying and I hadn't noticed it. I sympathize with women who are unaware of the problems around them. I sympathize, but I spend time trying to involve them.

The issue that I really regret was the no-fault divorce law. It
came early in my senate service. It went by me without my becoming involved. I was still busy reforming government. I remember
Arthur Neu being very active in no-fault divorce. It was a Bar Association proposal. I think their motives were pure because they were
tired of seeing people fight and damage each other's reputations in
order to get a divorce. We weren't as bad as New York, but almost.
Lawyers didn't like the fault divorce law, but in doing no-fault divorce we really hurt women after the divorce.

Women formerly used to use their kids to bargain for more
money or they bargained that they wouldn't give a divorce unless
they got something out of it. Now they have nothing to bargain
with. They end up with the kids. I'll never forget one welfare woman
who later told me that when she was married she had a husband
who had a business. They had three cars and five kids. She said,
"Now I'm divorced and he has a business, and he has three cars,
and I have five kids." When you've got five kids you can't work so
you go on welfare. Stories like that made me a feminist. Each one of
them made me more angry, and I started trying to change the law.
The most flattering thing that anyone has ever said to me was by
Clara Oleson when she was practicing law. She did family law and
she said, "Minnette, so many times I have searched that code to find
out the genesis of some law in my law cases and I always find your
tracks." I was a feminist before I knew I was a feminist. I believe
many other men and women are also feminist while rejecting the
label.

It was the abortion issue that probably was the thing that made
me go well over the line, if there is a line, into conscious feminism. If
women can't control such a basic thing as their own reproductive
rights then women can't be in control of much else. I chaired the
Public Health Committee in 1965 and that was when I really got the
letters. I've turned them all over to the University of Iowa Library. I
received letters from older women who told me how miserably they
had been treated by their husbands, how they had suffered through
painful intercourse, how their uterus was tipped and how they were
forced into intercourse, and how their husbands just controlled
their lives. I started getting letters from women all over the United
States after a news story that went nationwide. The letters dealt
with forced sex, and how they had been mistreated, and how they
weren't loved. They were abused women, and I just thought, Lord,
forgive me, I've been unaware of all of this.

Two letters I didn't turn over to the library were from a Catholic
mother from a small town here in Iowa. Her fifteen-year-old daugh-

ter was pregnant. She wrote, "I can't talk to my senator because he's Catholic and antiabortion, but do you know any place I can take my daughter for an abortion?" Fortunately I knew Rosemary Hawks, a Unitarian in Iowa City, who had just brought that subject up with me. At that time I was still unaware of the implications of Iowa's abortion law and Rosemary wanted me to introduce a bill to make it less restrictive. I called Rosemary and she had a number in Mexico, which I passed on to the woman who had requested help. I said, "I can't speak for the service but Rosemary Hawks has sent people there. This woman took her daughter to Mexico and wrote me afterwards that all went well. About four years later this same woman wrote me again. Her next daughter was pregnant and she wanted to know where she could take her. I said, "You can take her to the Emma Goldman Clinic in Iowa City." She didn't even know that it existed. I didn't give this woman's letters to the library.

Anyway, it was the abortion issue that really taught me how cruelly life dealt with women, particularly poor women. Rich women probably had the same kind of husbands in the same numbers but they didn't write. They were oppressed at a little higher level. As the national picture moved, my letters did, too. The letters changed to economics—women being harrassed in their jobs, women who couldn't get hired or promoted. I became a real feminist—inch by inch—as Iowa women told me their troubles and how they were treated, and asked for my help.

What were some of the most important pieces of legislation regarding women that I was involved with? I think the comparable worth law was one, but probably those earlier laws too, like the law Lipsky and I did, which was simply for welfare women having some of their own money and not being taxed 100 percent. At the time it didn't seem like that much but it was the first independence some of these women had. We studied the facts about Iowa women on welfare. We found the average stay on welfare was two years, a relatively short time. I sensed a genuine dislike for women as a group, if not as individual women. All this came out time after time, subtly, in the abortion debates. I remember how they scheduled the first abortion hearing at 7:30 at night so that hardly anyone came except for friends. We did not have public hearings at night in the sixties. Women's issues were very low priority early in my legislative career. But that's changed. Look at John Chrystal, Jo Ann Zimmerman, Don Avenson, and Tom Miller running for governor in the Democratic primary [1990] highlighting women's issues. Miller is now trying to say he's not a die-hard antiabortion proponent. The heck he isn't.

When I was in the senate, one of the more important pieces of legislation which I worked on was a law making the kindergarten through twelfth grade curriculum nondiscriminatory. I've forgotten how it was worded, but schools couldn't have special courses for boys and girls. Schools had to let boys and girls in each other's courses. The change was made when we were redoing the school standards law. Later we passed a law saying schools had to teach in a nonsexist, multicultural manner. That was when I was in the senate. Mary O'Halloran put the same requirement in the house bill and that's how we got it enacted.

I was in the house from 1964 until 1968 and then I went to the senate. I stayed in the senate through 1978. I ran for lieutenant governor twice, in 1970 and 1978. The first time, my nomination was a gift or somewhat of a "sentence" from the party. They couldn't get a candidate and I had a holdover term in the Iowa Senate. I had a total of $11,000 to run my campaign. Cliff Larson was chair at the time and he talked me into it. He promised me all kinds of help which never materialized. Lois Copple of Des Moines managed my campaign for nothing, and then the party headquarters was even reluctant to give her a desk at state headquarters. They treated her like an interloper. Doris Mandelbaum (later Doris Field) helped her a lot and the Democratic state office didn't help them at all. Lois finally got $500 out of the party. But the campaign was a disaster. All they wanted to do was fill the ticket.

That campaign taught me everything I didn't need to know about how sexist the world was. Everybody gave me this advice on how to hide the fact that I was a woman. They said a woman couldn't get elected. But I don't think that it was because I was a woman that I was defeated. It was the abortion issue. It was the first time that the right-to-lifers organized statewide. I campaigned in Dubuque and I had good reception but the right-to-lifers followed me around and told everyone my stand on abortion and how terrible I was.

In both my 1970 campaign for lieutenant governor and my second try for the same office, the press kept asking me "women's" questions, like, "How is it to be a woman?" That one really stumps me. I've never thought of a decent answer. I've thought of all kinds of facetious answers but never a good one. The reporter from the Des Moines Tribune said, "How are you going to overcome being a woman?" Questions like that are absolutely unanswerable. I was all prepped on what I was going to say on roads and bridges, which was a big deal, and on all kinds of issues that you deal with in a campaign, but all I got was, "You are for abortion and ———." I was the

Governor Harold Hughes signs a bill reorganizing county boards
of health. DODERER chaired the Public Health Committee.
Arthur P. Long (*right*) was Commissioner of Public Health.
*"Minnette, so many times I have searched that code to find out
the genesis of some law in my law cases and I always find your
tracks."*—Clara Oleson

abortion candidate. I couldn't get away from questions on abortion
and on being a woman. I had plenty of facetious answers that I
didn't think anyone would find very acceptable. I never thought
about not being a woman. I thought about not having opportunities
because I am a woman. When I was a kid I wanted to be a boy
because I could wear pants and do the things boys did. But I never
thought of changing my sex. You just don't. It's one thing you accept as reality.

When I ran for lieutenant governor the second time I was not a
holdover senator and I was defeated in the 1978 primary election. I
was out of the legislature for two years. At that time there was a job
open at the University of Iowa to teach newly elected county and
state officials how to do their jobs. I had been on those legislative
committees and I knew the laws, and I knew the job. I called Clay-
ton Ringenberg, chair of that department, about a job interview and
he said, "Minnette, do you think you can do that?" What a downer!
They still didn't take me seriously. I didn't get interviewed or hired.

Joe Johnston, a lawyer who had been a legislator, had devised a
computer software program for law firms and had started a business to market the program. He called me and asked me if I wanted
to come to work for him. I managed his office for a year. Otherwise, I

wouldn't even have had a job. My two kids were grown and there
was no point in my sitting at home.

In 1980 I ran for the house again. The reason I did is because
Dale Hibbs, a Republican who represented my district, announced
that he was not going to run again. This left my house seat open at
the same time that the man who had bought Joe Johnston's company decided he was going to move it to Colorado. I thought I might
as well take a flier at going back to the legislature. I liked politics,
the legislature, and working. I won in a three-way primary and was
elected in November. I've been in the legislature ever since and in
many ways I enjoy the house more than the senate. It's because
times are changing so much and the house changes faster than the
senate.

When I went back to the house in 1981 I organized the Women's
Caucus. We did a lot of consciousness-raising among ourselves
about how the men were going to treat us and how we were going to
avoid the traps that we often fell into in our experiences that when a
man feels he's been abused he goes to a woman and tries to get her
on his side and to do his fighting for him. During my years in the
legislature I had watched situations where if a woman took on a
man in a debate, he tried to get another woman to fight back. That
happened to me in 1964 during the reapportionment debate. I had
introduced an amendment which would put both houses on a population basis. At that time most people favored one house on area and
one on population, especially the Farm Bureau, which ran the legislature. When a bill came out of committee which would have put
both houses on area plus some allowance for population, I got up
and I gave what I thought was a good speech on what was wrong
with the bill and why it wouldn't pass muster by the United States
Supreme Court. The men were furious that I would do this so they
went over to Percie Van Alstine from Pocahontas and told her to get
up and answer. She gave the most foolish speech I've ever heard.
One of her lines was, "If you cover the land with water, what do you
have? You have nothing. So it's area that's so important." I couldn't
believe I heard this coming out of this woman. And they clapped.
The page bells started to ring to get the pages to come and take her
notes praising her from the male legislators. It was part of the men's
code that you didn't fight with a woman publicly. What they really
didn't do then was to take women seriously. Women would get up
and make a speech and no one would respond to it. Not so any
more.

While I was in the senate, members became so conscious of
their language because I had cautioned them both privately and

DODERER and Sarah Jochum, 1978. *"When the legislature submitted the ERA to a popular referendum in 1980 I thought we had it won."*

publicly about their attitude toward women that they never said the word *woman* or *girl* or *female* without looking in my direction to see if it was okay the way they had done it. Luke Dekoster always used the word *Portia* when he talked about women lawyers and he asked me one day if this was all right. I said, "Sure." I wasn't that nit-picky. Today the men don't necessarily vote with you, but they're not disrespectful, and they don't put you down just because you're a woman. There are too many sharp women in both parties. If you win an argument or the vote on an issue, the men don't hold it against you like they used to. When I would win the passage of a bill or an amendment, Jim Schaben, George Kinley, and some of the leaders at that time would get very angry even though I was a Democrat. It was sort of like, "That damn woman again." John Mowry used to call me that behind my back. And John and I get along great now. He's the one that did the reapportionment plan in the 1960s.

The thing that put the frosting on the cake, as far as I was concerned, was when we did the Iowa Equal Rights Amendment back in the 1970s. We had a terrible debate. Gene Hill from Newton brought up the subject of men and women sharing toilets and all that stuff, and I reminded him that we used the same one already. There's only one on the third floor behind the senate, and Senator Hill and I had offices on the third floor. The opponents used the toilets, drugs, prostitutes, marrying homosexuals, and all of the things that they could think of that were negative in our society in their arguments against the ERA. But earlier this year [1989], when I decided I was going to introduce the Equal Rights Amendment again, not one person said anything against equality for women or against having an ERA in the Iowa constitution. Eighty-nine of the

one hundred house members signed on and the only one that star-
tled me said, "Minnette, I'll sign on if you won't remind me later
when we do insurance equity that this is the way to get it." I promised I wouldn't remind him because he is very much against insurance equity. Another member had to check with his wife. A couple
of others said, "I don't think I had better." But there were only
eleven of them. That's a miracle. We didn't even get that many
votes the first time around.

When the legislature submitted the ERA to a popular referendum in 1980 I thought we had it won. What disappointed me about
the campaign was that we got into a Democratic-Republican thing.
This was because Peg Anderson, who headed the campaign, was a
Republican. She was a good speaker and doing a good job and I
thought that because Iowa was a Republican state it was better to
have a Republican as head of the committee even though I didn't
pick her. Some of the Democratic women objected to having a Republican head the campaign. I thought we had it made until Phyllis
Schlafly came into the state with those films of the San Francisco
gay parade. She spent $25,000 to put those on television and to say,
"This will happen in Iowa if you get the Equal Rights Amendment."
Maybe we wouldn't have won it without Schlafly, but I still resent
her coming here. A lot of people were not aware that women are still
not equal.

It took me years to become terribly aware of problems that I
wasn't involved in. Young women, particularly, now have that same
problem. They manage to get to college, they manage to do graduate work, they manage to be lawyers and doctors, and the only
thing that stopped them was their own ambition and intelligence
because money can be found to finish college if you're bright. Many
women step into very good jobs and they aren't aware of what happens to the fifteen-year-old who gets pregnant. It's just not within
their comprehension. Because they've had so many advantages,
they are also not aware of the kids who don't get to go to college.
When I was young the middle classes, which had the advantages,
were often unaware, but now those advantages have passed to
many more people so this means that more people are unaware.
There are just so many women now that have it easier than young
women in my day because of the opportunities that we're guaran-
teed by legislation and by equal access to education and equal job
opportunities. Reagan hasn't managed to make the entire middle
class disappear. The ERA campaign did an awful lot to bring the
women of Iowa together and to make us more aware of groups that
we were not personally involved in. For example, the older women

DODERER as president pro tempore of the Iowa Senate, 1975.
*"While I was in the senate, members became so conscious of
their language because I had cautioned them . . . about their
attitude toward women that they never said the word* woman *or*
girl *or* female *without looking in my direction to see if it was
okay the way they had done it."*

and the younger women worked together, and labor women worked
with pink-collar women and white-collar women. We didn't get the
job done, but I think we will the next time. Of course it's a long time
before an ERA has any effect. Maybe it doesn't even need to be done
any more. As Congressperson Barbara Mikulski said, "You do get
tired of going plantation by plantation, law by law."

Economics is the thing that holds women back now, like insurance equity. The insurance companies don't want to change. They
are satisfied with what they call "fair discrimination." I've heard
that if they treat women the same as men it will cost them some
money, or they'll have to admit that they are mistreating women.
It's the same way with comparable worth, equal pay for work of
equal value. They still get a lot of work out of women that they don't
pay for. We mandated comparable worth for all women employed by
the state and then we were going to move on to local government
workers and the private sector. Something else interfered and we
haven't done it. There isn't any big push anymore. Female employees of the state got about $20 million more a year because of compa-
rable worth legislation. Of course, the schools had comparable
worth because they had salary scales without regard to men and
women. We fall short in the schools in the administrative jobs,
which are the ones that are well paid. We can correct that by law but
it is a long process. Many women with families find it is easier to

teach when they start out because they do not have to do weekend work at administrating. By the time their families have grown up, they do not wish to fight the battle that it requires to be administrators. Nonteaching jobs are very unequally paid between women and men in the school system.

That about covers my involvement. We haven't talked about the organization of the Iowa Women's Political Caucus. I would like to hear what Roxanne had to say about it because that's sort of a vague memory. I remember coming to Des Moines and meeting at Roxanne's house. The caucus was effective in raising consciousness and eventually that affected legislation. It was very effective because it was the first time that a group of women who had standing in their communities were working for a common goal of improving the legal and economic status of all women. Individual women had always done this with their charitable work and with their church work but they didn't get together to move all women forward. One trouble with the caucus was that opposing political parties were joined together and it was a structure that was almost bound not to last. It was the caucus women who really managed the ERA campaign and then they got into fights because of the differences in the parties. They didn't want to see Peg Anderson promote the Republican party, and I'm not sure she did it, but maybe subconsciously. This is true with women in the legislature. Dottie Carpenter is a Republican. I keep forgetting that until we work on an issue like minimum wages for labor. Then she is a shouting Republican. Right now we are crosswise on insurance equity. She just thinks that's almost a sin. So does Julia Gentleman and Janet Metcalf. Even Elaine Szymoniak, a Democrat and a feminist, is a business candidate when it comes to economic issues. She was against the minimum wage, and my goodness, whom did that minimum wage help? Women, low-income women.

What about the status of the women's movement today? I believe that while progress may be slow, the majority of women will not choose to go back into the second-class citizenship of the past. Women have had a taste of better pay, better and broader education, and have observed the legal inequalities between men and women in the past. We have watched ourselves change; we've fought for our rights; we've expanded our horizons; and we've discovered politics and the glass ceilings. Each advance becomes more difficult, but as a group, women in the United States will never accept going back to a time when we were not entitled to an equal share of the social, legal, educational, economic, and political advantages of this great country.

III Employment Activists

Phylliss Henry

Mary Garst

Betty Talkington

Kay Stone

Ann Kelly

Barbara Mathias

Louise Swartzwalder

Clara Oleson

Sarah Hanley

EMPLOYMENT ACTIVISTS can generally be divided into three categories: (1) women who were pioneers in nontraditional work and who thus served as role models for others, (2) union women working to improve their status within their unions, and (3) women who used their positions in the work force to support feminist issues.

Phylliss Henry and Mary Garst fall into the first category. Henry was the first female patrol officer on the Des Moines police force. Although she was not a feminist when she joined the force, an unwelcoming and unfriendly chief of police soon made her realize that no matter how hard she tried to be an exemplary officer, she would never be accepted as other than an unwanted woman on the force. It was at this point that she became an active feminist, forcing the chief to treat her fairly.

Garst, the mother of six children, is married to Stephen Garst, member of a family that has extensive farms near Coon Rapids. When her youngest child started school Garst became involved in the family's cattle business on a part-time, volunteer basis. She eventually ran the entire operation full time and was paid a "real wage." In the early 1970s, when corporations were feeling the pressure to add women and agricultural experts to their boards, Garst was invited to serve as the token woman and agricultural expert on the boards of Burlington Northern Railroad, International Harvester, and the Chicago branch of the Federal Reserve. She also served on the board of Northwestern Bell, where she was one of two female members.

Betty Talkington, Kay Stone, and Ann Kelly championed the rights of working women through their union involvement. In 1972 Betty Talkington, director of women's affairs of the Iowa AFL-CIO (American Federation of Labor and Congress of Industrial Organizations), organized the first of several conferences of Iowa union women, which provided them with their first opportunity to come together statewide to discuss feminist issues. She also worked in other ways to encourage women to stand up for their rightful place in union management. Talkington also was one of a small group of women who founded national NOW in 1966.

Kay Stone, a member of the Communications Workers of America (CWA) in Cedar Falls/Waterloo, was so inspired by the two statewide conferences of union women she attended that she became a leader in the movement to include women in the management of her local. She soon became known as the "Gloria Steinem of the Waterloo phone company." Stone has worked at several nontraditional jobs at Northwestern Bell (now U.S. West), including the position of installer, which requires climbing telephone poles.

Ann Kelly, an operator at Northwestern Bell in Des Moines, took an enthusiastic part in electing the first woman president of the CWA in her local. Kelly, an African-American woman, came to her activism less as a feminist than as a minority member dedicated to the idea of fairness for all groups in society.

Barbara Mathias, Louise Swartzwalder, Clara Oleson, and Sarah Hanley are representative of how women in the 1960s and 1970s furthered feminist objectives in their disparate occupations. Mathias, who was director of the YWCA in Ames from 1973 to 1975, furthered feminist ideals through speakers, discussions, and especially in providing counseling and a referral service for women seeking advice about problem pregnancies.

Swartzwalder chronicled the progress of the feminist movement in Iowa when she worked as a reporter for the *Des Moines Register* in the late 1960s and early 1970s. The feminist movement in Iowa probably would not have been as successful as it was without the publicity given it by Swartzwalder and the *Register*.

When Oleson got a job as a technical writer at the University of Iowa she discovered that because she was a "student wife" she was not eligible for a higher-education retirement fund. After more than two years of research and writing, she finally was able to establish that student spouses were eligible for this fund. Oleson next led a successful effort to secure equal pay for maids and janitors at the university. A U.S. Department of Labor ruling forced the university to pay each maid two years back wages along with other remedies to insure that inequities would be avoided in the future.

Hanley, a founder of the Cedar Rapids Women's Caucus in 1971, caused a stir in the community by her outspoken espousal of the feminist cause. Since 1977 Hanley has taught at the University of Iowa, where she is a distinguished professor of history. She was instrumental in the development of the women's studies program at the university and chaired this program for four years in its early days. She has also been active in working for the improvement of the status of women in the university as a whole.

Phylliss Henry was the

first woman to serve as a patrol officer on the Des Moines police force. She was not a conscious feminist when she joined the force, but the unfair way in which she was treated by the chief of police soon changed her outlook. She now works as support services manager for the Iowa State University Department of Public Safety.

"Some officers on the force accepted me and some did not. But the chief openly didn't accept me, and so that said to the officers who didn't that it was okay to be vocal about this."

Okay, name, rank, and serial number—Phylliss Henry, born July 10, 1940. Grew up on the east side of Des Moines in "Snusville," over by Snusville J.C., otherwise known as Grandview Junior College. My mother's parents were Danish and she grew up in the Danish tradition around Grandview College. I identify my mother as a closet feminist, I think she just didn't know she was a feminist. She used to work at *Look* magazine and would come home and say, "How come we women train the men and they get the supervisors' jobs and we who do the training are still in the same positions?" I remember lots of comments that my mother made, but she was not an activist in terms of doing anything. Later some of her statements came back to remind me that it was okay to be a feminist. I was raised to have the kind of marriage that my mother felt she never had. I was prepared to raise children. My father grew up around Hull Avenue and Bowdoin. He was Swedish and Dutch. So my heritage is half Danish, a quarter Swedish, and a quarter Dutch. I went to Cattell Grade School, Harding Junior High, and graduated from East High in 1958.

I was going to be a nurse and go to Lutheran Hospital School of Nursing and come back for classes at Grandview Junior College like I watched all the nurses come for their classes every afternoon. I could watch them from my front porch because I grew up at 1301 Grandview, directly across from the college. Instead I got married right after high school and I worked on and off during my marriage. My first job was at Farm Bureau as an actuarial clerk. I worked there for a year and I quit for what I now recognize as sexual harrassment. I didn't recognize it as that then. One of the fellows on his way to being a full-fledged actuary would come to my desk and put his arm on my shoulder or around my back and I found it very uncomfortable. Instead of saying anything about it I found it easier to move on to some other place.

I then went to National Travelers Life, worked there for a year or two, then we moved to Indianola in 1960 because my husband had a job as deputy sheriff in Warren County. We moved into the sheriff's residence in the courthouse. The arrangement in almost all of the counties at that time was that the sheriff and his wife lived in what they called the sheriff's residence. In Warren County's case it was an apartment on the third floor of the courthouse in Indianola. The other half of the third floor of the courthouse was the county jail.

The sheriff had lived in the courthouse for about twelve years. His wife had the responsibility of taking care of the prisoners: feed them, wash their bed linens, and wash their jail clothes, and also to answer the police radio and the telephones when the sheriff's office was closed. So that meant that every noon between 12 o'clock and 1 o'clock, she had to be home to answer the radio and the telephones, and every night from five o'clock until eight o'clock the following morning she was responsible for the telephones and the radio. As she explained it to me, it was easier to find a babysitter for her children than it was to find a sitter for the telephone and the radio. The sheriff's office closed at noon on Saturday, so from noon Saturday until eight o'clock Monday morning, she again was responsible for the telephone and the radio. It was assumed that the sheriff's wife would do that for the large sum of zero dollars a month. After she had done it for twelve years she told her husband that if he ran for reelection and won, she wasn't going to do it anymore. So the next deputy sheriff that was hired had to come in on the condition that he and his wife would move into the sheriff's residence and that

his wife would take care of those "female responsibilities." This was
the agreement when we moved into the courthouse. We didn't have
children at the time and I was very glad to do this. I got a raise. I was
paid $25 a month. We also got free housing and there was a stipend
for groceries. I fed the prisoners every meal; cooked them breakfast,
lunch, and dinner. We had anywhere from two prisoners to maybe
ten or fifteen. Ten or fifteen was a big number. We did that for about
three and a half years. During that time our two children were born.
When the sheriff was not reelected, we moved out. I was certainly
not a feminist at that time.

After we left the courthouse we lived in various places in Warren County. At first I stayed home with the children and then went
to work for Bankers Life [now Principal Group]. Then I quit my job
because I again decided to stay home and raise my children. This is
what I told them at work but it was only partially true. I also stayed
home to see if it would help my marriage. It didn't. A year later
(1968), after ten years of marriage, I divorced my husband. I decided that we were not good for each other and that I wanted more
in life than I was getting.

That was probably the beginning of my feminism although nobody in their right mind would have labeled it that. I took the children and moved to California and managed an apartment building
in Isla Vista, a college community connected to the University of
California at Santa Barbara. This was the time when the Vietnam
riots were at their height. We had our own riots. Students destroyed
businesses, burned down the Bank of America, and fought the police. The National Guard stood ouside our front door with bayonets
and the children came home from their grade school telling me stories they had heard about all the gory things that soldiers did with
bayonets. They'd heard it at school and they believed that was what
was going to happen outside our building that very night. There
were helicopters flying overhead.

At that time I became involved with the church I was attending,
which was the Methodist church. We were working to calm the community down, to get the students, the activists, and the law enforcement people to talk to one another. I remember the community
gathering that the church sponsored and we had something like
three or four hundred students there. The sheriff had promised us
enough law enforcement people so we could break into small
groups. Two law enforcement people showed up. So the groups that
we broke into weren't very small and it was certainly an unproduc-
tive and frustrating experience. This was my first experience with
law enforcement in the community.

PHYLLISS HENRY at the police academy, 1973. *"My feeling when I joined the department was that if I was unopinionated . . . and did my job I would be accepted. Since then I've come to learn that this was a very naive opinion."* Photo courtesy of Iowa Women's Archives, University of Iowa

I stayed in California for a couple of years and then in 1970 came back to Des Moines and managed apartments for a person who owned several houses and buildings. I did that for a year. Then I decided that I needed to get out of the house and took a course in police-community relations at the Des Moines Area Community College (Area XI). The instructor asked me if I was going into law enforcement. I said, "No, I'm just here to get out of the house." He then told me about the Law Enforcement Assistance Administration (LEAA), which at that time was pumping a lot of federal money into police departments. A lot of this money was being pumped into education for police officers to encourage them to at least get an AA (Associate of Arts) degree. Area XI was one of those colleges receiving a lot of LEAA money. This money was called LEAP, Law Enforcement Assistants Program, and you could use it to go to school. For every year you were involved in law enforcement, after you finished your degree, a quarter of your loan would be forgiven. So I ended up getting money to get my AA degree from Area XI and all of it was eventually forgiven because I joined the Des Moines Police Department.

When I started school in 1972 I learned that there was a separation between policewomen and policemen. Policemen joined police departments as patrol officers. They worked on patrol and they could be transferred to vice, to narcotics, or anyplace in the department. They could be promoted to sergeant, lieutenant, captain, and eventually they could become chief. Women, on the other hand, were hired as policewomen. Their responsibilities were to handle

women victims and women offenders. They were limited, generally,
to the juvenile or the women's bureaus. Occasionally, they might
work for vice or narcotics on special assignment but they could not
be transferred. There wasn't a department around that allowed
women to be promoted to more than the rank of sergeant, and then
it was usually with the stipulation that they couldn't supervise
men. They could only supervise other women.

I had decided at that point that I was going to have to think
about a career because I was probably going to be raising my children by myself. So instead of just thinking about a job, I needed to
think about a career. A law enforcement career got me excited and I
decided that's what I wanted to do. So, at that time being a non-
feminist, being rather naive about the whole procedure, I began to
apply around the country for a job as policewoman. I probably sent
out a hundred applications and received about that many rejec-
tions. Some didn't bother to answer at all. Nobody said, "Oh, goody,
we'll take you." I characterized the responses as saying, "We only
have one policewoman's position and if you're still interested in
1995, please give us a call." That was twenty years ago. Most of
them said, "Gee, thanks for applying, and we will put you in our
file, and if we ever get an opening, we'll let you know." Well, those
openings didn't come up very often because the women, even
though they couldn't be promoted or transferred, started out at the
same salary as the men. They received a sworn police officer's salary. Where it became discrepant was when the men began to rise in
the ranks and their salaries increased and the policewomen's salaries didn't.

What I didn't know at the time was that the Police Foundation
in Washington, D.C., was doing a study of all the major departments
in the country. This study discovered that in 1972 not one major
police department was hiring women, but all of those departments
were hiring men. In fact, one of the responses that they note in their
report is exactly the same letter I received. It said, we are not at this
time hiring women, we are on a campaign to hire—I forget the exact
number—something like a hundred fifty or three hundred men, but
they weren't considering women.

I went to Denver, Colorado, and applied. They, too, split their
applications between policewomen and policemen. For what they
said might be five openings for women—more realistically one or
two—they had 119 applications. They apparently had 100 openings
for men and they had 115 applications. Now if they had just put the
numbers together they could have had the cream of the crop.

I applied in Davenport at the time that they had a woman

mayor, Kathy Kirschbaum. This was in response to an announce-
ment in the *Des Moines Register* that they were going to hire
women in Davenport. They said they would notify me when they
were taking applications and when the test would come up, but I
didn't receive any notice. They went ahead and gave the test and
there was an article in the paper the next day that said that there
were no women applicants because none of them met the height
and weight requirement. So I zapped back a letter and said, "It's
really strange that the only female applicant who met your height
and weight requirements was not notified when the exam was
given." I was about 5 feet 10¾ inches tall and weighed 149 pounds,
which at the time were the height and weight requirements for both
women and men. In the meantime Davenport found that they had
to regive the exam, so it was possible for me to go over and take it.
For the first time ever they instituted a psychological exam. I
flunked this exam. I should probably not advertise this or let you
put it in a book, but I flunked the psychological exam. They
wouldn't tell me why, but it was before the MMPI (Minnesota Multi-
phasic Personality Inventory) was split into two sections, male and
female, and they asked me such questions as would I rather go
hunting or stay home and knit. Well, I prefer to stay home and knit.
If I was a male answering that question, they would have scored it
differently than a woman answering the question.

One of the replies to the letters of application I sent out was from
Portland, Oregon. They said, "We have no openings for policewomen but you understand that this does not preclude you from applying for the patrolman position even though you are female." I
thought, Well, that's really a crazy idea. However, shortly after that
there was an article in the *Des Moines Register* telling about the
change in the Civil Rights Act and that it now applied to public
employers. For the first time police departments were going to be
forced to hire women as patrol officers. I guess that was the beginning of my saying, "Fine, I'll go where the openings are."

While I was sending applications to departments throughout
the country a man I knew at the Unitarian Church in Des Moines
asked how the job hunt was going. I complained that it wasn't going
well at all. He suggested I call Roxanne Conlin, who was then an
assistant state attorney general. When I called Roxanne I started
the conversation by saying, "I'm not a women's libber but . . ." Roxanne explained that I was being discriminated against and that it
was illegal. She did not overtly encourage me to file a discrimination
suit but her tone was clearly that if I wanted to she would help me.

Finally I said, "Why am I applying all over the country when

Des Moines has openings and I could apply right here? And besides, I can keep track of what's going on in Des Moines." At this time I had finished my first semester with the police-community relations class at Area XI and was taking another semester and had decided on law enforcement as a career. I decided to take every folio exam that the Des Moines Police Department offered. One of the police officers told me that the matron's exam was coming up and he said, "This is a way of getting your foot in the door." I believe now that it would have been a big mistake if I'd gotten hired as a matron. That would have gotten me into a position where the police department had control over me. They could say, "Your job depends on you not raising a ruckus." As it was it worked out better.

When I applied for matron, I also applied for policewoman. The ironic thing about the policewoman's position is that there were no policewomen on the Des Moines department. The three who had held the job had been appointed to a newly created rank called "detectivewoman." (There is a reason for that, which we cannot publish unless we can prove it.) But since Chief Wendell Nichols did not want any more women on the department (God forbid he should have six—three policewomen and three detectivewomen) the police-women positions were never filled even though they went through the routine of certifying the list every two years. I took the matron's exam and ended up number one on the list.

Applicants for patrol officer had to have a physical exam, a TB x-ray, a physical agility test, and a background check. Another woman, Nancy Moore, applied at the same time that I did. We were the only two people who did not get the notice of the physical agility test, but fortunately we found out about it and got there in time, otherwise we would have been disqualified. Nancy was rejected be-cause she was too short. I knew the matron's list was going to be certified on a Monday night at a city council meeting. I also knew that on the following Wednesday was the last day you could apply for patrolman. What I wanted to do was make sure that the ma-tron's list was certified before I applied as a patrolman because in certifying the matron's list, they were saying that my background was okay and my oral interview was okay. Those were two areas that could be very subjective and were being used to weed women out. So what I wanted to do was make sure that it was on record that those things were okay.

When I went to the civil service office for an application for the matron's job, I asked the fellow in the office what would happen if a woman walked in and asked for an application for patrolman. He said, "That is the law now and I would have to give it to her." Then he asked, "Are you going to do that?" I said, "Yes." He said, "Fine." He got this glint in his eye that indicated that he thought it would be wonderful if that happened. He called me a few days before the Monday when the matron's list would be certified and said, "Are you coming in or not?" I said, "I'm going to wait until after Monday. I want the matron's list taken care of first."

After the matron's list was certified, I went back to the civil service office and asked for three other applications: police patrolman, deputy court bailiff, and dispatcher. I had no chance of getting the latter two positions. The position of deputy court bailiff was under Sheriff Bob Rice (who was then chief bailiff) and he in no way wanted women in that position, and women at that time were not allowed to be dispatchers in the Des Moines Police Department because (they claimed) women get hysterical and scream when things happen. So, including policewoman and matron, I applied for five positions in all.

I placed first on all five written exams. I was second on the list of police officers after all of the tests were done and the reason that I got bumped down was because I didn't have veteran's preference. When I went before the Civil Service Board [Board member Marion], Cunningham asked me, "You've applied for five jobs. Which one do you want?" I said, "I want the patrolman's position." He said, "You'll probably get it." The night they certified the patrolman's list my mother and I went to the city council meeting, which didn't end until after midnight, and that was the last thing on the agenda. Russ Levine was on the council at the time and the only comment was by Russ who said, "I don't ever recall certifying a patrolman by the name of Phylliss." But by then everybody was tired and wanted to go home. Even the press missed it. I don't think it was in the paper the next day and it was a while before anyone caught on.

Roxanne Conlin was my advisor in this process, telling me what each next step would be. From the information I got from Roxanne, Phil Riley, the city attorney, probably told the chief, "Legally, you have to let her on, but she probably won't make it through her first year, so don't worry." Because of Roxanne we didn't have a court battle to get me on the department.

Some officers on the force accepted me and some did not. But the chief openly didn't accept me, and so that said to the officers who didn't that it was okay to be very vocal about this. Those officers who did accept me were pretty quiet about it because they knew that theirs was an unpopular position. It's like supporting blacks. If the top person takes the right position, the people under him or her will be supportive of that position and the others will be quiet. In this case, Nichols gave permission to be vocal against me.

On the morning of the day I graduated from the police academy, there was an article in the *Des Moines Register* quoting Nichols as saying that next he would be forced to hire pygmies because of reduced height and weight requirements. I think Nichols purposely timed his comments for the day that I would graduate. The only reason I was able to get on the department at that time was because I met the height and weight requirements which were the same as for men. There were currently court cases in Des Moines and else- where trying to knock down these requirements and ruling them as discriminatory towards women. One of these suits was brought by Nancy Moore, the woman who had applied at the same time as I did and who was rejected because she was too short. The officers in the academy, because we were all rookies and we were all in the same boat, were pretty receptive. If they didn't like my being there, they didn't say so. One was a sort of grumpy fellow who, it seemed to me, didn't want me to be there but over the course of my career he was a supportive person.

I remember the day in the academy [1972] when we were going through the English portion of our training and we were required to give a three- or four-minute speech and field questions afterwards. I specifically did not choose a feminist issue that was on the agenda because I didn't want to argue it in front of all those people. The instructor said, "Phylliss, why don't you take this women's rights issue?" I said, "I don't want to." But she practically ordered me to do it. When I stood up to give that speech, the people who were directing the academy—the sergeant, the lieutenant, the captain, and a couple of other officers who were probably standing around in the hallway—began to filter in. That was the only speech that they listened to. I thought it went pretty well and we didn't get into any great arguments but I certainly got a lot of, "How come you women don't like to have doors opened for you?" and the typical questions that were going on then.

My feeling when I joined the department in 1973 was that if I was unopinionated—heaven forbid we should have an opinionated woman—and if I just did my job, I would be accepted. Since then I've come to learn that this was a very naive opinion. For the year that I was on probation, and even into the second year, that was my attitude. If I disagreed with opinions about civil rights that officers would take, I pretty much didn't state my opinion. I just did my job. I knew that a lot of people outside the department were interested in what it was like to be a female officer on patrol and that there were requests for me to speak to various groups but the chief was turning

Patrol officer PHYLLISS HENRY
with Rosalynn Carter, 1976.
*"I've decided that my first love
is the criminal justice system."*
White House official photo

them down on the premise that I didn't have enough time or my
schedule wouldn't allow it. But he never asked me about it and I
didn't have the opportunity to say, "Oh, yes, I can arrange that."

In 1975 two things happened practically in the same week: one,
a sergeant in the police-community relations section called and
said, "We're doing a public service ad on one of the television programs and we need an officer who will go to the station tomorrow
and do it." I said, "Yes, I'd love to." He said that the script would be
at the station and I would have a little time to rehearse beforehand.
He called me back early the next morning and was very apologetic.
He said, "Phylliss, I'm really sorry. I thought this had been cleared
with the chief, but he doesn't want you representing the department." I said, "Okay, that's fine" (although it wasn't fine, I was very
angry). Then a lieutenant who was teaching the law enforcement
class at Tech High asked me if would talk to his students about
women in law enforcement, what it was like to be a female on patrol. It was still unusual for a woman to be on patrol. The chief
refused that request as well but he gave permission for one of the
detectivewomen to talk to the class. The lieutenant turned down
that offer because he didn't want information about what it's like to
be a female detective who did not work patrol; he wanted his students to know what it's like to be the woman out there on the street
and to be the only woman among three hundred fifty male officers.

After this I wrote a memo to the chief. Being rather dumb and
naive, I made some comments that I probably should not have
made but in thinking back it was certainly okay. The chief had said
that I didn't have enough experience to give me credibility to talk to
the law enforcement class. I pointed out to him that a police cadet
with less than six months' experience had been allowed to talk to
the police class about his experiences as a cadet. I also pointed out
that what the students wanted was not to hear from the policewom-
en but to hear from a female officer on patrol. I said, "As the only
female officer on patrol in the City of Des Moines I am therefore the

most qualified person to be talking to the Tech High class." The chief was irate about this memo. He saw me in the hallway one day and said, "Come in here, I want to talk to you." He asked who in the hell I thought I was to tell him what the people of the Tech High class wanted. Didn't I think that the chief knew what they wanted? I was brash enough to say, "No, in this case, sir, I don't think you do." I reiterated what was in my memo. I was probably in there about half an hour and the chief just got angrier and angrier.

He told me in the course of that conversation that I would never be able to prove to him that I was capable of being a police officer. I replied that I had been doing my job for two years. I had never been reprimanded. I had never been taken off the street for doing a bad job. I was doing as good a job as everyone else in my academy class and I was doing a better job than probably 50 percent of the officers on the street. I asked him what it would take to prove that I was capable. He said, "You haven't yet pulled a 300-pound man out of the river." (This referred to a question in my oral interview.) He also told me that I hadn't yet been confronted by a man with a gun in a dark alley and that he had no way of knowing if I was capable of handling that situation. I told him, "If that is a criterion for being a good police officer, then 98 percent of your department will never be in such a situation and will therefore be incapable of proving that they are good officers." "I know what a man will do, but I do not know what you will do," he said. The implication being that I'm a woman, I will therefore act differently and probably faint or scream or go running off looking for a cop to protect me. All this contradicted my belief that if I just did my job I would be accepted. It was now clear that doing my job would not be good enough.

Before the interview was over the chief was leaning over his desk saying, "You will never prove to me that you are capable of being a good police officer. Do you understand that?" I said, "Yes, sir," and walked out really angry. When I hit my hand against the door to his office to go out, my exact comment to myself was, "The son of a bitch is going to pay for this one." On the way through the outer office, I thought, "That man is going to come kicking and screaming into the twentieth century if I have to drag him in. He's not going to like the laws, but he's going to have to abide by them." Then, about the time I hit the outer door, I repeated, "The son of a bitch is going to pay for this." And that was the exact moment at which I identified myself as a feminist.

I challenged the chief in five different instances. I won them all. First, Gordon Allen, attorney for the Iowa Civil Liberties Union, and I went to see Phil Riley and told him that we would file charges of violation of my First Amendment rights if the chief continued to bar my speaking in public. I'm not sure what Phil did, but I do know that from then on I was allowed to speak. I immediately arranged to speak to the Iowa Women's Political Caucus and this speech was approved by both the chief and the police-community relations section.

Next, I challenged the height and weight regulations by filing a complaint with the Law Enforcement Assistance Administration (LEAA). I also went to the Police Burial Association, which is the police union, and presented a written proposal that they change the height and weight requirements before the federal government came in and forced them to do so in a way they might not like. The motion to consider this proposal was promptly tabled. Actually that was fine because all I was doing was trying to run it through the system so that we could take the issue to court. Next Phyllis Pearson, a lawyer, and I talked to the city personnel director, whose name was Jerry Thompson, about changing the policy. Thompson was also the EEO [Equal Employment Opportunity] officer. We again suggested that the rules be changed before the federal government stepped in and took away the city's LEAA money. He said, "That's a joke. Don't use that on us. We are not big enough for LEAA to bother with." Subsequently I contacted the LEAA investigator, who hadn't been doing a whole lot on the case, as was typical with lots of civil rights cases. I said, "By the way, we talked to the city personnel director, who is also the EEO officer, and he told us that you guys aren't going to mess with him, that Des Moines is not a big enough fish in the pond." He said, "We'll see about that." Within four weeks Des Moines received a letter saying that if you don't remove your height and weight requirements and eliminate your separate lines of promotion within a month, we are going to remove your federal funds. The chief of course was very angry but the height and weight requirements were dropped and the separate lines of promotion abolished. The LEAA also ruled that women had to be allowed to hire on as dispatchers. So here were four wins.

The other issue concerned the matron's position. To understand a little bit about the system: the male jailers were police officers who were transferred into the jail for a certain term of service and then they could go back out to the street or to some other duty. A lot of times officers were transferred in as punishment. It took five men to run the men's portion of the jail. There were five matrons as well who handled the female section of the jail. They were not female police officers transferred in. They were hired as matrons and they would retire as matrons. When one of the matrons quit in 1976, the chief apparently saw his opportunity to get me off the street and he transferred me to the jail. During that time, there was another matron in the jail who wanted to be a police officer but never quite knew how to go about getting there. It was not good to put the two of us together. The matron (Barbara Dennis) was not good at writing memos because she would get so angry that her memos would ramble and she would bitch, bitch, bitch. By the time you got through her memo you weren't quite sure what her complaint was. She was just an angry person because she had been prevented from being what she really wanted to be. I offered to write the memos for her and she signed them. We again wrote LEAA and said the Des Moines Police Department has separate lines of promotion. They have the matron's position and they have the jailer's position. The jailer is a police officer, the matron cannot go anywhere. LEAA came down with a ruling which said that women had to be allowed the opportunity to become policewomen and that they had to be transferred into and out of the jail on the same terms as the men. The matron I was helping was beyond the age requirement for police officers but the department was told to make an exception for her. She is now a police officer.

All this happened just at the time the chief signed an agreement that if male officers were transferred into the jail against their wish (e.g., as punishment) they would be transferred out after a year. Then the LEAA decision came down that said that women had to be transferred into and out of the jail on the same terms and conditions as the men. This meant that the chief could keep me in the jail for a year and my fear was that he was going to bury me there forever. I wrote another letter to LEAA and pointed out the folly of their decision; that there were approximately three hundred fifty male officers and it took five men to run the jail, that with the ratio of five to three hundred fifty, a man could be transferred in once in his career, probably for a year. If there were only four matrons and one female police officer, which was currently the case, how could rotation be achieved? But that was one time I couldn't get LEAA to listen to me.

After the year was up, I then wrote a memo requesting to be transferred out of the jail. My request was denied. When the chief failed to respond within the required time limit, the rules allowed me to send a letter to the city manager, which in effect forced the chief to answer my memo. The chief refused to transfer me out because he said he had no one to replace me with. I wrote back another memo that said in effect, "I don't care. I want out." This time I went to a different attorney; I don't remember her name. We again went to Phil Riley because when I was transferred in I asked

Phil, "What happens if I am still in here after a year and I can't get out?" Phil said, "Come back to me." When I went back, my first comment to Phil was, "Well, it's been a year. I want out." I don't know what he did, but the very next day I was transferred out of the jail.[1]

I was the first person out of my academy class to be promoted to sergeant. This was after about seven years on the force and only a short time after Chief Nichols left office. The new chief, Billy Wallace, was a relief after Nichols. He asked for my suggestions and even implemented a number of them.

After I had been on the force about ten years, I decided that I needed something more challenging. I looked at the system and decided that it had a lot of control over what I did. I looked at the promotional possibilities. If, for example, I was promoted to lieutenant, where would I be assigned? And if I was assigned in any one of those positions, would I like doing that kind of work? For instance, lieutenant in charge of dispatch. In most cases, I said, "No, it's not challenging enough." It seemed that people were already being groomed for the jobs that would have been challenging, and I wasn't in line for those. Besides, every time that you're promoted, the department can transfer you at any time. So even if you developed expertise in a certain area, such as arson, you could be transferred back to patrol where you didn't use your arson knowledge at all. What I wanted to do was to know that five years from a certain time I would be doing the same thing and doing it better than I was doing it today. It seemed to me that I couldn't do that in the police force.

Maybe it was just egotistical, but I decided I wanted more, and one way to do that was to go back to school. People normally go back to school in the fall, but Roxanne was then (in 1982) announcing for governor, and I worked on her campaign for a year and then went back to school in January of 1983. I got a master's and then a Ph.D. degree in communication studies.

After graduation in December 1988 I worked as a legal communication consultant with Starr and Associates in West Des Moines. However, I've decided that my first love is the criminal justice system so I'm looking at ways to reenter law enforcement. I am interested in the law enforcement system, how it affects those working in it, and how the system can be improved so as to improve work life and in turn improve the delivery of law enforcement serv-

---

1. Henry's struggles on the force are chronicled in detail in a collection of her papers in the Iowa Women's Archives at the University of Iowa in Iowa City.

ices. I am looking at private consulting or returning to law enforcement at the managerial level.

Phylliss Henry was diagnosed with breast cancer in November 1989. She underwent a mastectomy and spent six months in chemotherapy.

In December 1990, she began working for the Iowa State University Department of Public Safety as support services manager. The day after she started the job, she was told that her cancer had returned. She took a two-and-a-half-month unpaid leave and underwent a bone marrow transplant in February 1991. There has been no sign of further cancer since then.

In her current position, Phylliss works on a number of community education programs in areas such as crime prevention, sexual assault awareness, and victim assistance. She handles training and supervises the student reserve officer (SRO) program.

REFERENCE

John Van, "Midgets and Pygmies on Des Moines Police Force?" *Des Moines Register*, 23 March 1973.

Mary Garst managed her family's

cattle business in Coon Rapids from 1972 to 1988. She also has been the token woman/agricultural expert on the board of directors of several national corporations. She currently is president of the Iowa Civil Liberties Union.

"Although I was a feminist I was willing to stand for what happened to me, but it really hurt when I started to see things happen to my children."

I am totally an Iowan. I grew up in Jefferson, a small town in the western part of the state, the youngest of four children. My father was a country banker. He had a lot of power in the family but it was more a negative kind of power. He had a veto right, but my mother was very much the leader. She was a very strong-minded person and she was employed in an age when women generally did not work outside the home. She could be very manipulative as women at that time probably had to be, but she was really a power-house.

I entered Carleton, a small college in southern Minnesota, in August 1945, just when World War II ended. At the time I went to Carleton there were seven hundred women and only seventy men students. All of the men were in the service. Carleton had also lost a lot of male faculty members. One of the courses I took my freshman year was the History of Western Civilization. It was taught by Lucille Dean, head of the history department. She was the first woman to head a department at Carleton and she was a feminist. I didn't even know the word then, but you can be darn sure that I knew quickly that she was pleased to have her position but outraged that she had it only because all the men had gone. This was the first time I had ever met a woman of marriageable age who was unmarried and whose title wasn't preceded by "poor." In high school in Jefferson, there was a wonderful teacher who was unmarried. Even my mother, who was a supporter of women, always called her "poor Miss Jones" [a pseudonym]. The "poor" was because Miss Jones was unmarried in a society that said an unmarried woman is a worthless object. It would have been inconceivable that anybody at Carleton would have called my history professor "poor Miss Dean." There was nothing poor about her. She was a magnificent person. So there was a lot of feminist influence in my early college years just because men weren't there. If I had gone to college three or four years later it would have been a far different scene.

After I graduated from college I married my cousin Steve Garst of Coon Rapids, a town of twelve hundred about thirty miles from Jefferson. My maiden name was Garst, too. Steve was still an undergraduate at Stanford so I went to graduate school there. When I married I knew we would come back to Coon Rapids, where Steve's family are large landowners. There was no question about that. He was going to be a farmer. I remember coming into Coon Rapids in 1951 after we finished school—there was a gravel road that came in from a high plateau into the valley where Coon Rapids is located— and thinking, My God, what have I done coming into this town and moving into a little house? I'll never get out of this town again. It was a horrible feeling of being trapped. So then I proceeded to have six children, some of whom were probably conceived with the feeling that if I'm going to be trapped here I might as well top how things are done in Coon Rapids. If the average family has four children, I'll have six. I was determined to be part of the Coon Rapids community, so I became Coon Rapids with a vengeance. But I soon ran out of steam, partly because I was never totally accepted in Coon Rapids no matter what I did. In lots of ways it is a company town, and the Garsts were the largest employers in the community.

The family had always had a cattle operation which was sort of limping along—lots invested in it—not ever very successful because managers came and went and nobody paid much attention to it. So in 1969 when my youngest child started school, I got involved in the cattle operation. It was something I could do. I could see that some kind of organization was needed. I had also learned enough about genetics from just listening to people talk about corn to have an idea that those same principles had to be applicable to cattle.

MARY GARST, 1976. *"It occurred to me that parents of daughters ought to be ERA supporters."* Photo by Werthman Constable Studios, Omaha

Part of the problem with having managers come and go so fast was that there was no continuity in record keeping and genetics. You can't prove things in laboratories; you have to substantiate any thesis you have by just building up circumstantial evidence, and the only way you do that is to keep good records.

As I got into the cattle business I began to think it should be computerized because nobody can really milk all of the significance out of this collection of data without a computer. So I went over to Ames and found a private contractor who would write some software packages. Between us we dreamed up a package. Then I rented time on the mainframe computer at Iowa State University. (There were no personal computers then.) We actually communicated by mail; it was way too expensive to go on-line. The scheme worked.

I got the records in such a shape that I could understand them but they got so complex that nobody else could. I did all this for two years without pay because farm wives do not get paid. Then in 1971 I thought, This is ridiculous. It is not good for me because I don't take myself seriously enough and it is not good for the men in the business not to pay me because they don't value how good I'm getting to be at this job. So I went, not unpleasantly but firmly, saying, "You've got to pay me a real wage because I'm doing a real job and I will be truly responsible for this operation." A lot of times in the future I regretted that. There is protection in being an unpaid volunteer. It's a lot more comfortable.

I started out first with just the breeding records and then I started into sales work because we developed cattle good enough for other people to be buying them for breeding purposes. Before that we just had terminal cattle, which meant that we raised them for meat animals. Next I got into advertising and then I had to get into managing the cowboy crews because I now knew exactly how I wanted it done. When I relied on somebody else to do it, they couldn't see why it was important to do it my way. By 1972 I was running the whole operation full time.

It occurred to me that farming was getting to be fairly technical. Farmers had always been generalists—they had a few hogs, a few cattle, a few chickens—but now it was getting to be an age of specialization. There was a tradition that women worked on the farm, but their jobs were to keep the books and do the disking. Disking is the most god-awful, boring job in the world. The fun is planting or running a combine. So there were women who did have a tradition of working on the farm and they were being underutilized; there was no reason they couldn't take on specialized work. So I began talking with women's groups, mostly farm women's groups, saying, "Your husbands are in hogs. They can't know all about immunization programs to protect the health of piglets and you can become a specialist. You would become invaluable to them."

Although farm women keep the books, they are not really involved in production agriculture, making the buying decisions and getting into the management role. They are bookkeepers, not accountants. It is a rote kind of secretarial service. By management, I mean decisions such as, Do we or don't we buy the new tractor? What is our rotation going to be? Do we tear out this fence or do we rebuild it? It is the day-to-day decisions about how much capital to spend and where you are going to put it. That's what I define as management. There are some women I know who are getting more involved in decision making, particularly in hog operations, which tend to be a good profit center on farms. It takes quite intense and very specialized management. As far as I know, women are still not into crop production. Four or five years ago Iowa State University asked my help in locating a woman in production agriculture, someone other than the specialty kind of management. I made many telephone calls, wrote many letters, and never found one woman in Iowa. I found one woman in southern Minnesota. That was it. Women might be involved in production agriculture as widows of a farmer where they are the nominal head, but they really have some male who does the production part for them.

I don't like to talk about my experience in hiring cowgirls because it was not very successful. Only 1 percent of the men's work with cattle actually involves male-type muscles, 99 percent doesn't. There was absolutely no necessity to have only cowboys, so I determined we would have cowgirls too. The job required that you be able to back up a trailer and be able to ride a horse, but I was surprised at the kind of basic knowledge that you did have to have that the women didn't have, for example, how to use a crescent wrench. Somehow boys absorb the knowledge of what a crescent wrench is at their fathers' knees. Girls do not. When I realized this I thought, This isn't going to be as easy as I thought. There was just no culturalization for women to get into this kind of life.

To a great extent you can overcome this lack of culturalization, but there were other problems. A large part of a cowboy's work— why it appeals to people—is that it is largely unsupervised. Cowboys have to be out there alone, and the tradition is you never check up on them because you assume that what you have asked them to do will be done. They resent a lot of supervision. Despite low pay and miserable working conditions, the appealing part of the job is that it is seen as macho and the cowboys deeply resented the women. They took advantage of the fact that they were unsupervised. When I was there the women were treated okay but the minute I disappeared all hell broke loose. It was horrible—the sexist, discriminatory practices, and the demeaning kinds of experiences. I would find out after the fact what the women had gone through. I never could totally beat that.

I finally ended up with one really super woman, a very nice person, and she left as a basket case. She was an animal science graduate from a prestigious school who came with high recommendations from her department. She was victimized by the men from the day she appeared. It took the form of isolation mostly. The men sort of melted away when she appeared and they ignored her in general conversation. They always chose a male partner for any jobs that needed two or more. This is how they behaved when I was there. I later found out that they "pulled a joke" on her when I wasn't around, like sending her to the wrong pasture, giving her a fast deadline and then telling her to drive the pickup which they knew had a flat tire. She started out telling me some of the problems but soon quit that. I assume the guys called her a tattle-tale.

It was an unpleasant atmosphere when she was around. Our efficiency seemed to be dropping and she was acting droopy, even morose. Now that I think about it, it was horribly unfair but at the time I felt mad at *her* a lot of the time. Why couldn't she get along better? Ultimately I began to wonder what kind of service I really was doing because I could not give her the protection she needed without totally rewriting what cowpeople are like. So it is still a male's field.

About 1972 or 1973 there were lots of articles in the national press about agriculture being the new frontier in American business. Agriculture became recognized as important to the national economy. That trend came along with the trend about women's involvement in the social and business fabric of the country. So quite a few corporations began to think that they ought to have a woman director. They didn't want a lot of women, but they wanted to have their black and their woman, and they also began to think that maybe they should have somebody who knew something about farming. They didn't really want women and they didn't really want farmers, but if they could find a woman who had management experience in agriculture and who was safely middle-aged, they could get rid of both of these onerous burdens with one body. So they started looking around at women who had the right kind of credentials. They looked all over the country and they came up with me. I first went to Northwestern Bell. Jack McCallister, for whom I had great respect, was then the CEO (chief executive officer). He actually had two women on his board. This was, and still is, unusual in American corporations.

Then I got passed around from corporation to corporation because I was identified as a woman who "won't cry at board meetings." That literally was a quote given to me as the reason I was put on the Burlington Northern Board. The next board I went on was International Harvester, which at that time was a booming corporation. It later had a lot of hard times and is now called Navistar. I am still on that board. Next I was asked to go on the Chicago branch of the Federal Reserve Bank Board. I became a member of these boards because, fortuitously, I was at the right place at the right time with the credentials that they wanted. I was one of a kind. They really did want farming represented. I think I was a good board member.

Commensurate with my ability, the respect I got on these boards was small. I was quite isolated from where real decisions were made, which was not in the boardroom. They were made in places like a gun club in Arkansas and the Augusta golf course in Georgia. The men would go away for a golfing weekend and the only debate was, "Are we going in your jet or my jet?" I was never included in any of those; in fact I've had some miserable experiences. One board was planning a lot of jolly, ho-ho stuff for a weekend at a hunting encampment in Arkansas. I like to hunt so I thought, That will be fun. I'll enjoy doing that. The man who was

GARST managing her family's cattle business in Coon Rapids, 1989. *"I started out first with just the breeding records. . . . By 1972 I was running the whole operation full time."*

organizing the trip came around to me at the end of the meeting, patted me on the shoulder, which I resented, and said, "We are going to miss not having you with us, Mary." I had not realized until then that I wasn't included. Actually a very major policy decision was made that weekend. I didn't know anything about it until I went to the next board meeting. Obviously it had been set up and greased. A lot of board service is men being jolly and bonding together. When they get into trouble, then they value my contribution more because it becomes less Old Boys Social Club and more task-oriented.

I never joined any feminist organization because I was working sixty or seventy hours a week and also because the one or two NOW meetings I attended in Des Moines seemed like preaching to the converted. I did work for an Equal Rights Amendment to the Iowa constitution. I have five daughters and I was beginning to see from the older ones some pretty ghastly things that were happening to them. My daughter Elizabeth, who got a master's in agricultural economics, had one of the highest GPAs (grade point averages) in her department and the sponsorship of a very prestigious professor. She was one of three women in a department of 120 graduate students. They ran a job bank. She got zero interview requests. Then she changed her folder to read "E. Garst" rather than "Elizabeth Garst." Immediately she got ten interviews scheduled. When she turned up in person—in her female body—there was minimum interview time given and zero follow-up from prospective employers.

This is just a sample of what we were hearing, enraging in part because we were so helpless to intercede on our daughters' behalf.

Although I was a feminist I was willing to stand for what happened to me, but it really hurt when I started to see things happen to my children. It occurred to me that parents of daughters ought to be ERA supporters. This was also a time of exodus from Iowa agriculture. So I started watching the local paper and each time a birth of a daughter was announced, I wrote the parents a letter saying, "I have five daughters and I support the ERA. The chances are your new daughter won't always be in Iowa in agriculture and under the protection of a social structure which it provides. The ERA will give her the protection that she will need and which you will want her to have when she is out in the world." I wrote a few of those letters and got an irate call from a father who said, "How dare you try and tell me how . . ."—that sort of thing. So to protect myself and also to get more acceptance Steve and I signed the letters jointly. We never got another complaint. That effort was not very successful. The ERA was defeated pretty badly and Carroll County, which is where we concentrated, was even worse than the state average. It was a nice idea. I'm glad I did it. I still believe in the ERA.

I can't remember the exact occasion, but sometime in the early seventies women all over the country were trying to get organized on a certain day to present our case. One of my daughters who was in high school set up a card table on Main Street in Coon Rapids. She couldn't get any literature but she handed out something that she had written herself and tried to talk to people about the feminist cause. She said the old men would stop and talk to her because they were just wandering the streets and wanted to be sociable. The guys who owned the retail stores acted annoyed or just politely brushed her off. The high school boys really wanted to talk. She felt very encouraged because her generation was listening. I thought that the vibes she was getting were probably genuine. For the old men it was the novelty; for the community leaders, nothing; but the younger ones could hear what she was saying. The kids from that generation are now the leaders.

Betty Talkington

is a veteran worker for women in the labor
movement. At a statewide meeting for Iowa
union women that Talkington organized in
1972—the third such meeting in the United
States—women went home inspired to improve
their status in their local unions. Talkington is
one of the small band of women who can
claim charter membership in the National
Organization for Women (NOW) when it was
founded in 1966 in Washington, D.C., at the
time of a national meeting of commissions on
the status of women.

*"One of the first really big fights I got
into in the labor movement was
when I advocated an Iowa
Federation of Labor standing
women's committee."*

I work for the Iowa Federation of Labor as, first of all, the
women's activities director, and also the volunteers in politics director. My job as women's activities director consists of working with
women who have problems and who do important things, trying to
talk with them, to have them help the women in the labor movement. It also consists of being a part of a statewide Women in the
Labor Movement conference every year, and also reporting activities to the Iowa Federation of Labor women's committee at their
annual convention. My job with volunteers in politics is to prepare
the lists of the union members for work with elections and other

political activities. We work very hard at that and it probably con-
sumes about half of my time.

I was born in Illinois and brought to Iowa at a very early age. My
father walked away from my mother and me. Mother was subsequently divorced and married my stepfather, Atryl Johnson, known
by his nickname Spider, who adopted me. He was a very interesting
person: a fighter, a boxer, and a baseball player. He was called up to
go to the Cubs one time but when he stepped off the train in Chicago
he took one look around and said, "I'm not going to raise my family
here," and he turned around and got on the next train back home to
Iowa.

When I was fairly young they were building the dams along the
Mississippi and my dad was hired on as a laborer for a dam that was
being constructed at Muscatine, Iowa. At that time this job was not
unionized on this particular dam, but the chief engineer liked my
dad and taught him how to tie rods, which is a term used when you
tie iron rods together in a certain way to strengthen the dam. The
ironworkers had the jurisdiction over my dad's new job and I can
remember my stepfather coming home and saying that he had
made it as an ironworker. I also remember the difference from then
on in our way of living, because the pay was lots higher. He became
a loyal union member and from then on anyplace he went to work
he was a union member or he was organizing. He lost several jobs
because he was organizing for the union. That was not a popular
thing to do.

The button manufacturers had the town of Muscatine by the
throat. If they didn't like what you did, you paid hell doing anything
to help your family or anybody else. But the interesting part of it
was that we lived at the head of a dead-end street, at the end of
which was a button factory. The women who worked there all
walked to work. Nobody was driven to work in those days; you trot-
ted along on the sidewalk. They were trying to organize the button
factories at that time and the organizers for the button workers
came to my dad one night and wanted to know if he knew of anybody who would stand out on the corner in front of our house and
hand out literature. Dad says, "Well, I've lost many jobs and now I
have a pretty good one. I think this is one I'm going to pass but I
can't pass it totally." The guy says, "I really didn't expect you to do
it, Spider, but I wanted to know if there was somebody in the neighborhood who would do it." My dad says, "I got an idea." The next
morning, quarter after six, my brother (who was about a year old)
and I were playing on the sidewalk out in front of our house. The

women who worked at the factory all knew us and so it wasn't unusual that we were there. What was unusual was that we were there early in the morning instead of later in the day when they went home. My brother was in a little wagon and I would pull him around and make corners and turn circles and everything to keep him entertained so it would look as though we were really playing there. But what I was really doing was handing out literature. That was my first union activity. The workers lost the election and many people lost their jobs. Finally, about ten years later, they did manage to unionize a small portion of the button industry.

I did political work in Muscatine for a long time. In fact, I got to ride on the Truman train that went through Iowa in 1948. I rode from West Liberty to Davenport. I had a new fall outfit for this trip and thought I was something else. I had a sign on a stick and I was standing next to the end of the train waving my sign and all of a sudden I realized that there was a bunch of big guys behind me, all of whom were cursing the president. They were students from the University of Iowa, which is thirty miles away, who were angry because Truman had vetoed the raise in the help that was given to the men who had come home from service. Now I don't think you should curse the president; I think the office is owed respect. If you don't like the man, wait until he is out of office, and then you can cuss him. I got mad at these guys and said, "Don't do that," and one of them said something smart, so I hit him with my stick and all that kind of stuff. It ended up that I was being escorted away to the pokey along with about four of the fellows because we were making so much noise. Just then the sheriff, who was a friend of mine, came along and said, "Where are you going, Betty?" I said, "I don't know where the guard is taking me. Should I put my feet flat and make him carry me?" The guard said, "You had better not do that." He told the sheriff that he was taking us all to jail and that we would be kept there until fifteen minutes after the train had left. The sheriff told the guard that he should explain to his boss that I was one of a group which was supposed to meet the Trumans and Margaret and ride to Davenport with them. The guard said, "Do you promise not to go back to the end of the train again?" I said, "Of course." So he let me go. Because I had been on the gravel, my hose were ruined. Margaret was kind enough to lend me a pair of hose. I rode on into Davenport and enjoyed the speeches and then went home to Muscatine. Alberta Metcalf Kelly, a member of the state Democratic Central Committee from the First Congressional District, had gotten me on the train. She had gone somewhere out West to get on the

train and ride the whole way and I thought that was exciting. This
was one of my very early political experiences and I've been a rabid
Democrat ever since.

In 1939 I married Harold Talkington and had two children, two
girls. I worked in the button factories in Muscatine when they
weren't organized. Later, I worked in the ordnance plant in Burlington and drove back and forth from Muscatine. There wasn't an organization down there then. It's now Machinist. When I was divorced
in 1954 I went to Cedar Rapids and worked at Collins Radio. I
started working for the AFL-CIO in 1962 when I was still in Cedar
Rapids and I didn't move to Des Moines until two years later.

I served on the Governor's Commission on the Status of
Women, which was formed by Governor [Harold] Hughes in October of 1963. I had the privilege of being appointed the secretary to
that organization. There were twenty-five members and we didn't
have any money. In fact, we paid for our reports by digging into
our pockets and getting organizations to help us. The chair of
the commission was Marguerite Scruggs, who was then on the faculty of Iowa State University. Part of her duties were in the extension department and the rest were in the home economics department. The vice chair was George Moore, who was in charge of the
Iowa Employment Security offices. We had both Democrats and Republicans on this commission and we broke up into several committees.

I was notified that I was a member of the commission in a very
strange way. I was coming home from a meeting in Council Bluffs
and listening to WHO radio and they announced the officers. I about
drove off the road. It seems the governor's office had contacted my
boss, who was president of the Iowa Fed, and he had agreed that I
would be allowed to work on this committee. We did a great many
things for the commission out of the Iowa Fed office. Our job was to
try to find ways to help women in all areas and all economic strata
of the state. The members of the commission were varied. We had
extension service people, Margaret Yoder and Marguerite Scruggs;
we had lawyers, Dr. Ruth Updegraff and Patricia Duckworth. Duckworth was a very militant feminist. There were also several men,
including the vice chair, George Moore.

One of our tasks was to get the state labor laws changed and we
did get them cleaned up. For instance, we thought it was an abomi
nation that the state law still had the words *earth closet* instead of
water closet. We thought we were really way back in the hinter-
lands with that outmoded wording and we managed to get that
changed. While that probably was not the most important achieve-

BETTY TALKINGTON, 1989. *"In August 1972 I organized the first of three or four conferences of labor women. We wanted the ERA, of course, also maternity leave, equal pay—you name it . . ."*

ment, it certainly gave us a feeling of having accomplished something in updating state laws.

The need for changes in laws affecting employment practices was very important, especially in regard to laws relating to wage collection protection and maternity protection for working women in both public and private employment. Women needed to be given reasonable maternity leave, but we were unable to get most of our recommendations passed. Basically, the whole legislature was male and they were of the opinion that women should either stay at home or forego the chance to bond with their children and go back to work as soon as the employer insisted. We weren't able to get any good ideas into those male legislative heads at that time.

The Governor's Commission on the Status of Women was a member of the National Organization of States' Commissions on the Status of Women. I attended several of those meetings. They occurred annually and were very effective. We lobbied and worked for several of the issues that we had talked about on the state level. I certainly learned a great deal about the difference in state laws. I'm an Iowa girl and I had never ever realized that there were so many differences in how the states dealt with these issues. When we talked about various issues, one state would say, "Oh, but we have that," and another state would say, "We'll never get that through." The gradations were from the best to the least.

The first meeting of the national organization was when [Lyndon B.] Johnson was president. We always were invited to the White

House, which was very nice. We had tea in the Rose Garden with Mrs. [Lady Bird] Johnson on the day that her first grandchild was a year old. That just happens to be something that sticks in my mind. Several of the women talked to her about the fact that it was Patrick's birthday. She was always a very gracious hostess. I was there twice and both times we got to be in the Rose Garden. Very, very impressive.

The speakers at these national meetings were very interesting. We had people from all parts of the government talking to us about the various things that they thought they should be able to do in their departments. The secretary of labor [W. Willard Wirtz] came in and that particular secretary was very gracious. He had Esther Peterson as an assistant secretary and I'm sure he would have been in ill repute if he had not been interested in all of the things that we were concerned about.

The National Organization for Women came out of one of these meetings [1966] and my recollections don't exactly match what's printed in the NOW literature. We went in to this meeting and the chair was the editor of the *Ladies Home Journal*. There were several of us who wanted to put a resolution on the floor endorsing the Equal Rights Amendment but the chair would not allow it. She was acting under instructions from the Department of Labor. The planning committee had decided prior to our meeting that there would be no resolutions from the floor. This was to keep the issue of the ERA from coming up for discussion. So a group of us, mostly labor women, got together one evening in someone's room. I can't remember whose room it was, but I do know that Esther Peterson was not there. She was horrified when she found out what we had decided to do. Our decision was that we would send a telegram on the equal rights issue to the lady who was chairing the meeting. Someone who claimed to know the chairperson well said that she would read the telegram to the delegates. We would be sure that it was given to her while she was on the podium and she would then read it without having it censored in advance. So we did that. Everybody in the room chipped in a little money to help pay for the telegram. When the telegram was read, pandemonium ensued because people who didn't want the subject of the ERA to come up were terribly unhappy. It was ruled out of order and so we decided that we needed to do something else about this.

We got together that evening and the person who had done the final writing and shipping off of the telegram said that we had a little money left over. Somebody else came up with the idea that we needed an organization for women. As I remember, the lady who did

The Feminine Mystique and made a lot of money out of women's issues—Betty Friedan—was there as a journalist. She was sort of circling the outside of the room and was not a part of the group. She wanted to know what was going on. Somebody said, "We need a national organization and we've got enough money to put out a mailing." So we decided we would do that. Somebody else spoke up and said, "What are we going to call this organization?" Someone else said, "We need it now and it's for women. How about calling it the National Organization for Women, NOW. Everybody uses initials." There was much clapping and one of the girls even knew how to whistle by putting her fingers to her teeth; there was a lot of whistling done. When other convention delegates heard about what we had done, women from all over the United States said, "We want to give you some money so that we can get the mailings."

In 1972 the Governor's Commission on the Status of Women was succeeded by the Iowa Commission on the Status of Women. Members of the governor's commission met with staff members of Governor Robert Ray, who had succeeded Governor Hughes. We asked that since we were a bipartisan body perhaps, just on the basis of continuity, Governor Ray would at least invite the Republican women who had served on the governor's commission to serve on the new commission. Governor Ray did not heed our request and he chose not to ask any former member of the governor's commission to serve on the new commission. By then it was a statutory commission and they did have a little money, not a lot, but I understand they did have a little.

I helped organize the Des Moines chapter of NOW in 1971 but my boss asked me not to hold an office and so I was there as someone who had a place where they could meet and we could mail from there and that sort of thing. My boss allowed this. I have been a longtime member of NOW, but one time I got very angry and didn't like something the national organization was doing so I wrote them a letter and said that I wasn't going to pay my next year's dues because of their actions. That was the only way I could express my disapproval. I can't remember what I was angry about.

Will I talk about my work within the labor movement? Okay, you mean you want me to be honest about how chauvinistic my bosses were? We have our stinkers and we have our chauvinists and we have our good people and bad. When I went to work I had a boss who has now passed on, and all I had to do was to ask to do something and I was given the go-ahead. Now you have to understand that I do put some thought into most things I ask for because I don't want to embarrass this organization any more than anybody else.

For instance, the first president that I worked for thought it was a marvelous idea that I serve on the Governor's Commission on the Status of Women. He thought it was something that I should be doing as an employee of the Iowa Fed.

In August 1972 I organized the first of three or four conferences of labor women. It was here in Des Moines and we had a great many things on our minds. We wanted the ERA, of course; also maternity leave, equal pay—you name it, those women brought it up that day. We thought we'd be done about 2:30 but we didn't walk out of the hotel until about 4:30 or a quarter to five. The women were excited. The second conference was held in June 1973. This and subsequent meetings were pretty much reaffirmations of what we had done earlier. Perhaps they'd bring in a new subject but I am sorry to say that the minutes and tapes are not at my fingertips at the moment. If they still exist, they are down at the historical society in Iowa City where we give all of our papers on a periodic basis. They are not available to the public because the immediate past president of the Fed asked that the various financial records not be made available until a certain time, and somehow this request got tied up with other records and, as I understand it, not many of the records are available as yet.

One of the first really big fights I got into in the labor movement was when I advocated an Iowa Federation of Labor standing women's committee. The president who succeeded the man who had hired me didn't think that this was important. In fact, he was horrified. Other states had organized women's committees and once you hear about what other states have done and think it a good idea, you go for it. When the idea of a women's committee was first brought up I was told that it wouldn't pass. I said I thought it would. So we had it introduced, and under our rules we have to send in a proposed resolution prior to the convention. I worked a lot with the women and they understood what I was trying to do, so I called a couple of friends and said, "Here's a resolution, how about getting it passed through your organizations to be sent to the Fed?" And it worked that way.

When the resolutions hit the desk of the president, the roof almost went off the building. He had told me that these resolutions wouldn't pass and he just didn't want to waste the convention's time or his time as chair of the meeting trying to discuss these things. I said, "I don't know how you do this, but I'm sure there's a way for you not to send them to convention." With that I turned and left the discussion. I was through. I had done what I could. Since I have never had a union contract and I've always worked at the pleasure of the president, I decided it was time for me to back up a little.

As a way of killing these resolutions, the president assigned them to a convention committee that would send them out with a "don't pass" response. The president told me that if I worked for these resolutions when they hit the floor that I was gone. So I called together the women who were depending on me for help and told them what the boss had said to me and then I told them what to do. They decided who would do what. But with the "don't pass" as a report from the committee and not having a whole lot of women on the floor as delegates, they didn't make it. So we lost that one. This was at the 1972 convention in Cedar Rapids.

The next year when we went to convention a couple of the women said, "Betty, we don't see any resolutions. How come? Aren't we going to try again this year?" I said that I was specifically told that I should stay out of it and I have done this so that I could look at the boss and raise my right hand and say, "I swear to God, I did not involve myself." If resolutions come out, they come out without my help. Since no resolutions had come in within the prescribed time limit, the cause was lost for that year.

In 1974 I had lung surgery in the spring and was only working very minimal hours when, the Friday before the convention, a man brought me a resolution and handed it to me. I read it and said, "Do you think this is the year for it?" He said, "It is time. It was time two years ago and now it's going to pass." This is interesting because before I had been talking only to women. I went to convention knowing the boss was madder than hell at me. He didn't say anything but he was really angry. He again assigned the resolution to a committee he knew he could influence. When the women started coming to me for advice (not just the women either, there were fellows who were really interested), I told them, "This resolution is going to come out with a 'don't pass' again." I repeated, "I have got to stay clear of it. I just can't stand the strain."

The committees all met in the ballroom in Sioux City where they had curtained booths all the way around the room. I was there for another purpose but I saw the people come out of one of the committee meetings and one of the girls looked at me and threw up her hands as though we lost. Somebody came to me and said, "What do we do now?" I said, "Get a committee to bring it out. That's all you can do. Just work each committee and see if there is one that will bring it out." Those are the words I used and that's as much as I said about it.

The women worked the committees and they found a committee that had the courage to bring the resolution out and the president did not know it was going to come. When the chair of the convention committee took the podium and read the resolution, the president immediately left the platform and I saw him go from vice president to vice president and I knew what was happening. He was saying to them, "Talk against it." One of my friends went by and said, "Betty, what is Hugh [Hugh Clark, president of the Iowa Federation of Labor] doing?" I said, "He's killing our resolution. You need to find somebody that can influence each one of these men he's talking to." At that moment he was talking to a man who was very active in one of the large internationals in Iowa. My friends asked, "Who would you have talk to him?" I said, "Ask the international rep." So as soon as the vice presidents got in line, somebody went to each one of them and by the time the debate came, there were about eight people for the resolutions and three stood firm against them. We won. That was in 1974.

The women's committee meets annually. It is part of the convention procedure. The members are named by the president with the help of the other two elected officers—the secretary-treasurer and the vice president—all of whom are full-time officers who work here, and on some of the committees I will be consulted.

You asked me to talk about the women in the labor movement in Iowa. There are women in many unions and thanks to the equal work for equal pay and some of the other laws that have been passed, and because of the directives from the federal government, the construction trades unions must have some women involved in every construction job. We have women in practically every local in Iowa.

The largest union in Iowa is an IBEW [International Brotherhood of Electrical Workers] local in Cedar Rapids and there is a woman who has been president of that local for about ten years. She is running again this year [1989] and doesn't even have opposition. We have another woman who has been president of a CWA [Communications Workers of America] local in Davenport for many years. She is well liked and seldom has opposition. We have lots of women secretaries. Somehow they seem to think that is a woman's job. I quit taking pencils or pens to meetings quite some time ago so I don't always have to get stuck.

You asked me if it was an uphill struggle for women. Yes, it is, and I want to cite an example. I thought that once we got equal pay for equal work and women were in the construction trades and doing their jobs that construction trades men from those unions would realize it wasn't a bad thing, that it was something that needed to happen and was late in coming. However, four years ago I went to a meeting of just construction trades people. It was an all-male audience and I started talking about some of the women who were working. There is a carpenter who is very good, a bricklayer who is doing a beautiful job, and a laborer who really pulls her weight every day she works. Well, when I started talking about these women, I was literally booed out of the meeting. I thought that once the older fellows retired, the ones who had been around for so many years, things would be better, but I find that in some areas the younger ones have the same feelings. It's just as strong. It seems to me even a little bit stronger because they're a little younger, a little more vociferous, a little more frightening to me because when they stand up and start waving their arms, they're usually half again as big as I am.

It isn't just building trades. I don't want you to think that. It's the whole labor movement. Lots of the fellows, especially when they have wives who don't work, are terribly antiwomen in the work place, especially if they work for the same money in the same jobs. Now if they have a woman as a secretary or a timekeeper, or the little person who stands out there and turns the stop and go signs as construction's going on out on the highways, that's something different. But it's still there and I tell you it's going to keep going. I think one of the ways that would help change attitudes a little would be if we had not only maternity but also paternity leave. I think men see maternity leave as an advantage that women get and if women have that then they should stay home.

I come out of IBEW, a union where way over 50 percent—at one time it was 70 percent—of the members were women. This was at Collins Radio in Cedar Rapids. The men were the highest paid. They were the technicians and the test people and that sort of thing—not that they had stronger backs; that had nothing to do with it. It was that they were more highly trained. Many of their wives worked in the same unit. When it came time to negotiate a contract, those women would not fight for their own salaries; they fought for their husbands' salaries. It divided the women into two groups, those who wanted a percentage raise across the board and those who wanted a flat raise on an per-hour basis. A percentage raise across the board meant that women's salaries kept getting smaller and smaller in comparison to the men's. If women got a flat raise, say 50 cents an hour, their men would not have as much money in their paychecks. It really was a self-defeating thing for all women because the number of spouses who worked together in that plant outnumbered the single women or women whose spouses worked elsewhere. This condition is still true in that plant.

Some women are active in their unions but they also have another problem that has never been addressed and I think it should be. I've been thinking about having a resolution this year and seeing if I can't sell it to some of the younger gals. This is to have child care at union meetings. So often women working in a plant or in an office not only have that job, but they also have the job of being mother, spouse, church worker, whatever. They don't have the money to pay a babysitter for all of these things and the easiest one for them to drop when there has to be a choice made between their church work or their family or their union is the union. That's the easiest one to let go because it doesn't seem to be affecting them as much as the other things.[1] As an extension of that idea, I think we should have some good day care for which the employer puts money in, the employees pay according to their salary, and it's on-site so that a nursing mother who has to work can do those things and then go back to work. There are a lot of things needed for the mother who is a single parent and has her kids twenty-four hours a day except for the short time they are in school. I'm not suggesting that schools should be day care centers. They should be teaching institutions, at least for the period of time they now operate, but we could extend the hours and use the buildings for other programs. At least at the moment this is a great deal of pie-in-the-sky, but wouldn't it be lovely? I'm being real honest about it.

CLUW [Coalition of Labor Union Women] is a very exciting organization formed in 1974 and is doing many things toward helping women who are presently working. CLUW started out just women but they now have opened their membership to men. There were some wonderful people who led the fight for this group. It was marvelous to go into a well-planned meeting in Chicago where they expected three hundred to five hundred people and over two thousand showed up. Women were sleeping in the halls of the hotels because that was all the room that was available. We met Friday night, all day Saturday, and Sunday until four o'clock. Because of good advance planning we came out of this meeting with a constitution, bylaws, officers, and literally no fights. The men couldn't do that. That CLUW conference was really very special and when we all held hands and sang solidarity at the end everybody had tears.

---

1. Since 1989 child care has been offered at state union meetings.

Kay Stone has worked for Northwestern Bell Telephone Company and its successor, U.S. West Communications, since 1965. She has held a variety of jobs ranging from operator to installer (climbing poles) to her current position of tester of installations for business customers at U.S. West Communications. An ardent feminist, she was dubbed by her male co-workers in Waterloo the "Gloria Steinem" of her union.

"I decided to try something I had no idea I could have any chance of success at and that was being an installer/repair technician. They made a lot more money than clerks made."

I grew up in northeast Iowa. I lived on farms and moved to town when I was about ten. I'm the oldest of seven children; there were four boys and three girls. My mom was a homemaker and she also worked as a waitress. My dad was a union man; he worked at John Deere. I went through schools in Waterloo, Iowa. My interest in the women's movement and feminism was just a result of a search for a solution to something I always saw in my family while I was growing up, going to school, working, and being married: women weren't very important, they didn't matter, they weren't listened to. They didn't have any power, but I didn't see that in terms of power and powerlessness. I saw it in terms of men could do anything they wanted and women were helpless.

All my relatives used to gather at my grandmother's house on

Sundays and when I was about three years old I began to be sexually molested by my grandmother's husband. This horrible violation of my trust and innocence led me to conclude that the world was a hurtful place in which I needed to find ways to protect myself and survive the pain. When I told my parents they said to just keep away from that man. This solution to my problem made me feel guilty, ashamed, enraged, emotionally abandoned, and terribly alone. I continued to suffer sexual abuse for several years because my parents continued to take me to Grandma's on Sundays. My mind blocked all memory of this sexual abuse until I was nearly forty. The sexual abuse made me feel unlovable and bad and unworthy of anyone's attention, and certainly untrusting of all men.

When I was a kid I had a real hard time talking to people. I thought a lot but I didn't talk about what I thought. I read a lot. When you have nine people crammed into a house it's pretty noisy and I was a pretty sensitive kid. I found out that if I read books, I wasn't there in that house. So that was my salvation when I was a kid and I read lots of books. I remember reading about the first woman doctor. I was too young to understand what they meant in the book when she was told in school to examine this woman and report her condition to the class. The woman student said, "Well, the symptoms indicate pregnancy but, of course, she's not married, so I don't know what's wrong with her." That didn't make any sense to me then. I didn't know anything about that. I started reading Zane Grey books when I was seven years old and once I discovered the public library that was just wonderful. I liked reading stories about women who did things with their lives. A lot of these women were teachers and social workers, or beauty shop operators. After I got bored with those I started reading metaphysical books and then I changed to European history. I loved reading about those queens, Elizabeth and Mary, and depending upon which author you read, one of them always had the upper hand.

I had made up my mind when I was about twelve years old that I wasn't going to have any kids and I was never going to get married. I thought I would like to be a nun. I grew up in a neighborhood where there were a lot of Catholic families and so I found out about nuns. When I was eleven or twelve I found out that the church I belonged to didn't have any nuns. I thought being a nun was a neat solution for women. They could live with other women and never have to worry about what they wore. They wore the same thing every day. They never had to get married and they never had to have kids. My mom told me that when you had children that was the end of your dreams. She didn't go to school beyond the tenth or eleventh grade.

There was one strong woman in my life when I was growing up. Her name was Peg Mullen. She lived a half mile down the road from us when I was a child and she had a son, Michael, who was my age. My mom liked Peg because Peg spoke her mind and my mom was afraid to. But Mom was kind of fearful and I sort of was, too. Mom would say, "Peg went to the school board meeting and she spoke up again about something," or "Peg wrote a letter to the editor and she just shouldn't do that." I liked what Peg did. Her son was killed in Vietnam in 1970. At that point I reconnected with her. I was no longer Peg's friend's little daughter. I was an adult woman. I listened to her, sat in her basement with her and read letters about her son's death. I thought, Peg might be crazy but she might be right. She was important in my life. She wasn't like the other mothers I knew. She took me to my first peace rally.

I went off to a church college in California in 1963 when I was eighteen because I wanted to get as far away from home as possible. Various people talked to me about going to the University of Northern Iowa, which was called Iowa State Teachers College then, but that was too close to home. I didn't want that. The church college proved to be more of the same. The idea was that they would train men to be pastors for churches and I don't know what else, but the women had only two roles; if they couldn't be a minister's wife, they could be single and go off to Africa and be a missionary. Neither one of those roles appealed to me and I was real unhappy there.

The school was really into protecting the women. You couldn't drink, you couldn't dance, you couldn't play cards, you couldn't go to movies. So everybody went up in the hills and screwed, except me. Nobody asked me. There were lots of early marriages. I was at this school for a year and I was real unhappy. I came back to Iowa in 1964.

When I came back to Iowa from California I had the idea that I would get a job for a couple of years and then I would continue my education. I didn't know what I wanted to do. There was something in me that said it would be good to help people. Well you grow up being the oldest of seven kids and you're told, "You're such a good helper." Maybe that was early programming. My neighbor lady, who was the personnel director at Allen Hospital in Waterloo, said, "Why don't you come over and apply for a job as an aide?" So I did. I worked in the old people's home. That wasn't new to me because when I was a child, twelve or thirteen, I had worked in an old peo-

ple's home feeding patients after school. After a couple of months
the personnel director told me that they were going to start something new. They were going to teach people to be surgical technicians who were going to assist doctors in surgeries. I thought that
would be real exciting. There were seven of us, six women and one
man. We had classes learning about instruments, what they looked
like, what they were used for, how to make a surgical pack, how to
prepare them for sterilization, how to set up a sterile field for surgery. But they didn't tell me what to say to patients when I went to
get them. One time I was trying to reassure this guy who was real
nervous. He said, "What are they going to do to me?" I forgot what
his surgery was, and I said, "They'll perform your surgery and
probably while they are at it they'll take your appendix out." He got
real agitated and said, "I hope not. I'm here for a nose resection."

I worked as a surgical assistant for about six months. I have a
hearing loss in my right ear and that was the ear that was always
toward the surgeon. He wore a mask so I couldn't read his lips and it
took too much energy to follow his instructions. Besides which, I
had some women friends who worked at the phone company, Northwestern Bell, and they made $60 a week and I only made $48 a
week. So that was a big incentive to change jobs.

I started as a telephone operator in 1965. I got my job by accident. They asked me if I knew anybody there. I played tennis with
this guy whose mother worked there, and I said, "His mom works
here." What I didn't know was that she was one of the very few
management women and it was by who you knew in 1965 that you
got a job. It's mostly not that way today. But that's the way it was. I
remember they asked me what my dad did, what my mom did, how
much money he made, who were my brothers and sisters, how old
they were, those kinds of questions. Was I a member of the Commu-
nist party? Which I thought was really silly. I didn't have any notion
of the McCarthy hearings. I didn't have a sense of any of that and
what it all meant. I didn't have any thoughts about anything outside of myself when I was twenty years old.

I did notice right away that there was a big difference between
men and women at the phone company. My brother was also offered
a job at the same time. They were going to hire him as a lineman for
$90 a week. He was just as ignorant about the phone company as I
was. I thought that was real unfair. My brother screwed it up and
got arrested for drinking under age in a bar. He never did work for
the phone company. He took off for California.

I started as a telephone operator because that was where
women started in 1965. I didn't like the regimentation. The rebel-

KAY STONE at work in the employment office, Northwestern Bell, 1972. *"I wanted a desk. I wanted to use my own words."*

lious part of me delighted in playing games—passing notes when you weren't supposed to, chewing gum. I had long hair which I would let fall forward on my face and I would chew gum and they couldn't tell. I only had one good ear so it was real sensitive to the change in transmission level when the management monitored, so at those times I did everything just right. I had a terrible attendance problem. I didn't like going to work. Sometimes I was too drunk to go to work. I didn't realize it then but I already had a problem with alcohol. All my friends stayed up late and drank and smoked marijuana and listened to wild music and wished we were in California. That's before I got married.

I married in 1968 and for a while I was okay. However, marriage radicalized me and I found out that it did a whole lot of other women, too. There's one incident that comes to mind that I can't believe I did it, but I did. My friends Cynthia and Julie and I had husbands who all worked at the same place. They were all service technicians for Sears: electronic technician, washer/dryer specialist, and refrigeration technician. They had to wear these uniforms which included long-sleeved white shirts with the Sears emblem on them. They were given to them by the company and they were a pain to keep clean. These men were doing work where they got just filthy every day, and each of them only had three shirts. This meant that Julie, Cynthia, and I were all the time not only washing these shirts, but starching them and ironing them. About this time I started going to union meetings and wanting to spend time with people I was meeting at work, because mainly that's where I was meeting people at that time. I thought my life was getting sort of limited and I had been reading anything I could get my hands on about the new women's movement. This was late 1970 or mid-1971.

I started getting ahold of the idea that my husband worked eight hours a day and I worked eight hours a day, but yet I did all the laundry and I did all the cooking and I did all the shopping and the housework and he told me that was fair because he took care of the car and did the yard work and the sidewalks in winter. I told him that I could pay the neighbor kid to do that, too, and I could take the car to the local station for service, just like he did. It looked like he had a pretty easy time of it. I was starting to feel real angry about how unequal that was and I talked it over with Cynthia and Julie and their solution was to just do it. I could hardly believe that of Cynthia. Julie I could, because Julie had kids, a herd of cattle, ten thousand laying hens, and no job outside the home. I never had children so I didn't have that to deal with, but one day I just sat down on the job. I said to my husband, "I'm not going to do your shirts anymore. You want clean shirts, you do them." He put up a big fuss and he said he wasn't going to do them. He wore them dirty. Then I started feeling guilty. I was really feeling angry so I decided to write the local store manager. I said, "Here's my situation and the situation of some of my friends. We work outside the home. We have these other responsibilities. Give these guys five shirts and a spare because they aren't going to do them themselves and I'm not going to do them."

The next thing I knew, I came home late from work one evening and there's my husband with Tom and Elbert, the two friends he worked with. Cynthia and Julie were also there jumping up and down and grinning from ear to ear, saying, "This is so great." The men were just madder than hell. They were saying, "You had no right to do this. We could lose our jobs." They were just overreacting. You know what happened? They got more shirts. I felt really good about that. It was something I did to solve a problem and that was before I hooked up with women who knew anything about the feminist movement; women who were trying to band together and do something in the way of a common solution. Usually back then I only did individual little things, and some of them were real crooked. They came out of my anger. They were passive-aggressive type things. That was in dealing with my husband and men in general. I didn't know any other way.

I cleaned up my act my fifth year at the phone company. I had a year's perfect attendance. I had the best count on calls per hour. I wanted out of traffic. I didn't want to be an operator anymore. I wanted a desk. I wanted to use my own words. So I got a promotion to a clerical job. I inventoried equipment in the toll room, which meant climbing ladders and counting channel units and amplifiers and things I didn't know what they were. I was putting numbers in columns and making reports, using my own words. I was real angry with men at that time, 1970–1972. I have recently come to the realization that inside of me I believed that all men were responsible for all the pain that women and children suffer and that all men hurt all women and all little children. It was a belief that was so deep inside of me that it was hidden from me, but that's what I operated my life on. My anger covered my fear. I took my anger out on the men I worked with. There were fourteen men in the area where I worked and one other woman who was a clerk. I would read something and then argue with the men. One of the men I worked with was Jim Gallagher, who was the senator from Jesup. Bless his heart. He would give me information. He gave me stuff on the Commission on the Status of Women before I knew it existed. But he would argue with me. Our union editor, Jim Davis, a very thoughtful man, tried to be reasonable and used logic with me, but I was just into blaming men for all my pain and trying to make them see what was right.

One of the men in the toll room was an editor of the union newsletter and he asked me to write something for it. So I did. I spent hours agonizing over this piece. I wanted to say just the right thing but I didn't know what to say. That article reflected what was on my mind: there ought to be something that I was interested in but I didn't know what it was and I wanted to find it and get involved. So that was what my article was about—there are all these social problems in the world today so do something about them.

When I was working in the toll room with all those men, a strange woman came up to me in the bathroom and said, "Do you type?" I said, "Yes." She said, "How would you like to come and work in the employment office? I need a clerk. Of course you'll have to take a downgrade." I was ready for a change so I thought, What's eight dollars a week? That's all it will cost me. So I said, "Okay." It turned out that this woman had been sent to Waterloo to start an employment office in the phone company. This was part of the company's way of carrying out a consent decree that AT&T had signed with the EEOC [Equal Employment Opportunity Commission] as a result of a sex discrimination suit. This was late in 1971.

Some changes in employment practices were made rather quickly. No longer could employees bring in their relatives and neighbors and say, "Here's another perfect employee." There had to be procedures for AT&T to demonstrate to the federal government that they were trying to utilize minority men and women and other women in the work force in proportion to their representation in the community. Promotion policies were also revised. I started typing reports which categorized men and women by job title, numbers, race, and sex. It's like, How many three-eyed, green-toed, blue-haired men were operators in Waterloo? There weren't any. I talked about these reports to my friend Cynthia Hutchins at the Human Rights Commission and said, "What do you think of this?" She said, "Bears looking into." She was of the opinion that the phone company discriminated against black people in Waterloo. Blacks were about 8 to 10 percent of the population but it certainly wasn't reflected in the work force. There were black janitors. There were a couple of black operators. But in 1965 when I started at the phone company, that's about all I saw.

Cynthia Hutchins was important to me. She was a black woman whose husband and my husband worked together. She came to Waterloo to work at the University of Northern Iowa, getting money for minority students. Then she worked at the Waterloo Human Rights Commission. At that time I was tired of being married. I was tired of being a telephone operator. I just didn't have any purpose in life and on my days off I would clean my house and then go to bed and sleep. I wouldn't answer the phone. Once Cynthia came out to our house in Jesup with her little daughter and dragged me out of bed and made me get dressed and took me to town and took me with her wherever she went that day. She was working with welfare mothers on a project. She was also involved with the Urban Campus of the University of Northern Iowa on the east side of town, which was the black area. She introduced me to people who had lived there all their lives. Mostly I had lived in Waterloo since I was ten and I didn't even know they existed. I was pretty overwhelmed by it. Cynthia always put all of her energy into what she was doing. She said, "There's a world out there and there's stuff to be done." I remember one night at three o'clock in the morning she was trying to teach me to play bridge. She was intense. She was that way with her friendships and with her work. She died because she was too busy speaking out one night on the problem of black children graduating from Waterloo public schools who couldn't read. She thought she had enough time to get to the hospital for a shot for her asthma, but she waited too long. She died. Something happened inside of me, I don't know what it was. It was like being afraid to take risks didn't matter anymore. Anything I did couldn't hurt me.

I was even more insufferable [at the phone company] after I got into the employment office because I could act on some of my ideas, which were just beginning to become real to me. I got to go to black churches and meet black ministers and tell them to send people to apply for jobs. I met really neat gay men in the Democratic party headquarters who were just working their butts off for the Democratic party. I had them come and apply for jobs and they became telephone operators. I encouraged women to apply for nontraditional jobs. The first woman installer/repair technician in Waterloo had hair so long she could sit on it and she was married. They paired her up with one of the two or three black men who were installers. It was wintertime and they had parkas on and they were in their truck eating lunch in an alley on the north end of town. They got a real undesirable area to work in. Somebody called the phone company and reported this black employee who had his white girlfriend in the truck, in an alley. They were just eating their lunch.

I got excited about women doing things they'd never done before. There was a male supervisor for the installer/repair technicians and he would come in the office frequently and say to my boss, "Give me Kay, let me make an installer out of her." I knew that he didn't have that as his true motive at all. He wanted to humiliate me, find a way to make me fail and shut my mouth. I'd stand up in union meetings and confront sexist talk. I wouldn't plead a case nicely. I would demand in very ungracious ways for participation of women in the union. I fought with male union members over the rightness of the company's affirmative action policy. I was real angry and hostile. I worked in the employment office for four years. I enjoyed it. I got to go out to schools on career days and show slides of women climbing poles and black people in management. It was an exciting time to be alive.

Right after my thirtieth birthday in 1975 I decided to leave my husband. By this time I had met several women, some were married, some were single, some were lesbians, some were straight. I met them through the Black Hawk County Women's Political Caucus and the Democratic party and the union. They were my support. I was starting to believe I could be whoever I wanted to be. I didn't want to be a fraud anymore. I didn't want to be married. I thought I had the world by the tail. It was such freedom. I was active in the union. I was going to school. I was in a bowling league. I couldn't bowl worth diddly, but it was a great excuse to be out drinking with the women. I met lots of interesting people.

I was first exposed to the CWA [Communications Workers of America], the union at the phone company, and to the women who were the union stewards when I was a telephone operator. I signed up right away when I got my job in 1965. I knew that was what I needed to do because I was not management, I was a worker, and I'd been exposed to that in my home. I didn't want to go to meetings and the only time I did go was when we talked about contracts to find out what the issues were so I could decide if it was a good contract. I have voted no on every contract since 1968. I think that just shows what a rebel I have been through the years.

I started going to the regular union meetings in 1969 when we moved into town from Jesup. I don't know why I wanted to. It could be partly that I was looking for something I could put my energy into, where I could meet some people who might think like me so I didn't have to have those conversations in my head. One of the first things that happened was that I went to the yearly state CWA legislative conference. I remember being surprised at being asked to go. When I look back on it, I've been surprised a number of times when people have asked me to do things or consider taking on a leadership role. What happened was that when I started talking at union meetings, I had some ideas and some thoughts. They may not have been agreed with but I was speaking up and maybe that's how I came to a leader's attention. That's the only thing I can think of.

Since the CWA was such a male-dominated union as far as the leadership went nationally, regionally, and locally, there were some things in operation that some of the older women who used to be active in the union told me about. What they told me was that whenever they tried to do anything to be a part of union activities such as serving on committees, never even hoping for an officer position, some men would get their heads together and gang up on them. They would assign somebody to go after this woman sexually. If the woman went along with that, then she was compromised in that they always held it over her. I didn't learn about that until after it had happened to me. I chose to deal with it by lying to the men that it ever happened, saying, "Were you there? Do you know what happened?" Just getting right up to their faces and denying it. I wasn't even honest enough to tell the women it had happened to me. But I repeated the stories that the older women told me and said, "Don't let it happen to you. Don't let them get anything on you." That's how I dealt with it. Again, it was an individual solution. I had a number of individual solutions along the way.

One of the things I noticed was that whenever there were national conferences, the men officers got excited and always made a show of having an election of delegates. There were four male officers and these guys just kept rotating. "You two will go this year and we two will go next year," and that's the way it worked. So I was real surprised one union meeting when my union president said he had this communication that there was going to be a conference in Des Moines for union women. He pointed to me and said, "Kay, you and Betty see me after the meeting and we'll talk about it." He sent us off to Des Moines and we didn't know what we were going to.

This was the first meeting of the Iowa Conference of Trade Union Women, which took place on August 12, 1972. It was only the fourth state conference in the nation sponsored by the AFL-CIO. That's where I met Betty Talkington and Katherine Clarenbach [a prominent Wisconsin feminist], and some other women whose names I don't remember, but they were from unions around the state. Some of them spoke out about what they thought. This was my first exposure to trade union women getting together and talking about issues of importance. What surprised me is they they didn't talk about just stuff at work, they talked about larger things outside the home like the Vietnam War. I was frightened because I thought you could get in trouble over doing something about what you felt deeply. They said if you want to make any changes, you have to work together. The notion of working together with women was real foreign to me. I was a teenager in the fifties and I heard lots about how you have to have a good personality and good hygiene because it was necessary to attract a man. All women were competitors. That's what I learned. That conference was pretty exciting. I went home and didn't know what to make of it. I tried to talk to my union members at union meetings about what I'd heard there but I forgot the first rule of public speaking—know your audience! Women were sixty percent of the membership but barely three percent in attendance at local meetings.

There was a second Iowa Conference of the Trade Union Women in Des Moines on June 9, 1973. My union president did the same thing again. At a meeting of our local he said, "Kay, we'll send you and somebody else off to that conference. Tell you what, Kay, I'll give you some money and the union will pay for you and whoever else might want to go down to Des Moines the night before and stay in a hotel and have a nice meal and go out and have some drinks. Have some fun and we'll pay for it." I got really angry and said, "That kind of money would pay for a lot of registrations. It's only five dollars. I would like to see ten women go. I would like money for registrations for ten women and mileage for two cars." He said, "You won't find ten women." That made me angry. It seems like a lot of things I've done is because people said, "You can't." I was just mad enough to prove him wrong. That was on a Thursday night and I worked real hard on it over the weekend. At that time I was working in the employment office of the phone company and it is fairly small. There were four hundred union members at that time in Waterloo, so I had a good idea who the people were. I thought of women I admired because of their mouthiness. They weren't afraid to speak up and challenge what was going on, whether it was in the workplace or in their personal relationships. I admired that. I wasn't real good at that but I was wanting to get good at it. I was also aware that we had a number of black women working at the phone company who weren't real active in the union and I wanted to pull them in so I found three black women. On Monday I called the union president and said, "I have ten women's names. I want money for ten registrations and for two cars." He said, "Okay," but he didn't think it was a good idea.

One woman at the last minute couldn't go but the nine of us went off to that conference in Des Moines. I remembered Betty Talkington from the year before. Florine Koole, assistant vice president for CWA's region, spoke. There were workshops. One of them was how to participate in your union local and why as a woman you ought to do that. God, that was pretty exciting. We started putting our heads together and counting numbers and since Florine was there we asked her, nationwide, what percentage of the union did women represent? She said, "Sixty percent." We said, "If that's true then why are our leadership positions filled by men in our local?" We decided we wanted to do something about it but it was such a new idea that we asked everybody, "What can we do? We don't have any power." Betty Talkington said to me, "What do you mean you don't have any power? You walked in here with nine women. There is no other union local that sent that many women. Now obviously something's going on. Look at what you've got and try to use it." That was a real challenge.

We heard that day from a woman who talked about women's auxiliaries in unions and even though we weren't auxiliary, we could take some of their ideas and put them to use. One of the ideas that we came up with was starting a women's caucus for our union local with the primary purpose of getting women involved in the union. One of the things I did that night was I took a risk. It was only a one-day conference, and I said, "Let's go back to Waterloo and meet at a restaurant and talk and plan. I'll pay for dinner and submit a bill and have the president pay for it." I was real surprised, but he did.

The next meeting after the conference, the local president said, "Kay, tell us about the conference." He acted really bored. I said,

"There were nine of us who went and we all want to talk. Peggy's going to start off. Peggy Morgan was a big black woman with a big mouth, real intimidating in presence, and angry, too. She had gotten so turned on at that conference that she was just giving them what for! Then we told them we had formed a women's caucus and that we were going to get involved.

Those us us who went to the conference decided that one of the things we could do was talk up attendance at union meetings. We would meet at the Pizza Hut right after work and we would eat and then go directly to the union meeting. That way the women didn't have a chance to go home and get caught up in other things. We did that for a long time.

At union meetings, while they were doing reports of various committees, women would pop up and say, "What is that committee? What does it do? What do you mean, finance committee? When do you meet the next time?" I wanted to know where I could get a copy of the bylaws. Their answer was there had been so many changes over the years that they hadn't typed them up. "They are in the file drawer cabinet." I said, "I'm a typist. I'll be glad to type them up. Get me off work, pay me through the local." They paid me to do that and I got them run off. The next few meetings we passed them out so that everybody could see what the standing committees were, what they were responsible for, what were the officers' positions and how long their terms were. We thought, Wouldn't it be neat if we could elect a woman president, vice president, secretary, or treasurer? It didn't happen for several years but by 1975 we put two women on the executive board as vice president and secretary. That's pretty exciting. Eventually a black woman was elected head of that local. This was sometime in the early eighties and I was real excited to read about it. So maybe it took seven or eight years but it happened.

There were lots of interesting things happening in the early seventies. The Iowa Women's Political Caucus started in 1973 and I found out about it in a couple of ways. One was opening the *Des Moines Register* one Sunday morning and seeing an article talking about an upcoming conference. Another way was through women I had met, like Erma Wiszmann, the president of the local union in Davenport. I had gotten really excited when I went off to those two state conferences of union women put on by the Iowa Federation of Labor. There seemed to be strong women who knew what they believed in and who were willing to take risks. Inside, I felt real scared but I wanted to see some things change. I wanted to hook up with those women who seemed to know how to do that. Some of the

same things that I had observed among the women at those two
conferences, I sort of was getting from that article in the paper
about the Iowa Women's Political Caucus. They were interested in
changing the laws and supporting women's rights. I hardly knew
what that meant. I just knew I was for it. So I went to that first state
convention of the Women's Political Caucus in September of 1973. I
remember meeting union women that I had met at these other two
conferences I went to. They said, "Did your union send you?" I said,
"I am here as an individual." They said, "Go back and submit a bill
for your lodging and your meals and your mileage and tell them
what we are doing." I didn't know about using the system but I was
learning fast.

Before I went to the state convention I paid attention to the
Waterloo newspaper and found out about a meeting of the Black
Hawk County Women's Political Caucus, which I attended. When
that conference was over I faithfully attended the Women's Political
Caucus meetings at the county level and I was elected secretary. At
one point we got incensed over radio stations playing "Having my
baby, what a wonderful way to say you love me." I mean we spent
an hour discussing the pros and cons of whether it was right to ask
radio stations to stop playing it. We made an issue of it locally and I
liked that. This was a start. Maybe we could make some changes.

The political caucus met at the YWCA. It had big double doors
to the room that we met in. One night, in the middle of the meeting,
the doors burst open and in came Lyle Taylor, union representative
from the packinghouse workers. He had two or three very fright-
ened-looking women in tow, and he said, "I want some of your time.
These women have a story to tell." I'm used to men being unpredict-
able in the union setting, but the caucus women were ladies whom
we needed, who didn't have jobs outside the home but felt responsibility to their community. They had experience working in the Junior League and also church and school organizations. They had
what it took to get this thing started because the rest of us who were
working jobs were too busy to do it. Most of the women in that room
were quite surprised, to say the least, when this big, beefy man
arrived. I had never seen him in a suit before and it didn't look like it
fit him very well. He strode to the front of the room with these
women, who were members of the Hotel-Restaurant-Bartenders Union of the Cedar Falls Holiday Inn. They were on strike and they
wanted some support. They wanted money for one thing, but basically they wanted to know that somebody cared about what they
were struggling for. These women talked about how the Holiday Inn
folks, the union-buster folks, within that organization had hired

thugs with dogs and guns to harrass them. It was galvanizing to hear their story. That had never happened to me and probably never will, but here it was right in our own backyard. The most amazing thing happened that night. Women who had never heard anything like this before were ready to throw their bodies on the line. But I think this guy's main purpose was to get some bucks out of us and so he calmly talked them down and then made the pitch for money. I think we gave him $50 or $100 and adopted a resolution supporting the women. I took a copy of the resolution back to my union local and asked for approval to send it to corporate heads and to say, "We're in support of these people and you ain't doing them right." That was an action. It was really kind of heady.

Soon after the Black Hawk County Women's Political Caucus was formed there was interaction with other women's organizations in the area, such as AAUW [American Association of University Women] and WEAL [Woman's Equity Action League], and we started talking about forming our own women's space with desks where representatives of these various groups would work and all the information would be in one place. At one time there was a small church for sale on the west side of town and we thought that would be just great, but we didn't have the money. Then the University of Northern Iowa offered us some space and the Waterloo–Cedar Falls Women's Center was born. Diane Young, who was a coordinator over at the Hawkeye Institute of Technology, was real active. At one of the meetings the speaker asked, "How many women in this room have been raped?" Of the fifteen or seventeen women there, nine women raised their hands, only I didn't, so that would have made ten. I was shocked by this response. I wasn't alone. It was important to me to learn that I am not unique and I'm not crazy for what I was thinking.

By the time the second Women's Political Caucus convention in Iowa happened in September of 1974, I was a little smarter than I had been and lobbied the leadership of my local for money for me and other members to go. I also took two of my friends, Julie and Susie. Their husbands worked with my husband and they were glad to get away for a weekend. They got so radicalized, Julie became some sort of a representative-at-large because she lived in the country and they needed rural women to be involved. She was a rural woman who had stayed home and raised children, livestock, and was a strong woman all by herself. Susie got so radicalized she didn't go home after the convention. I dropped her off in her front yard and about 10 o'clock that Sunday night her husband called and said, "Where's Susie?" I said, "The last I saw her was standing in your front yard." Well, she got so radicalized at that conference she went off to spend some time with a friend and didn't go home for days. Before we knew it, Susie was saying to Sears, "I'm tired of being a clerk. I'd like to make the bucks the men do. I'm interested in washers and dryers, I know all about them because I use them, so train me to be a technician." She became the first woman in seven states to be a washer/dryer repairperson. Julie left her husband shortly after the caucus convention. She left her children in his care because his parents had money and she didn't have a dime. That was real hard for her to do but it was the only way she could see to do it. She filed for divorce and asked for maintenance money and tuition money and she became a nurse. She realized her dream. And I left my husband. All kinds of things were happening.

After I got my divorce in 1975, Peg Mullen said to me, "You never were meant to be married, Kay." That shocked me, coming from her very strong Catholic background and my having known her since I was five years old. I kept my married name and the reason I did was that I had gotten so used to the men saying, "That damn Kay Stone is raising hell again." I identified with that name. I thought about changing it but then I thought about my ear doctor, my eye doctor, my family doctor, my gynecologist, my dentist, my orthodontist, on and on, and it was just too much. I thought about changing it to my mother's mother's maiden name, the one who homesteaded in South Dakota, but I found out it was Murphy and there were just columns of Murphys in the phone book. I experimented with several different names. My mother's name was Amy. Perhaps I'll be Katherine Amyschild, or Kay Amysdottir and spell it like they do in Iceland, *dottir,* but in the end I just kept the name Stone.

Shortly after I got divorced I took a job as a clerk traveling on the road with the Yellow Pages sales crew in northeast Iowa. What an interesting subculture! (That's what Nicholas Johnson said when he was taken to a bowling alley when he was running for Congress in the third district.) There I was, traveling around northeast Iowa, just having a wonderful time, drinking myself to death for two and a half years. I would meet the men on the sales crew at the door of the motel in the morning with a pot of coffee and a bottle of aspirin. They would take the aspirin, drink their coffee, say they had to get off to appointments and then go find public parks to sleep in until they could get it together and go to work. I would keep it together until they left and then I would flop across the bed, because we had our offices in motels. The first year they were all men. We were on the road eight months of the year and home on weekends.

One night toward the end of that first year when we were drinking real late up in Decorah my boss said, "I didn't want you on this crew. But the employment office said I had to take you. We didn't want women traveling with us. We didn't want anybody carrying tales back home to our wives and sweethearts, but you're all right." I don't know why I was all right. It was probably because I was in there doing the same things they were. Hit the bar at 5 o'clock; it was a good day, it was a bad day, we felt good, we felt terrible, there's nothing else to do, there's too much to do, whatever—all the reasons why any of us ever drink.

My boss supervised sales reps and me. I had the job of clerical worker. We were an experimental group and the company was looking for women to fill sales jobs, too. My boss was on the phone day after day calling every little dolly he'd ever met in every little bar along the way, saying, "It's a great life, why don't you apply?" They would come in and talk to him and they all looked alike. There was one type he liked. They all had big boobs, little faces, and lots of blonde, teased hair. I got angrier by the minute because I would sit there, slaving away as a clerk, listening to him say, "There just aren't any woman who want this job because women don't want to travel." Because I was so angry and so pissed off at him, I didn't apply for a sales job.

At the end of two and a half years the experiment of clerks traveling with sales crews was over and the job I was doing as clerical support was done away with. I was told that if I wanted to keep working for the phone company, I had to come to Des Moines, where they would find a job for me. I was devastated. I liked my life in Waterloo. It was comfortable and it was familiar. But I had no choice if I wanted to stay with the phone company. I had been with the company thirteen years. I had been an operator, and I had been a clerical worker in several departments, and I had sat on my butt, and I was convinced that physically I was a wimp and unable to do anything. I came to Des Moines and decided to be real reckless. I decided to try something I had no idea I could have any chance of success at: being an installer/repair technician. They made a lot more money than clerks made. Besides, the company trained you. One of those things I discovered was that the company used to get men to work on line crews and cable crews and installation crews who were farm boys, because they were used to hard work and they knew how to use small tools. But things were changing. I became an installer in 1978. They had these little schools where you learned which direction to turn a screw to tighten it and to loosen it. That's very useful information. It wasn't just because women were coming into the job; those urban boys didn't know how to do it, either.

My first day on the job I was told to ride around all day with an installer, a man, and watch what he did. As we were walking to his truck he said, "We've heard about you." I'd never met this guy before in my life, and I said, "Who's we?" He said, "Everybody here." I said, "What have you heard?" He said, "That you're the Gloria Steinem of the Waterloo phone company." I said, "What does that mean?" He replied, "It means that you're a troublemaker. It means that you're always sticking your nose in where it doesn't belong. Of course some people don't like that and so they won't like you. As for me, I'll make up my mind later." That was news to me and I was real scared because I thought, Wow, I'm coming to Des Moines and here's this union local that has all these women, and you go to meetings, and there are more women than men, and they seem to have their act together, and I can rest for a while. Then he said that.

I learned to climb a pole and when I didn't fall off I was pretty excited. I learned to do lots of things—haul a sixty-pound ladder around on my shoulder—it's all a matter of balance. I learned to drive a truck. I found out that the insides of a telephone were very simple, that men had kept quiet about it for years, making me and other women believe that it was all very complicated and mysterious when, in fact, it was very simple. I was mad when I discovered that. I was mad at how many years I had been kept out of a higher-paying job. I remember in 1970 arguing with my boss in the toll room about why women weren't allowed to climb poles. He told me that a woman would hurt her breasts climbing poles. When I learned to climb poles in 1978 I discovered that if a woman was hurting her breasts, a man was hurting something else. Because if they were hugging the pole, they weren't staying there, they were sliding down it. That's one of the things I had to discover for myself.

I worked as an installer for a while. I was real lonely in Des Moines. I was working six days a week, ten and twelve hour days. I didn't have time to go to school or make new friends. So, I said, "I don't want to do this anymore." Twice I got talked out of it. The third time I said, "No, I'm not going to do this anymore. I want to sit behind a desk, I want to be a clerk and work eight to five. I want a normal life." Sometime after that I got a money award from the company because I fell into a category of women who held a traditional female job prior to a certain date who then went into a nontraditional job during a certain time period and who worked at the job a determined length of time, and therefore qualified for some of the money that AT&T had to pay because the federal government had

STONE as Northwestern Bell telephone station installer/repair technician, 1978. *"I learned to climb a pole and when I didn't fall off I was pretty excited."*

ruled that the company had discriminated against women. So indirectly, I benefitted from the lawsuit. I was very surprised.

When I was an installer I didn't know anything about electricity and I was afraid of it. They told us we didn't have to know anything except how to check your pole so that you wouldn't get electrocuted in case there was electricity running where it shouldn't be. So when I stopped being an installer I took a course on basic electricity. That's when I discovered that I didn't know much about algebra, so I took an algebra course. Then I wanted to find out about these electrons that made electricity, so I took a chemistry course so I could learn atomic theory. I've done everything backwards it seems. Just because of following my interests along the way, both with those courses outside the phone company and that nontraditional job inside the phone company, I qualified myself for the job I have today. I'm a controller-tester. I test specially designed circuits. Actually, I'm controlled by everything outside myself. I have projects where circuits are going to be taken off of old equipment and put on new equipment and my job is to coordinate that activity, get everybody where they're supposed to be at the same time, get permission from customers to take those circuits out of service for the time period involved. Then I use a computer program and I test through their work. I'll look for opens, grounds, shorts, foreign voltage, anything that won't make the circuit work. Then I turn it back to the customer. I've learned to talk, and it's something I do a lot of today.

When I came to Des Moines I discovered that more women than men went to union meetings here. Then we got Marian Moffitt as president of our local. Boy, I admired that woman. Ann Kelly is another woman I liked. Ann came to me one day and said, "We're going to be cheerleaders over at the statehouse and it's going to be a kickoff for the Iowa Equal Rights Amendment campaign. We're going to wear these T-shirts and carry this torch and we're going to lead cheers." We did that. And then, somehow, Moffitt was introducing me to Betty Talkington and Peg Anderson, whom I had known in Waterloo. Peg was head of the ERA campaign. Here's Moffitt introducing me as the chairwoman of the women's committee of my local. There was no such animal. I could see her and Talkington sort of exchanging eye signals. The next thing I know I'm on the steering committee for the ERA campaign. Once again, I saw that you just have to have your act together, know what you want, and just move through.

Something happened in the early eighties. My alcoholism got out of control. It probably contributed a great deal to my choosing not to be involved so much, not really caring anymore. I wrote a little for the union paper. I did a little committee work. I haven't been to a meeting at the union hall for a long time. I used to love to go to meetings, sit in the back and check everything out, see who was talking to whom, figure out what was going on, and stand up and yell about the topic under discussion. I loved it. I don't know how productive that was. I don't know how much of a contribution I ever made. I know I had some fun. I know I grew as a woman. I know that some of my beliefs crystalized. I know my involvement changed me.

I can say today that I'm more assertive than aggressive. I've calmed down a lot. Part of that was sort of getting burned out, going through so many years in too many directions at once, trying to figure out who I was, and trying to run away from who I was. It takes its toll. I wound up in treatment for alcoholism in 1985. I've been sober four and a half years. A great deal of my peace and calmness is a result of dealing with my incest issues. My desire to work with women and help women is still there. For a year I worked as a volunteer facilitator at a treatment center for a weekly aftercare group of chemically dependent women. For over three years I've lectured once a month at a women's treatment center. I tell them all about a twelve-step program for recovery from chemical dependency and how it got started. I found out I like standing in front of groups and I like being a ham and I like making material interesting to people who are detoxing and falling asleep on their chairs. I make myself available to support newly sober women. I'm looking forward to doing some volunteer work with a new recovery house for chemically dependent women. I have some ideas about that.

Ann Kelly is an enthusiastic,

dynamic woman who brought her energy and
enthusiasm to her union activities while
working at Northwestern Bell telephone
company in Des Moines. Her dedication to
combating injustice wherever she finds it led to
her work for fair treatment for women and
minorities both within her union and within
the telephone company. Her interest in politics
has led to her current position of VIP director of
the mideast area of AFL–CIO COPE (Volunteers
in Politics director of the mideast area of the
American Federation of Labor-Congress of
Industrial Organizations Committee On Political
Education).

*"There was an advantage in being a
black, female laborer because every
time they needed a token, I was that
token."*

I was born at the Still Osteopathic Hospital in Des Moines.
My family moved to Seattle, Washington, when I was two or three
while my dad finished law school. When I was eight or nine, my
brother and I lived with my grandmother in Hollidaysburg, Pennsylvania, while my dad set up his law practice in Davenport, Iowa.
My brother and I joined my parents about a year later, in about
1958 or 1959. At first we lived with our parents in a tiny apartment

in Davenport, but they were looking for a house to buy. Because no realtor would show them houses in an area they wanted to live in, they had to buy a house across the river in Milan, Illinois. My mom worked in my dad's law office as a secretary when he was first getting started but she has a degree in home economics and she is just a couple of hours short of a master's in chemistry.

When we were growing up Mom tried to work a couple of times but it was always a big problem. The right blue shirt was never ironed and dinner was either too early or too late. When my youngest sister was in seventh grade, Mom finally put her foot down and said she was going to go back to work. One Sunday morning my dad was having coffee with a bunch of Illinois political cronies and he was raising hell with them about how they didn't have any blacks in the driver's license bureau. They told him, "You find us a qualified black and we'll hire him." When he recounted the story to my mom, she said, "You just found one." She went and took the test and they issued her a uniform on the same day. She still works for the State of Illinois in the driver's license division.

Mom can also sew like you wouldn't believe. She makes clothes and drapes and slipcovers but she says her eyes are not what they used to be, so now she has to sew early in the morning when it is real light.

One thing my parents taught me was that you have got to learn to do for yourself. If you have a question, you ask it. We were brought up to be pretty independent. Our home environment was relatively strict. On Saturday morning we had to be up and dressed before my dad went to his office. We were told, "Get your work done, and then you can do what you want for the rest of the day," but to my recollection we never got our work done. My dad was active in the NAACP [National Association for the Advancement of Colored People], that was the early seventies, and he was around when things were real rough. I'm sure I got part of my rabble-rousing from him.

I had the privilege of going to an all-girl Catholic school, which was very much in the tradition of the old guard. Social activities were having teas where you wore white gloves and the nuns were always saying things like, "Nice girls don't do this," and "Nice girls don't do that." If the nuns are watching over me now they are probably turning over in their graves. Most of the girls in the school were from very wealthy families and my family wasn't particularly wealthy, but my dad had a falling out with the Davenport public school system soon after my return from Pennsylvania and he took me out of public schools. This was because of racial discrimination.

We lived at that time in a very poor neighborhood and they had special rules for my grade at Lincoln School, things like you couldn't take books home. Furthermore, I was repeating work which I had had in the East. My dad wanted me to have more work. He and the school principal had a big fight and the next thing I knew I was in the Villa, an all-girl school in Rock Island.

There were some real benefits to the girls' school. I think as a black growing up in Iowa I learned how to live with white people and that's real important. I found how important it was when, later in life, I had a girlfriend who was very nervous around white people. She had grown up in an all-black environment and she didn't want anything to do with white people. She was just very much a recluse because of that. I was fortunate that I learned how to get along with the other race. In fact, people tell me I never knew I was black until I got out of high school and went to college. I never realized what discrimination was until I came to Des Moines. Going to the girls' school was a plus because you learned discipline and the emphasis was on education. You were in the "in" crowd if you got good grades. I protested a lot at the time because I wanted to go to the public high school where all the fun happened. In the long run, it was all to my benefit.

When I got out of high school in 1966 I went to Bradley University and ended up with two black roommates from Chicago. That's when I figured out that I was black; actually I was a black person with a white mind. I didn't know anything about the music and the traditional things of the black culture so it was a real shock. In fact, I ended up going into a room by myself because I was having trouble dealing with it. I was involved in things like the Newman Club [a Catholic campus association] while everybody else was partying in fraternities but I just wasn't into that. I decided college wasn't exactly the thing I wanted to do, so I ended up coming back home, much to my father's dismay. I was the only one of his four kids who never finished college.

I went to work for the telephone company [Northwestern Bell] in Davenport in the spring of 1967 and got involved in the union. My parents were having a hard time with me not going to school so my dad saw this ad for AIB [American Institute of Business] in Des Moines and decided that I ought to be a court reporter. I ended up leaving the Quad Cities and going to AIB. I lived at the Young Businesswomen's Home at 1111 Woodland. That was a rude awakening. There were four girls to a room. One of my roommates was from Nevada, Iowa. She was a farm girl and a great person. She had never been around black people so this was a big experience for her.

Another roommate named Laura had gone to school in Turkey and lived all over the world because her father was in the diplomatic service. We bonded pretty quick.

The housemother at the Young Businesswomen's Home was Mrs. Shinners. I will never forget that we called her Shitty Shinners. This was kind of a do-good establishment run by Des Moines society women. The advertisements said, "Two full meals a day." In my estimation, when they give you eggs on one day, and bacon on another, and cereal on another, it wasn't what I call a full breakfast. Laura agreed with me that this was kind of a continental breakfast, not a full breakfast, and that we were the victims of false advertising, except we didn't realize then that it was false advertising. All we knew was what the brochure said, and this ain't what we're getting. I think we paid $19 a week to stay there and that was a lot of money. We were getting ripped off, so we organized the dorm to have a protest about these meals and complained to the board. The phone system had six-button sets, and I listened into the conversations Shinners was having with the dean of students at AIB: Laura and I were rabble-rousers and spoiled brats and the dean was just going to have to do something about us because we were creating problems in the dormitory. That was my first experience with being rowdy.

The Young Businesswomen's Home had this large parking lot attached to it but none of the residents were allowed to park there. It sat empty most of the time. I began questioning why we couldn't park there because at the time I had a nearly new Firebird which I parked on the street. My roommate's car had gotten banged up in a hit-and-run accident so I was concerned about my car being on the street. I couldn't understand why we couldn't use this parking lot. I was telling my dad about it and he said, "You had better check this out." So I went to the city hall and looked at the records and checked building permits. I can't believe that at twenty I was doing this kind of stuff. I found out that when the residence was built, they were supposed to be providing parking. Then I went to Mrs. Shinners and said, "I have been to the city and you're supposed to be providing parking." She kind of brushed me off, so Laura and I went to the board. They got real upset and the next thing we knew we got kicked out of the Young Businesswomen's Home.

The parking was just the icing on the cake because I had not been a model resident. Our room was on the ground level and we figured out that if we knocked the screen out and buried it in the snow, we had our own private entrance and exit and we didn't have to worry about hours. So our room became the after-hours entrance and exit for the entire dormitory. We weren't very smart because when spring came and the snow melted, they found our screen and they also found a bottle of wine, which they were not thrilled about because you weren't supposed to drink in the dorm. So I ended up getting kicked out of the Young Businesswomen's Home and my dad threatened to sue. He was real upset because he thought it was discrimination. I thought it was the greatest thing since white bread because we could now move into an apartment and not have to deal with hours. About seven of us from the home moved into a big apartment on about 18th Street. We had our own little private dormitory and we could do our own thing.

I ended up going back to work at Northwestern Bell in Des Moines because I had a falling out with the dean at the school. They had this course called Nancy Taylor. It was bullshit. It was grooming and makeup and all that kind of stuff. They wanted you to pay $25 for this Nancy Taylor kit and these books. These books were high school crap that told you about grooming and makeup and all that etiquette crap, but the makeup was for white people. It wasn't for black people and I said, "This is stupid. Why do I need to pay $25 for this stuff when I can't even use it?" The dean and I had a falling out about that and I ended up leaving school and the dorm at the same time.

When I went back to work with the phone company in 1971, I was a telephone operator, and not exactly a model operator because I was still very young and very much into partying and having a good time. I had not decided that working at the phone company was the way I wanted to go but I needed a job to pay the rent. I found the job very boring and tedious and so I got mildly involved in the union [the CWA, Communications Workers of America]. I was real concerned about what was happening in the 1974 contract negotiations because when we got the contract back we found that house services people and janitors were being paid more than operators. That really ticked me off. I called the union to find out what was going on and nobody would answer any questions. What I did not realize then was that they hadn't had the contract explanation yet so they didn't know what was going on. In my mind, they just refused to answer my questions. So I said, "This is crap." I rabble-roused among the operators and got them together.

We had a little meeting down at Bishop's cafeteria when Bishop's was downtown, and we decided that if they weren't going to answer our questions we were going to drop out of the union and look for another union. While we were in Bishop's a couple of reporters I knew came up to us and asked what we were up to. When I

ANN KELLY (*left*) with fellow Communications Workers of America members, Mardell Duden and Rita Carlson. *"I didn't realize that we were feminists, we were just being oppressed and we needed fair treatment."* Photo courtesy of CWA, Local 7102

told them, they asked, "Can we print that story?" I said, "I don't care," because my dad had told me that sometimes if you can't get answers from the people, newspapers can get answers for you. So the paper ran a story about us. At that time our local president, Dutch Kleywegt, and the officers were in Omaha, Nebraska, getting the contract explanation. One of them picked up the newspaper and says to Dutch, "Hey, you got some problems at home." He showed him this article about how the operators in his local were going to desert if things weren't taken care of.

When he came back to Des Moines Dutch called and tried to explain that what had happened was that they were trying to beat the EEOC [Equal Employment Opportunities Commission] because they had been paying female janitors or house services people less than they were paying the males. Rather than reduce the males' income, they brought the females up to where the males were. This made them be paid more than operators. I found that offensive. Operators are the backbone of the company. When there's a snow-storm they don't come and get house services people, they come out in vans and pick up operators. I was real ticked off. What came out of that was that Dutch decided that these operators were too much for him to handle, so he loaded us all in a car and took us over to Omaha to meet with the district vice president, the guy who had negotiated the contract, to let him calm us down.

I was a directory assistance operator in 1974 when all of a sudden there was a spot for me on the executive board of the union.
They created a spot for me and then they assigned Marian Moffitt,
who was then secretary-treasurer of the union, to watch over me to
make sure that I didn't get out of control. That was very clever on
Dutch's part because here he had a person with some energy, a
basic radical, and what he did, instead of letting me be on the outside making him angry, he brought me in and then tried to channel
that energy. That was my entrance into the big-time activites of the
union. I was chief steward for operator service. For years the union
was guilty, just like the company was guilty, because the position of
operator was traditionally a female job. They just didn't think it was
worth very much. We operators were also partly guilty because the
union is a political establishment and in politics, the one who yells
the loudest or creates the most problems gets taken care of first. We,
as operators, had not done much to promote ourselves. We referred
to ourselves as just operators. That's crap, because operators are
the backbone of the telephone company as well as the backbone of
the union.

If it weren't for telephone operators and women we could not
conduct a successful strike because on any picket line you look at,
the majority of picketers are women. Operators have a tendency to
be the tough cookies of the union. They were just then emerging.
This was happening across AT&T and not just Northwestern Bell. It
was in 1975 that I started getting active in the union and ended up
going to conventions. At the convention in San Francisco in about
1976 or 1977 everybody was boiling inside. It was a bargaining year
and there was a rule that you could not talk about bargaining issues
on the convention floor. But the operators had a point to make and
at that convention I organized people who were willing to get up and
say we want to be treated better in bargaining. All the operators
from across the country who were at the convention got up and
went to the floor mike to show support. There was a line all the way
around the room, because we got other people to stand up with us.
We were the controlling factor in many of those locals if we exer-
cised our voting rights. The union president at that time was Glen
Watts and he let about three of our folks speak before he ruled us
out of order. He could have ruled us out of order from the get-go, but
if he had done that he would have had major problems the rest of
the convention. So he let us have our say.

It was either that contract or the next that things started to get
better for the operators. We got short-hour tours and we were getting financial bumps that were putting us more in line with the

boys. Negotiations were usually done on a percentage basis, which meant that everyone got the same percentage raise but operators were down there so far that the boys just kept getting farther ahead of us. So they started giving us the percentage plus a cash bump to try to bring us more in line with everybody else.

We were just fighting for operators but actually it was women asserting themselves. That's just the way we handled things. That was the start of my involvement in the women's movement or in a movement making myself equal with everybody else.

I remember when this operator thing happened that Sally Hacker came to my house. She had on this black leather jacket. She informed me that I was a feminist and tried to get me involved. She asked me all kinds of questions about Northwestern Bell and she had me do an interview for her. She was writing some paper on AT&T and how rotten they were. So I was telling her all this stuff and she was loving every minute of it. I didn't realize that we were feminists, we were just being oppressed and we needed fair treatment.

After the 1977 convention we operators saw that we had some clout; maybe we ought to organize ourselves to get within the system. A woman named Annie Crump from Milwaukee headed a local that was all operators. She got some folks together who decided they would have a conference for operators from all across the country to talk about our common problems. The international wouldn't have anything to do with this conference. They said we were segmenting our people even though every convention and every union meeting is a plant meeting with the boys from the plants in control because we let them be in control. The international called our conference a "rump" conference, although there were three or four folks from the international there as observers. We sent eight or ten people from our local to that first operators' conference, which was held in Milwaukee. We got a van and drove it up there and shared rooms so more of us could go.

The conference was fabulous. They didn't need the doggone international; they had workshops on stress and all that kind of stuff. The international thought the conference would meet an early death but it turned into a big thing. It only stayed rump one or two years. Many locals now participate and pay for people to go but many people come on their own because they can't get funding elsewhere. It's another form of networking within the union. This year [1989] the operators held their ninth annual conference. Over four hundred operators from across the country were there. Notices are now sent out through the international and international people are on the program. Even the president of the union comes.

Everybody should have to start as a telephone operator, first, because it would give you an appreciation for the other jobs and, second, because it's good discipline and training. It is the most regimented job in the phone company although more and more jobs have gotten that way. The service rep job and repair clerk and a lot of those jobs have picked up a lot of stuff from the operator jobs. Our contention is that if you had helped us fight that stuff then it wouldn't be spreading like it is now. I am talking about things like secret monitoring, the regimentation, and the discipline. Back then you had to call the supervisor and ask to go to the bathroom. She would bring you a little green card to put over your position so that someone would know that you were gone. They timed how long you were there and wrote down how many times a day you went. If you went to the bathroom too many times they asked you if you had a problem. No other job was treated that way. The women finally raised enough hell so that the bathroom stuff is somewhat diminished. Now there is a little light that you turn on when you're out of the room but they're always rolling their eyes because only one person is supposed to be gone at a time.

A lot of the crap that's happening now has been going on for a long time with operators and it should have been stopped a long time ago, but it was just operators and the union didn't worry about it. This is not to say anything negative about the union. The union is a reflection of society and that's the way society treats women. If we don't scream about it, then they figure it's not a problem. It's not a problem until somebody tells them it's a problem. The operator movement is still going; they're still fighting for basic rights and the union has decided that maybe operators are a force to be reckoned with. It helps now that we have our first female executive vice president within the CWA who happens to come from the operator ranks. CWA is now pushing legislation to end secret monitoring. They want legislation to require that you have to notify the consumer and the operator that there is another person listening in on your call. The law isn't passed yet. The biggest opposition to the law is not from AT&T and the phone companies; it's from telemarketing firms—the Sears, the J. C. Penneys, and the large catalog sweatshop operations like the hotel reservations people. They are saying it's good customer service. Our studies have shown that customer service improves when there isn't monitoring. Part of this is because of lack of stress. If you know somebody might be listening in, the pressure to be always perfect doesn't allow you to provide good service.

KELLY (*right*) with George McGovern and CWA member Florine Koole, 1979. *"I had a basic feel for politics [and] I just happened to be in Iowa at the right time."* Photo courtesy of CWA, Local 7102

I got involved in politics because of the union. Dutch was the first local president I served under. He got beat by a guy named Bob Boudreau, who was a chauvinistic, racist son-of-a-buck. He was a Yellow Pages salesman and your typical, big-headed union guy. I didn't support him for president, but I was an entity he had to deal with because I was on the board. His vice president, who was another jerk, says to me, "Now I want you to go to your caucus (this was in 1976) and I want you to try to be a committee person, or get on the platform committee, or be a delegate to the county convention. You probably can't do any of those, but try for them anyway." I went, and I ended up with all three. It was a lot of work but he pissed me off so bad, telling me you can't do this. What a way to inspire people! Telling them, "You probably can't do it but go ahead and give it a shot anyway." That was my entrance into politics. I found out I liked it and I have remained active in politics ever since.

I got involved with labor folks, Don Rowen and the boys over at the Iowa Federation of Labor, because Marian Moffitt, who was my guardian, kind of hooked me up with them and before I knew it I was secretary of the Polk County Democrats. When I look back I realize that they wanted me to run for the job because they wanted to beat somebody else. How could anybody vote against a black, female union person? Jerry Crawford was chair of the Polk County Democrats at that time. He was well liked and could accomplish things.

When Don Rowen ran for president of the South Central Fed in 1976 I voted for him. Bob Boudreau and the rest of the delegation were against him. They were having enough trouble with me at the

time so that I was no longer a delegate to the Fed. I was only an
alternate but they weren't smart enough to realize that one of their
people never showed up for anything, so that I was a going to be
able to vote. As any good alternate would, when this guy didn't
show up, I had to cast a vote. Because I didn't vote the way he
wanted me to, Boudreau tried to castigate me there in front of everybody. He screamed and yelled and said, "You'll never go anywhere
with this union, you'll never go to another CWA function. You are
done." I said, "Okay, we'll see." But he couldn't stop me. When he
wouldn't pay for me to go to things, I would volunteer on my own
time. If I wanted to go to a legislative conference, I would take a
vacation and go. He could not stop me.

In 1978 we paid Boudreau back because he was such a tyrant.
We ran a woman, Marian Moffitt, against him as president of our
local. We organized her campaign as we would any political campaign. About three months ahead of the nominating convention we
started organizing our campaign within the building. Most of the
people on that campaign were women because in the union the
membership is predominantly women. We went through our building floor by floor and ID'd our people. Just prior to the election we
did a GOTV [Get Out the Vote] program. I had the scathingly brilliant idea that Marian's supporters should show some organization
to really scare Boudreau, so on the afternoon before the election
several of us ironed letters on a box of T-shirts that said, "Members
for Moffitt." The operators who came to the meeting that night wore
these shirts under their regular clothes and when Moffitt was nominated they ripped off their other shirts and here's all these people
with "Members for Moffitt" T-shirts. We had other people throwing
confetti just like in a regular Democratic nominating convention. It
was great! Boudreau was such an egotistical maniac that the night
of the election he called all the media to let them know that it was
his election and that the ballots were about to be counted. We beat
him two to one. We had the highest number of returned ballots in
the history of the local union. Marian at that time was in transition
to a new job so she was away in a training class. Basically, I and
another woman ran her campaign. As a result I developed an ulcer.

Moffitt named me legislative and political chair in the local. I
was no expert on anything and I did grunt stuff like lit drops and
door knocking. There was an advantage to being a black, female
laborer because every time they needed a token, I was that token.
That was okay because it gave me exposure. I continued a long time
as legislative chair and I worked in presidential campaigns. People
came to see me because everybody wanted union support.

I got to Washington because of that exposure in Iowa. I got to know Loretta Bowen, director of political affairs in AFL-CIO COPE, and in June 1987 she picked me out to ask, "Do you want to come to Washington and help me through this cycle?" She told me that the reason she picked me was that she knew I would work because whenever they needed a hundred bodies somewhere, she would just pick up the phone and call me. I might not have a hundred bodies there but I might have fifty or seventy-five on short notice. She knew she could count on me and and she also knew that I had a basic feel for politics. She didn't want to have somebody that she had to start from scratch.

I was supposed to be in Washington until December [1988] but Loretta hasn't sent me back to Iowa yet. She runs a very successful department but until I came she was the only person in it. If she had been one of the boys she would have gotten more help. Basically, I'm Loretta's assistant although that is not my official title. I screen candidates for the House of Representatives and I am her eyes and ears in the field. I do training workshops on politics and try to raise money. I have no special skills. I just happened to be in Iowa at the right time. Loretta says it wasn't because I was black that she chose me. She says I just happened to be black, which was a plus.

Ann Kelly is currently based at the AFL-CIO COPE headquarters in Rolling Meadows, Ill., a community in the Chicago area, but she spends most of her time on the road.

Barbara Mathias

was director of the YWCA (Young Women's Christian Association) on the campus of Iowa State University in Ames from February 1973 to February 1975. As director of the Y, she was particularly interested in programs relating to women's health and reproductive freedom. She now has her own firm in Des Moines, Mid-America Leadership Group, specialists in personal and management development. She also serves on the legislative affairs committee of Planned Parenthood and is active in the Metro Women's Network, a Des Moines business organization.

"In the middle of the seventies we at least knew we didn't have it so good, and it seemed like more young women were in touch with that and were willing to work for some changes."

I've been a feminist for a long time. I was born in Atlanta, Georgia, and raised in Richmond, Virginia. My mother did not finish high school because when she was in school in 1915 or 1916 the influenza was prevalent in Richmond. A couple of her sisters died and they took most of the other children out of school. My father completed high school and began work as an elevator operator at the Chesapeake and Ohio Railroad and he stayed with the Chesapeake and Ohio until he retired in 1965. He rose to be freight traffic manager. He had a nonstop, steady career, which we hardly see anymore. My brothers, sister, and I were the first in our family to go to college.

I was raised in a very sexist society, though not necessarily in a very sexist home. My parents were quite liberal and understanding. Nevertheless, there was great pressure on me as a southern girl child to grow up to be a southern lady. And yet, it looked to me like the black women I knew, who either worked in our home or were friends of women who worked in our home, had more fun and had a neater life than the white ladies. So my earliest concepts of myself as a girl child were that I did not want to grow up to be a southern lady. I had a lot of support from my father and some from my mother. My dad seemed to think that southern ladies were kind of useless and never really accomplished much. He seemed to believe my mother to be an exception. I remember that at an early age he allowed me to drink coffee. Now I was allergic to milk, but somehow he associated drinking coffee with being a fully functional person as opposed to drinking tea.

I had a lot of battles throughout my childhood and my teenage years with my mother, who really was split. She was a kind of feminist herself but also really a southern traditionalist in a lot of ways. She wanted me to adopt those ways and I simply couldn't. They seemed to me to be dependent, insufficient, and false—mostly false. One of the things that I equated with being a lady was a false set of social values. I was supposed to say things that weren't true and I just couldn't do that.

We moved north in 1946 when I was in fifth grade. I went to the Hinsdale, Illinois, high school and about 94 percent of the people who went to Hinsdale High went to universities afterward. It was considered a finishing process. If you grew up in a family like I grew up in, you did not end your education at the end of high school. Yet, as a woman, you weren't supposed to do much in college. You were supposed to get grades, participate in the social life, and find a husband. I did all those things.

I was quite a liberal and quite an outspoken worker for women's rights when I was in high school and college. My freshman year I went to Michigan State. That was in 1953. Women couldn't wear Bermuda shorts in the student union because Michigan State was just becoming a university and they felt that their image would be improved if the women always either wore skirts or full-length slacks. I remember I just railed at that; I thought that was so false. After Michigan State I went to Northwestern where I proposed to the dean of women that we eliminate women's hours. That was in 1955

or 1956. We had, I think, 2 o'clock hours, which were fairly late for
the Big Ten. Nevertheless, I said in a meeting that I didn't feel that
women were any more the responsibility of the university than men
were and men didn't have hours and ours should be eliminated.
Well, it was just out of the question.

I married as soon as I was out of college and had children immediately. I have three children born in 1958, 1961, and 1963—two
sons and a daughter. I also struggled in the work force. I had majored in English and Spanish in college as something to fall back on
and I went to work as an English teacher in Lafayette, Indiana. My
husband at that time was studying agricultural economics at Pur-
due. I remember struggling with the idea that my job was something to fall back on as opposed to a career and yet I didn't have a
concept of a career. I taught for a couple of years, and then did
substitute teaching as my children were coming along.

I began to see that teaching wasn't going to be what I wanted in
life. I didn't want to spend the day with children and also evenings
with children at home. I got interested in business and pursued
business quite a bit in the early to mid-sixties as my children were
getting into grade school; became a focus group leader for a market
research company; and did some work in St. Louis.

We moved to Ames, Iowa, in 1972. My next-door neighbor was
Kay Holmberg, who was a counselor at the student counseling service at Iowa State. She came over shortly to tell me that the job of
YWCA director was open and that because of my background in
human service volunteeer work and also because I had some business orientation I might be interested in applying. The Y was in
serious financial trouble and they were looking for someone who
was a fund-raiser or who was at least a little bit knowledgeable in
business and who also understood the concept of building a Y. In
1972 they had a part-time director who worked about twenty to
twenty-five hours a week. The total Y budget for the year was about
$7,500 and the director made about $7,200 of that. So I applied for
that job and went to the interview.

To my surprise, I was interviewed by seven women, all at the
same time. I had never been so shocked by an interview. First of all,
I thought it was overkill. I thought they might have selected their
two or three best. These women seemed so confused about their
own goals that when I left that interview I didn't want the job. A few
days later I found out from the chairman of that committee that I
was one of the two finalists. I thought, Well, that's more interesting
than I thought it would be. If I'm one of the two finalists then I
would really like to be considered. I went back and reapplied and

talked to several of the members of the personnel committee and got hired.

I was hired in February of 1973. *Roe v. Wade* legalizing abortion had just been decided by the United States Supreme Court and women's issues were very prevalent. Iowa State had, in fact, been the site of quite a bit of disruption. YWCA members had protested on the steps of Alumni Hall and, I think, Beardshear Hall in favor of women's rights. It was really a very fertile time to come to work there. I set out to accomplish several things. I knew that if the Y had only raised $7,500 the year before, it would be easier to raise $15,000 or $18,000 than it had been to raise the $7,500 or $8,000; that we had to make a mark on the community and really stake out what was going to be our territory.

One of the issues that I wanted addressed was women's health issues. It happened that at that time a man who was a conscientious objector had been assigned to the Iowa Clergy Council and to the campus ministries at Iowa State for his conscientious objector stint. He was doing abortion referral at Frisbee House. Abortion had been illegal in Iowa until the end of January that year and there was no place in the state to send women. The most desirable place, I believe, was a medical center in New York City. I met the conscientious objector through Open Line, another volunteer service, and so, as his tour of duty was coming to an end at the end of that winter, he and I went together to the government of the student body, to the Campus Chest, and to the United Way and got funding for a woman's position in the Y, to be called women's health coordinator. This position started out at about twenty hours. Then we funded an office coordinator through the United Way and then we funded my position as director.

So we raised donations to the point where the YWCA had a viable life for at least the next year. I figured that if we could get programming started, and this women's health coordinator could begin to set up really functional programing, we wouldn't have any trouble getting funded next year. I was hoping for a couple of things: help from the student health service, which it turned out we got, and help from Bill Layton, vice president of student affairs, which we got. At that point even birth control information, or any kind of counseling regarding women's health service, was still a real sticky subject for the university to handle. Yet, problem pregnancies, like any issue that has to do with women's health, was an issue at the university at that time. So I worked with Gail Proffitt, the woman who was the director of the student health center, and with Bill Layton, who was very supportive, and we set up what was a reasonable program of counseling and referral for women students. This program was funded through the YWCA instead of through the health center or student affairs, whose hands were tied by just trying to appeal to the breadth of alumni and their concerns about their own children and their sexuality.

I feel like the biggest part of the Y program at that time was the health care. We had a volunteer staff of abortion counselors who had been trained by Iowa Clergy Counseling Services, by the university health service, and by just about anybody else who had been working in that area. We also trained counselors at the Y. They would come in at a moment's notice. We would probably have at that time three to five calls a week from women who had pregnancies that came as a surprise to them and they hadn't decided how they were going to deal with their situation. Of these women, three to four would end up having abortions; one or two would go ahead and have their babies. But they needed to have somebody to talk to during that time and we had volunteers who would come in at any time of day or night. This group of people met frequently to discuss the ethics of abortion and the ethics of how to counsel women with problem pregnancies. By no means were all of the calls from students. Maybe three-fifths of the calls were from students and the rest were from community women, some married, some single. We counseled quite a number of married women with problem pregnancies. Some of them decided to terminate the pregnancy, some decided to have their babies. Abortion referral was an important part of the Y at that point.

We also served as a call-in service for a lot of people who felt strongly about the abortion issue and wanted to talk to us about it. We always had somebody during office hours who would talk to people who were either antichoice or prochoice. Some of those led to very good conversations. Sometimes antichoice people would call in very angry at us, and then find out that we were really quite reasonable human beings, and that we were not trying to counsel in favor of having abortions. We were trying to listen to what the women's situations were, to question them as to what choices they wanted to make, and then give them the information they wanted.

One of the things I noticed in those years is that a problem pregnancy almost immediately resulted in the relationship in which that pregnancy was conceived ending. Many of the young women, especially the unmarried women, would not tell their partners that they were pregnant. A fair number of those were not partners with whom there was a long-term relationship. In the case where it had been a long-term relationship, if they were not married, the relation-

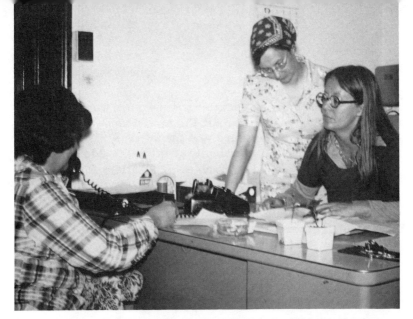

BARABARA MATHIAS (*right*) as executive director of the Ames YWCA, with Kay Carey (*center*), and Georgene Shank, 1973. *"We were trying to listen to what the women's situations were, to question them as to what choices they wanted to make, and then give them the information they wanted. . . . We truly believed that all things were possible."*

ship seldom was able to withstand the disruption of an unexpected pregnancy, whether it was carried to term or whether it was aborted. I think maybe that hasn't changed very much. In the case of the married women, some chose to tell their husbands, which we really encouraged, before they made a decision; others chose not to tell them. They may have told them later without our knowing it. We usually tried to do one follow-up with every decision and some women took advantage of that. Most of them did not. Most of the married women, once they either had the abortion or decided to go ahead and carry the pregnancy to term, just incorporated that into their lives and didn't particularly want to talk to us again. We understood the political ramifications of what these women were doing. They understood it only as a personal decision and so we had to monitor the difference between what we were hoping for and trying to make possible and what they were suffering from.

One of the things we did was to lobby the university health center to provide birth control to single women students. I personally lobbied McFarland to do abortions when abortions first became legal. McFarland Clinic was the large medical clinic in Ames, which was very paternalistic and judgmental about women's health choices at that time (but not now). McFarland at that point refused to do abortions for anyone except married women who already had two or three children. Meanwhile, Emma Goldman Clinic in Iowa City began doing abortions in about the fall of 1973, so we had a clinic in Iowa to refer to. Also shortly after that, Claude Koons, who was a doctor in Des Moines, began doing abortions within his private practice and we could refer to him. Dr. [Paulino] Fong also began doing abortions in Des Moines and we could refer to him. The result was that quite a number of the Y staff, including me, left McFarland Clinic as patients and came to Des Moines to Dr. Koons. Not long after that, Dr. Koons associated with Planned Parenthood here and then the whole situation opened up a lot more.

The YWCA and Iowa State at that time were not at all active in social issues and so the Y delivered services to both women and men students. We did two different programs that I remember were very eagerly accepted. One was called, "Sex and Your Head." That was a sexuality program where we would go out to both women's and men's dorms, to sororities, to fraternities, and talk to them about sexuality. We would talk to them about sexual intercourse and what birth control was. One of the most frequent questions asked was, "Can I get pregnant without having intercourse?" The answer to that is long and complicated because, yes, in some cases you can get pregnant without having intercourse. There were not a whole lot of acceptable birth control methods at that time. The student health clinic was not excited about giving pills to single women. They could get them, I believe, at the McFarland Clinic. At any rate, we simply talked about sexuality and answered questions. We had a panel of four women (sometimes three women and one man) who were comfortable with their own sexuality and could answer questions. The kids loved it. Those sessions would sometimes go on for three or four hours.

We also put out another group of panelists that I was real proud of. That was a group who simply went in the fall and talked to the students about basic health care. That had to do with the difference between dorm food and home food, that they would face more carbohydrates, and that the average freshman gains weight. If they didn't want to gain weight, we told them some things they might do about it. We even told them how to take their temperature and when they needed to call a doctor. This program was set up in combination with the health center.

One of the Y speakers at that time was Phylliss Henry, who I now work with on a volunteer basis at Planned Parenthood in Des Moines. Phylliss was the first woman police officer in Des Moines. She came to Ames and did a program for us on police work and her experiences on the police force. That was an interesting experience because the staff at the Y was very political and Phylliss wasn't political at all. She just wanted to be a good police officer. We were speaking different languages. I've since talked to Phylliss about that and she said, yes, looking back it wasn't a political act at all for her. It was much later that she realized the political ramifications of what she was doing.

I stayed with the Y for two years. After I left the Y in 1975 I ran small businesses in Ames, called Hardware Etcetera and The Frame Shop, for twelve years. This was sort of a natural transition into doing supervisory and personnel leadership training. Now I am a consultant for a management company in Des Moines and I work with companies, using a lot of my human potential background and a lot of my business experience.

When I look back, I think women had it better in some ways in the sixties and early seventies than they have it now. I'll tell you why. The administration at Iowa State was resistant. However, we had the emerging forces and the emerging excitement of the time. We truly believed that all things were possible and that it would only be a few years, maybe just a few months, before women had a more equitable situation. Also, the men weren't as organized as they are now to defeat us. That's a very delicate matter to even phrase, but the resistance on the male part was tentative. They were kind of knocked off base. For me it was a very exciting time, a very growing time. Women were coming into their own in terms of new careers and in possibilities for grants and scholarships that hadn't been known before. I see it in many ways as a lot more exciting time than we have right now because there is so much resistance now to the gains that women have already made. It seems like the establishment is so well entrenched. The glass ceiling is on tight. I think we will go through another period of growth, but what has happened is that we have had to pay the price for a lot of growth in a short time. I also think that the conservatives in the late sixties and the early seventies really got caught short. As much as I disagree with many of their philosophies, they weren't prepared to stand up for their own rights and they got trampled on. So what we have seen lately has been a counterbalance. I think of them coming back and saying, "Wait a minute, we didn't like that time and we're now going to impose what we want." I hope we are getting to the point where we can work out equitable rights. When I became director of the Y sixteen years ago, I certainly would have thought in some ways we would have been farther along than we are now.

In the middle seventies we at least knew we didn't have it so good, and it seemed like more of the young women were in touch with that and were willing to work for some changes. Now it seems almost as if the younger women think that the women over forty were kind of foolish to have worked so hard when we were going to get our rights anyway. In fact, we don't have them yet. We don't have equitable pay. We don't have equal earning ability. There are just many ways in which we are prejudiced against in our society. I hope that it is almost the calm before the storm. Eleanor Smeal, former NOW president, said last night that we will have the third wave of feminism as a result of the *Webster* decision on abortion. I hope we do.

Louise Swartzwalder

reported the progress of the feminist movement in Iowa when she worked as a reporter for the *Des Moines Register* in the late 1960s and early 1970s. She now runs her own business, Takoma Kitchens, a catering and bakery company in the Washington, D.C., area.

"People would have no idea of what to make of a woman in the news-room . . . and if you were one who stood up for what you believed in and went out and did your job then you were doubly strange."

I live in a suburb of Washington, D.C., and became famil-iar with Iowa by working at the *Des Moines Register* starting in 1968. I grew up in Ohio. My parents were farmers. Mother was a high school English and home economics teacher. I had two older sisters. When I went to Ohio State University I became the the first of my family to attend a college that was farther than twenty miles from home. I chose Ohio State because I was interested in journal-ism. I had summer jobs at local newspapers starting with my sopho-more year, and then at the *Cleveland Plain Dealer,* which was one of the major newspapers in Ohio. After that I went to work for the *Des Moines Register,* starting in the fall of 1968. I worked at the *Register* until July 1979.

Early on I did not realize what influence my mother had on me. John Hyde, who is my friend, says that there are some people who have real mothers. By that he means the kind of mothers who tell you how to tie your shoes and who call you up and make sure you're wearing warm clothing in winter and tell you you're not taking care of your own kids right. They are people who worry about you incessantly. John says that my mother is not a real mother because she's none of those things. She never was judgmental about anything I did but always very supportive. When I would ask my parents' opinion about something, the reply would be, "Whatever you think is right." I never thought about it very much, but that obviously had a very big effect on the way I do things now. They always were supportive, even when I wanted to do things that they probably didn't approve of. They just let me do what I wanted and had a lot of faith that I would do it right.

When I was at Ohio State I asked several professors what newspaper I should apply to because I was interested in working for somebody that did hard news. I was given a list of about ten newspapers which were said to be the best in the country and the *Des Moines Register* was on the list. I applied to a number of these places and the *Register* hired me. This was in 1968. I ended up replacing a woman named Julie Zelenka, who had been sort of the token woman on the *Register* staff. She was a phenomenon because they had hardly ever had any women covering hard news but she was one who did. I remember being told stories about what a tough person Julie was because she would cover the courthouse and deal with the police, using their language, and all these men would say how shocked they were that this person would actually do that. I thought, What's so hard about that? In those days the *Register* had a slot for a woman to cover "X" and that's what I was to do. So I started in covering courts and suburbs; I went to the courthouse during the day and at night I covered the suburban council meetings, such as West Des Moines and Urbandale. I never had anyone train me, which is quite a common practice now on newspapers. If a reporter comes in somebody will at least take them out to the beat they're supposed to cover and say this is who you talk to. Nobody showed me anything. From the minute I walked in the door I was on my own and I figured out who I was supposed to talk to at the courthouse and who the judges were and what kind of stuff I was supposed to find out. I just did it. There were not a whole lot of people working as editors then who were terrifically helpful either. They sort of expected you to just go out and forge your own way. So I did.

Every Friday or Saturday the *Register* had an entire page devoted to coverage of the local schools. There was a reporter who did only that page and this person was supposed to go out and find a story for each school and take pictures and do the layout and do the entire school page. The young woman who had this job decided she wanted to leave, so characteristically they decided that another young woman had to take over and so [in 1969] I was assigned the school page. I was really upset. I told them it didn't interest me at all and essentially I was told I had no choice, so I did it. It was terribly boring. It took me no time at all to do it and it was not a challenge. I could do it blindfolded.

Then we had a switch in city editors and in 1971 I ended up back in hard news. I was sent up to the hill [the Iowa legislature] to cover state government. I was the first woman to ever do that. At that point there were probably four reporters for the *Register* who covered the hill plus two or three for the Des Moines *Tribune*. I was sort of allowed to go up there and carve out my own little niche. At that point you could do that. You could find yourself an agency to cover, which somebody else wasn't covering, and I did that. I remember one time after I had done this for a while and it was becoming clear that I was successful, Jerry Szumski, who is still at the *Register*, came up to me and told me, "Of course, they sent you up here as an experiment and they don't intend for you to stay." I thought, Well, gee, thank you, Jerry. Let's just see who is going to be around here longer. I ran into all that kind of stuff because they thought it was odd for a girl to be up there. I ended up covering the house, the first woman ever to cover either side of the legislature.

About this time I became interested in the women's movement. Roxanne Conlin was in the attorney general's office and somehow I made contact with her. The Women's Political Caucus was just getting started [1973] and lots of things were happening in the area of women's rights. It was fascinating to me because I believed in all of these things. I ended up writing a lot of stories about the formation of the caucus. I can't remember the sequence, but I wrote one story about discrimination in Iowa. That was early on and Roxanne may have helped me with some of the information because she was fairly well tied into statistics and numbers, such as salaries at the universities. I think the caucus had begun to do some studies about salary levels. That story changed a whole lot of practices at the *Des Moines Register* because I managed to get into print some things that were fairly shocking to some of the editors. They ended up getting a lot of phone calls from their friends who were astonished that we would dare to put something in print that would talk about the salary scales of state employees. Actually, one of the figures involved a woman editor in Des Moines who worked for the *Register*. The editor who handled the story was quite supportive and he fought all the way to get this story in because he thought it was substantiated and was worthwhile. He ended up taking a lot of heat for it. But everything stood up.

I began doing a lot more with women in politics because the caucus was getting very involved in that regard. There was a period where the caucus was responsible for a whole lot of law changes and that showed a lot of clout. I found it to be pretty impressive. Some of the men who were covering the hill didn't think it was all that important, but I thought it was very important. It was incredible what happened in the space of a couple of years in the legislature because they changed all those laws including inheritance taxes and state taxes and other things. That was one of the things that was fascinating to me because little Iowa at that point was way ahead of a lot of other states due to this very active group of feminists who were able to lobby successfully on the hill and to be taken seriously.

When Roxanne ran for national head of the Women's Political Caucus, that became sort of controversial because Iowans had the reputation of being brash about how well we had done. Caucus members would go to regional meetings and to the national meetings and march in and talk about all the legislative successes and all these wonderful things they had accomplished. Roxanne is full of vim and vigor and there was a period where it began to rub some people in feminist circles the wrong way. You're not supposed to be too proud, I guess. I ended up writing a series of stories about the status of the women's movement and where we had all come. This was right before the International Women's Year celebration in 1977.

I had a four-part series which I thought was pretty good. It covered everything that was happening nationally in the women's movement and also in Iowa. It also covered the activities of Phyllis Schlafly. The city editor looked at the story and said, "I think this is just one story, this isn't four stories." I said, "What? This can't be." The editor was a person who was not terribly supportive about any of these things and he didn't think that this was worth getting into in such detail. I said, "It is worth getting into because Iowa has had an important place in the women's movement. There has been a hard core of activist women here and Iowa has always had a reputation for that. There are many things changing here and I think we should do some stories about it." My editor didn't want to do anything and so I appealed it to the next person above him, who said, "Fine, this is great. We'll print it." He told me I should sell the story to Ms. magazine, which I tried to do, but Ms. didn't want to buy it. Part of what I did was a lot of research into the financing of Phyllis

LOUISE SWARTZWALDER as reporter for the *Des Moines Register*, 1975. *"I ended up covering the house, the first woman ever to cover either side of the legislature."*

Schlafly and her types. I went to the legislative records in Missouri and to the Illinois legislature, where we were fighting for the ERA. I attempted to get into financial records on lobbying in those states but essentially there were none. I called Joseph Coors because he was one of the big backers of Schlafly. I also called the woman in Texas who has this company [Mary Kay] that sells cosmetics and who rewards her salespeople by giving them pink cars. She was reputed to be a big backer of the anti-ERA groups. But by the time I got around to calling people like that, they were smart enough to have a canned response to questions. They would say, "This is our statement regarding that." My four-part story was about the last thing I did as a reporter because at that point [1977] I became an editor and was put in charge of other people covering politics. I don't think there have been any other persons who covered the women's movement at the *Register*, partially because it died down after a certain point. There was a real heyday and then it became less important.

What about my association with NOW? That was something that I did sort of clandestinely because I shouldn't have done it at all. But I did. When I first began talking to people like Virginia Watkins and Roxanne and some of the other activist types, I clearly identified with everything they had to say. I felt like I was one of them, that I was not really a reporter at that point. A bunch of people got together in 1971 and decided there should be a NOW chapter and I said, "Yes, absolutely." I think our initial meeting was in a union hall. I remember a small group of us being there and that was how it all got started. I took an active part in NOW at the beginning and then essentially I had to back out because the *Register* had this unwritten policy about reporters being involved in organizational politics, which NOW would have been. However, I was able to always be involved in all these organizations by virtue of being a reporter covering the meetings. I didn't ever take an active part but at least I was there and knew what was going on. At some of the first meetings there was a lot of uncertainty in the entire group because not only were we getting together talking about things people didn't talk about before, but also some of these people didn't necessarily want anybody else to know they were there. Some people felt really uncomfortable. In those early days it was hard for people to get together and talk in a revealing way. But people did just that.

Was my job ever in jeopardy because of my involvement with feminism? I think the *Register* probably thought I was a little too much involved, but they also put up with it. I don't know whether that speaks about them or it speaks about me. Everybody recognized the fact that I was a feminist although they probably didn't know what that meant. But they recognized that I believed all these things and a lot of times they didn't know how to take me because I was always professional and I always attempted to act professionally and dress professionally. A lot of people bought into the stereotypes of the activist-feminist women and you were supposed to be grubby and unattractive and poorly groomed. I had a man say to me one time, "That really looks nice, isn't this inconsistent with being a feminist?" I would get things like that which were really bizarre. We got a lot of that in the very early days. People would have no idea what to make of a woman in a newsroom in the first place and if you were one who stood up for what you believed in and went out and did your job, then that was doubly strange. If you managed to persist, then you were really an oddity. You were supposed to get married and go off someplace.

At one point I did get married and I kept my own name. I didn't tell anybody at the *Register* that I was married. It ended up being somewhat embarrassing because a managing editor had to come around to me and say, "Excuse me, Louise, are you aware that under your health insurance coverage your spouse can be entitled to coverage, too?" It was one of those totally bizarre conversations because he didn't know what to do. The poor guy should have just come up and said, "You got married, right?" I would have said yes. But he had to go at it in this very strange fashion because I wasn't about to tell him anything. I figured, why should it matter if I'm married? It should have absolutely no impact on what I do. I treated it that way. There were people at the *Register* who were really supportive and there were people there who thought there was absolutely no news in the subject that I was dealing with. But I pretty much won.

SWARTZWALDER (*right*) with Mary Ritchies, 1976. *"A lot of people bought into the stereotypes of activist-feminist women. . . . I had a man say to me one time, 'That really looks nice, isn't this inconsistent with being a feminist?' "*

Some of the stories I wrote brought in lots of criticism. There was an incident when a woman friend of mine called up a brokerage house, probably Merrill-Lynch, and asked for information on investments. The man who answered her call asked her to give her husband's name. She said, "I'm not married." He said, "We don't send out any information to people unless you can give us your husband's name." This was terribly blatant. It was one of these ridiculous things where it was you either have to be married or there has to be a man involved or you couldn't possibly handle this complicated issue. I put that in the paper and the brokerage house was just purple. They called up and said, "This could never have happened." I said, "It did. Do you want me to have this person get on the line? She can tell you how it happened." There was a lot of heat. After my story about discrimination in state schools, people from the universities called up because I had quoted disparities in wages and I talked about problems with insurance rates and insurance coverage, and everybody was pretty much livid about that. First of all, they denied it was so and then they denied the accuracy of how it was portrayed. They were unhappy but the story stood and we did not have any corrections on any of these stories.

After I became an editor I pretty much stopped writing stories although on occasion I would persuade them to let me do something. One of the things that I did after I had become an editor was to get permission to cover the International Women's Year Conference in Texas. That was in 1977. This conference came at a strange point. It was sort of at the end of people being initiated into the process and there was a lot of divisiveness at that conference. There was a lot of evidence of splits in things that the caucus and NOW had initiated. Everybody seemed to have their own little interest area: the lesbian women, the low-income women, the Hispanic women were all there. It was a very eclectic group. Everybody from about every country and every interest group was there. It was phe-

nomenal that so many people could get into one city and function
under one roof. I don't know that the conference accomplished anything except that everybody got together in one city and talked.
That was the end of my covering any feminist events in a very
direct way. After the conference, a whole lot of organizational things
in the women's movement sort of fell apart.

Where is the Women's Political Caucus now? What do they do?
NOW is still there and it is a constant, which is reassuring because
that is an identifiable group that keeps going. Other groups are not
as visible as they used to be. For a while I thought the Women's
Political Caucus was a great idea, something that got a lot of people
involved. Maybe it was something whose time has come and gone.
It was an attempt to get women politically involved and maybe now
it's more of a situation where other interest groups are taking up the
slack, groups like Planned Parenthood or NARAL [National Abortion Rights Action League], for instance. That is reassuring because
after the Supreme Court decision in the *Webster* case, it is wonderful to see Faye Wattleton, president of Planned Parenthood, out
there doing what she does. She is a real catalyst. A lot of people
have probably been sitting on their duff for years and now they are
going to get geared up again.

I left the *Register* in 1979 to go to the *Detroit Free Press,* where
I was hired to be an editor. They did actually have women working
there, which was nice, but the paper is an entirely different animal
from the *Des Moines Register.* Whereas the *Des Moines Register,*
when I was there, would cover anything that moved in state government, the *Free Press* would go out of its way to avoid any story
except those that dealt with three-legged dogs or some other bizarre
incident. They had absolutely no interest in women in politics. The
political climate in Michigan is much different, too. The Women's
Political Caucus would never have happened in Michigan, for instance. Partially, I attribute this favorable situation in Iowa to the
Des Moines Register when the caucus was formed. Roxanne used to
ask me about that and I said that if it were not for the *Register,* the
caucus probably couldn't have accomplished what it did. This was
because at that point a reporter like me could pick a subject area
and write about it and get it into the paper. That gives a movement
credibility. You couldn't do that at the *Register* now. In other states
and other newspapers you couldn't have done it then. I was lucky
enough to seize upon feminist issues and decide that they were
important and to get them published.

Why couldn't they do it now? First of all, the *Register* would not
devote enough space to that kind of an issue; secondly, there is no

one reporter who is interested enough in that area to write about it;
and thirdly, the editors probably wouldn't do it. Maybe, also, there is
not any news on that score anymore. You have to have all of the
elements there. First of all, we had the right climate. We had people
like Roxanne, who was willing to go out and be a front person. Then
there was a group of hard-core activist women who were waiting for
something to do. They believed in all of these things. Then I was
able to get stories in the paper. That is partially how it happened.
For instance, we used to go to Women's Political Caucus regional
meetings and Roxanne would be there. I used to get away with
everything. I can't believe how many things I would persuade them
to let me cover. I got to cover all kinds of regional meetings and just
about any conference at which Roxanne would be speaking. Roxanne would pick up copies of my newspaper articles and start reading them to people and she would be talking about how to get yourself going with free coverage in a newspaper. I think that sort of was
true.

I was in Detroit from July of 1979 to March of 1981. I worked
there as an editor so I didn't have an opportunity to get into anything that was happening with women there. I left Detroit to come
to Washington to hunt for a job, which is what almost everybody
does. I found a job with Tom Railsback, the Republican from Illinois,
who was pivotal in the Watergate hearings. He is a good, moderate
Republican and his heart was in the right place on almost all issues.
I worked for him until he got beaten in a primary 1982 and then I
decided to work in a political campaign. I went to John Glenn's
office and said, "You need to hire me because I used to work for the
Des Moines Register and I can give you real good help." I kept beat-
ing on their door until they finally gave me a job. I was the deputy
press secretary in 1983 for Glenn's presidential campaign.

That got me back into Iowa in a different way. I had previously
not been able to be involved and had to keep at arm's length from
political issues. This was my first chance to do things from the inside. It was a whole lot of fun. I did that until the Iowa caucuses,
when it became clear that John Glenn was not going to be able to do
very much. After that I didn't work for several months. I tried to
figure out what I should do and at that point I decided I should bake
pies. Everybody else said, "You should bake pies, Louise," including
Sue Kaul, who was always a big fan of my food. I said that I'd always
wanted to do this but how should I do it? She said, "Well, you just
start doing it." And so I did.

I took a lot of my mother's recipes because Mother was a tremendous pie baker. She taught me how to roll out my first pie

dough. She gave me my first rolling pin and she also told me how to make preserves. I took all those things and decided that I would see if people cared, and they did. I am now using my mother's pie recipes and all the things she taught me. We are a wholesale bakery called Takoma Kitchens. We distribute to about twenty stores in the Washington area, including as far north as Baltimore and into northern Virginia. We also have a retail store where we sell our pies and breads and condiments. We do a lunch business and we make sandwiches on our own breads, which is what makes them unique. We do catering. The catering came out of the bakery business because people were very interested in our breads and the other things we did and they would say, "Can you fix me up something besides some of your bran muffins for breakfast?" I would say, "Fine." I sort of took the bakery business as a background and started developing the catering business. This part of the business is something that has grown by word of mouth. It's all through referrals.

Do I think it is a feminist thing to run a business like mine, or is it reverting to something from the past, back to cooking? Maybe it's a combination of the two. I've never blown my own horn about this but other people tell me that they think what I'm doing is just incredible. I took an idea and have built an empire. I don't know whether it is an empire but it is a viable business. Sometimes when I look at it now it really scares me. I started off with absolutely no money. I had a very small mixer and I had some ideas, and I decided, I can bake. Let's just see if anything happens. I kept doing that, putting everything I earned back into the business and I kept expanding slowly. We are now at the point where I have a fleet of three vehicles. I have about seven employees and a number of catering clients who are regulars. I have never thought about how feminism relates to my business, but I think feminism trained me to be independent, to have the stamina to do this, because this is all about stamina, creativity, and conviction. If I didn't believe in any of this it would never have happened.

I think my parents have had an incredible amount to do with my success because I have felt in recent years as though I've become more like my parents than I ever thought I would. My mother is the strongest woman I know. She is eighty-three and she keeps on going. She has had illnesses and she just keeps perking right back up. Growing up on a farm makes you tough. You always have something to do, you never sit around all day. My father also is a very good businessman. He always had this sense about how he should govern himself in business and how he should treat people. He would never sit down. In that sense, whether you want to call it feminism or whatever, I think that's a very good thing to have in your background if you want to be in business. I have a very firm sense about how I should be treated as a businessperson and how I should treat other people. I don't take any guff from anybody and I have a very firm sense about what you should do to maintain yourself in business and how you should deal with people. That is what I have done. It helps to have my background because it makes you uniquely suited for all kinds of things.

Some people will start a business and put a whole lot of money in it at the beginning and go through all these elaborate plans and then hope it works. I did it the other way. I went at it without a whole lot of knowledge and no money and a couple of products. I have just taken all these other steps and it is now to a point where it is pretty respectable.

Clara Oleson, a leader in the
radical/feminist community in Iowa City in the
1970s, has wandered far from her conservative
Catholic girlhood in Brooklyn, N.Y. She led the
successful fight for pay equity for maids at the
University of Iowa, then attended law school
and in 1976 opened the first all-women law
office in Iowa City. She now works as a labor
educator for the university.

*"I became a believer in offering
honoria to women speakers! Talking
to service clubs did not provide a
living wage."*

My full name is Clara Elena Rodriguez Oleson. I grew
up in a working-class section of Brooklyn, New York. My father, who
was born in Spain, came to the United States in 1919. He was a
bartender. My mother's name was Helen Zadistowski. While her
background was probably Polish she grew up in a Spanish-speaking
household and was known as Helen Diaz. She was a telephone operator. My mother's mother died of a self-induced abortion at the age
of twenty-nine, leaving my mother and her two sisters all under the
age of eight. I didn't find out about my grandmother until I was
involved in the feminist movement in the seventies. I had always
been told that she had died of tuberculosis, because in a Catholic
environment her death was considered a disgrace. The truth of her
death greatly affected me and ever since she has been a strong inspiration for me on this basic feminist issue.

I attended a Catholic girls' high school in East Rockaway, New

York. My parents hoped I would be a secretary. When I graduated from high school there was a lot of pressure from my extended Spanish family—mother, aunts, and cousins—to get a job and get married and have two kids and live around the corner and come home every Sunday for dinner. I complied in part. After high school I worked for Ma Bell [Bell Telephone] as a business office representative for fourteen months while I attended night classes at a community college. Then in the fall of 1960 I enrolled at St. Joseph's College for Women. The first year was an intellectual paradise. After that it seemed oppressive and less challenging, but now I appreciate the classic liberal arts education the school provided, and the friendships I made there remain very important to me.

When I graduated from St. Joseph's in 1964 I enrolled at the University of Pennsylvania in the American Studies department. In the course of the year I met and fell in love with another graduate student, Jim Oleson. We married and moved to Iowa, Jim's home state, in 1965. The plan was for me to work in Iowa City while Jim finished his Ph.D. at the University of Iowa. Then he would get a job teaching and we would have a daughter named Mabel and we would all live happily ever after. I worked at Northwestern Bell in Iowa City for nine months until I quit because I was disciplined for not wearing a charm bracelet of touch-tone telephones which I had been awarded for outstanding sales.

My next job was at the College of Pharmacy of the University of Iowa as a technical writer. The salary was a disgrace but I was told that I would be eligible to join TIAA-CREF [Teachers' Insurance and Annuity Association-College Retirement Equity Fund], a nationwide retirement fund for higher education which was much more substantial than the IPERS [Iowa Public Employees' Retirement System] state retirement plan. At the end of the first week I went to a universitywide personnel department meeting to sign up for TIAA and was asked, "Are you a student wife?" When I said yes, as did all the women present, the response was, "You are not eligible for TIAA. You will have to go into IPERS." I thought this was unfair but that if I simply educated people as to why it was unfair they would correct it. I had a gut feeling that this was something that happened to women but not to men.

I went to the university's human relations committee and argued that the TIAA-CREF exclusion had a negative impact on women. I gave my moral persuasion pitch, saying that the data I had accumulated showed that 96 percent of the people who were excluded were women and indeed that until 1965 this rule had explicitly applied to student "wives." Then the wording was changed to "spouses" to comply with the Civil Rights Act of that year. At the end of the meeting a male professor approached me and said, "The reality of the situation is that there is no way without power that you are going to make me share my piece of the pie. Why should I give it up to you?" That sticks in my mind as a watershed of my political education. It took me thirteen months within the university committee structure and another year of researching and writing to finally establish eligibility for student spouses under TIAA-CREF. When the TIAA-CREF retirement issue was finally resolved in 1967 it cost the university about $400,000.

In the course of the TIAA-CREF controversy women began calling me up, saying, "I'm in the same situation as you, perhaps we should get together." This led to the founding of SWEAT (Student Wives Equity Action Team), which met every week. The university, under the impulse of the sixties free speech movement, had established the Action Studies Program, a type of free university program. Anyone could set up a class and the university would give you a classroom and free campus mail privileges. SWEAT started a class called Sex Discrimination at the University of Iowa [held 1966–1968]. We were a group of seven or eight women, occasionally expanding to several dozen on particular issues. Most of us were student wives and all underemployed. We began accumulating information about sex discrimination at the University of Iowa. After several months of investigation we decided to file a complaint against the university with the United States Department of Health, Education and Welfare under Executive Order 11246.

We held four days of open hearings off campus at which women told their stories to three federal investigators. We provided the investigators with two hundred pages of allegations of sex discrimination on campus, including information about departments where you had to sleep with the professors to get graduate assistantships. The federal investigators were impressed, filed the report, disappeared, and did nothing. But the local efforts of the women themselves to improve their work situation could not be stopped. Each woman in our troupe tended to spin off and find a new issue and we would all work on "reforming" the institution by attending innumerable committee meetings and writing for the *Daily Iowan*, the campus newspaper, about what we had found.

Our Action Studies class devised a questionnaire about what it was like to be a woman employee at the University of Iowa. It was very biased. We asked questions such as, "How long have you been underpaid at your present job?" We duplicated, collated, stapled, folded, and mailed it to over four thousand women workers at the university. The response was terrific. The ones that got to us the most had been filled out by the maids. All of them reported that they did the same work as the male janitors and got paid between $100 and $125 a month less than the men. I was aware that this was a big-bucks problem and that our little group, no matter how articulate and bright, was not going to win this one alone. We were particularly concerned that the university would fire these women if they started complaining. If we could put this reform in the context of a union-organizing drive, the women would have the protection of labor laws. So we cut a deal with the organizers of AFSCME [American Federation of State and County Municipal Employees] in Chicago who were wanting to run an organizing drive at the university. We would research the issue, write the complaint, be present at every contact with a maid, but all the complaints filed with the federal or state agencies would be under the name of AFSCME and they could take all the credit for it. The deal was struck.

I began learning the Equal Pay Act and the Iowa Civil Rights Act in earnest. Dan Fitzsimmons and Peter Benner from AFSCME were true feminist comrades on this issue and we had hours of sessions, plotting and planning and investigating. I used the Iowa open records law to get the information from the university as to the number of maids and custodians going back five years; how many in each maid classification, how many in each custodian classification, what the average pay was, and how much overtime had been worked. I computed that the back pay award would be well over $500,000. I wrote a complaint of over one hundred pages, which took me a long time because I did not want to rely on any information which did not come from the university's own statistical base. I figured that once we got the complaint in the system the university would be damned by its own statistics.

We selected names from each of the building areas on campus and we interviewed these women extensively, detailing what they did every shift, what tools they used. Then the union organizers got us the male counterparts and conducted similar interviews. It was an extraordinarily complex and interesting task. We filed the complaint with huge fanfare and began fighting our way through the enforcement agencies. The federal Department of Labor came through for us in 1972 and forced the university to settle for two years back pay for each maid, to create a new job classification of custodian, and imposed other remedies.

Everyone who had worked on this action was at the personnel office when settlement checks were passed out and it was incredible to see the maids' reactions. The average back pay award approached $2,000, which is a good chunk of money when you are working at minimum wage. One woman waved her check above her head and shouted, "I'm going to buy myself a mink stole and when I empty the wastebaskets and clean the toilet bowls I'll wear it." I don't know if she ever did it but I loved that rebellion against the academic caste system.

In the late sixties or early seventies I joined a consciousness-raising group which met at Wesley House. I was the only straight woman in the group and I was regarded as the conservative nonradical reformist because I felt that sex discrimination in employment was the root of women's oppression. *The* revolutionary issues for this group were gender politics, socialism, day care, rape. Out of that group came many local actions, including WAR (Women Against Rape). We wanted women police officers, advocates for rape victims, better street lighting, an escort service for women who were traveling at night. We were very loud and noisy at innumerable city council meetings and did street corner handbilling.

A good friend of mine, Mary Weidler, was very interested in the women's health movement, which was blossoming at that time. We had secret meetings in her home and performed pelvic self-examinations and became educated about other health care issues which have now become part of the majority medical culture. This was before *Roe v. Wade* and so we also took up collections to help pay for abortions for financially needy women.

I was fortunate to have worked with such a talented and dedicated group of feminists. Most continue to do good and lead lives of conscious involvement with their world. Barbara Bordwell went on to become a union organizer/educator for the National Education Association. Mary Weidler left Iowa to lead NOW in Alabama and to work with the Civil Liberties Union in Montgomery. Judy Gibson went on to be very active in the radical co-counseling movement. Dale McCormick became the first master carpenter in Iowa and is currently a candidate for the Maine legislature.[1] Vida Brackwell and I went to law school.

By 1972 my seven-year relationship with Jim Oleson was being transformed and ended in divorce a year later. Jim had struggled with wanting a gay relationship for a good many years. He also had not worked in the seven years we were married, which for me was a bigger issue than his sexual preference. I had quit my job in desperation, thinking that if I quit he would have to get a job because he was also not doing anything about completing graduate school. We

1. McCormick was elected in 1990.

(*From left*) Jane Eikelberry, Linda Eaton, CLARA OLESON, and Victoria Herring after a Civil Rights Commission hearing in Iowa City, 1979. "*The most notorious case in my legal career involved Linda Eaton, the first female fire fighter in Iowa City, who won the right to breast-feed her young son at the firehouse.*"

remained friends and over the years he has been a tremendous support to me.

Meanwhile, I applied to the University of Iowa Law School in 1972 but was not accepted until the following year. So there I was unemployed and with no money. I began going around to women's groups in Iowa talking about affirmative action and civil rights. I must have hit every PEO [a women's organization] and Altrusa [women executives] club east of Des Moines as well as other types of service organizations. I became a believer in offering honoraria to women speakers! Talking to service clubs did not provide a living wage and I could not get a white-collar job in Iowa City because I was a "women's libber." Finally I took a full-time job at the Lazy Leopard Lounge as a bartender. It was a working-class neighborhood bar by the railroad tracks with black velvet nude paintings on the walls and much good cheer and alcoholic desperation on the bar stools. I would tend bar at night and then during the day I would do community action events.

There were lots of things going on. Elizabeth Diecke, Mori Constantino, Molly Eggers, Carol Spazziani, and I worked on a complaint we filed against the City of Iowa City when they came up with a new job classification scheme which had all the women's jobs at the bottom of the pay scale. We got the EEOC [Equal Employment Opportunity Commission] to investigate and got the city to sign a consent decree in 1973 which required that a certain number of women be hired in various departments, including the fire department.

We were also trying to start a women's center and there were
endless meetings about whether the center should be associated
with the university or whether it should be an independent community group. The Women's Center was established as part of the university and I was fortunate to help plan its tenth year celebration in
1980.

When Shirley Chisholm ran for president of the United States in
1972 I worked with a group of local Democrats to elect Sylvia Johnson—a black woman who was a statistics Ph.D. student, a mother,
and welfare recipient—to be a national delegate. The Chisholm
campaign was great fun and Chisholm got four votes from the Iowa
delegation at the national convention.

To this day I have no idea how I ever got into the University of
Iowa Law School in 1973. What seems most likely is that they were
scared to death that I would sue the pants off them if I was rejected.
In any event, I received my notice of acceptance the night before the
fall semester began. I arrived at law school at 7:30 A.M. after a night
of work and partying at the Lazy Leopard. A classmate said, "Don't
go to class. We're sitting in at the dean's office." I said, "Okay." So
we went up to the dean's office and there were forty or fifty students
literally sitting around. What had happened was that the law school
had posted a letter from an attorney in western Iowa asking for a
summer intern. The letter said that they wanted somebody who
was capable of carrying a canoe five miles, was a good swimmer,
and was capable of enjoying a good time with the boys. It did not
explicitly say, "No women need apply," but there was certainly that
implication. The protest was to bring to the dean's attention our
concerns about this. The dean was a classic liberal guy and I think
he was amazed at all these students sitting in his office. I remember
sitting there thinking, This is a strange way to start law school.
Maybe I should at least go to my second class, which met at 10
o'clock, which I did.

The sit-in was symbolic. I went through three years of law
school with great humor, much trepidation, and lots of confrontation. I helped found OWLS [the Organization of Women Law Students and Staff], I participated in planning national conferences for
women law students, and I worked on curriculum reform. At that
time there were no courses in discrimination law and the faculty
was almost completely unenlightened.

In the fall of 1976 Jane Eikelberry and I opened the first all-
women law office in Iowa City. When Jane left Iowa City three years
later I joined a group of lawyers in an association of solo practition-
ers and my last year of practice was with two other male attorneys.

CLARA OLESON on a peace march in Iowa City, January 1991.
*"I was fortunate to have worked with such a talented and
dedicated group of feminists."* Photo by David Greedy, courtesy
of *The Daily Iowan*

The most interesting and economically viable class of cases I
handled involved denial of tenure and failure to promote disputes at
institutions of higher education. Those types of cases took incredibly long hours and were factually complex. I very much admired
the tenacity and commitment to principle of those clients. Their
legal fights did much to bring procedural due process to the tenure
process.

Divorce cases were a constant, and I represented mostly
women. The quantity and range of cases involving physical abuse
of women and children depressed and enraged me. I became an
expert in the medical aspect of beaten women and children. Those

of us in similar practice saw this as emergency room law.

The most notorious case in my legal career involved Linda Eaton, the first female fire fighter in Iowa City, who won the right to breast-feed her young son at the firehouse during personal time when other fire fighters took care of their personal and biological needs. The case was conducted in two main phases: the first in 1977 with international and national press attention; the second, several years later, in almost complete obscurity. Jane Eikelberry and Victoria Herring, an attorney with the Iowa attorney general's office who was assigned to the Iowa Civil Rights Commission, were stalwart advocates in the first phase. My main contribution was devising the legal strategy which kept Linda on the job, breast-feeding her baby, while we established her right to do so. The second phase of the case, which I did by myself, involved a trial alleging job harassment and seeking monetary damages for the months Linda worked before she finally quit in complete exhaustion. We lost that phase of the case and did not have money to appeal.

Interacting daily with people who were dispossessed from economic, political, or social power contributed to my decision to leave the practice of law in 1985. I thought of it as battle fatigue and took a year off and moved to the country, where I recuperated.

In 1986 I began a new phase of my relationship with the University of Iowa by accepting full-time employment as a labor educator at the Labor Center, a part of the Division of Adult Education. My responsibilities include devising, planning, and teaching noncredit programs to union members and officials throughout the state. I am presently investigating and pushing for reform on the issue of migrant labor camps for corn detasselers in Iowa. Once again, I have the benefit of using my talents in a politically and socially useful manner.

Sarah Hanley

Sarah Hanley lived in Cedar Rapids in the 1960s and early 1970s, where she was a leader of the feminist movement. She was known for her audacious espousal of feminism at a time when the word "feminist" was a pejorative term. Since 1977 Hanley has taught at the University of Iowa, where she is a distinguished professor of history. She has been instrumental in the development of the Women's Studies Program at the university and is also active in working for the improvement of the status of women in the university community.

"One of the chief virtues of this movement (was) that we did not allow anybody to divide us along any lines, whether they were political— Republican or Democrat—whether they were straight or gay, whether they were married or single, whether they had children or not."

I grew up in Milton, Massachusetts, a town outside of Boston. My mother worked as a secretary. She was always very feminist because she was upset at the way that women didn't get the same chances men did, so I think I always thought that there was something askew. I went to Katherine Gibbs School and then worked in a law firm. I married when I was twenty-one. By the time I was twenty-five I had three children under the age of three. By the time I was twenty-seven I had lived in a number of different places; we were living in Pittsburgh when I decided to go back to school. I went to the University of Pittsburgh and did my bachelor's degree there, feeling very old because at that time older women—my being an older woman at twenty-seven—were not back in college. I went two years at night and then I went three years in the daytime. I got a degree in philosophy and history and graduated magna cum laude.

I had gotten so excited about university life and thinking and intellectual life, I wanted to be inside the university. I hardly dared admit that because I didn't think I could ever do it, but I wanted to get a Ph.D. I had a grant and was ready to go for the Ph.D. at Carnegie Mellon in Pittsburgh in 1957 when my husband to whom I was married then (I'm now divorced from him) was sent to Cedar Rapids and so that's how I ended up at the University of Iowa. I got my Ph.D. here. Then I taught at Coe College in Cedar Rapids for one year and two summers (1974–76) and I've been on the faculty here at the University of Iowa since 1977. I'm now a full professor of history and dean of the faculty.

When I was in graduate school there were very few women. As a result, very few women have Ph.D.'s and of those who did get their Ph.D.'s very few lasted or got jobs or tenure in big research universities. As a result, we now have very few women in academia, especially in the research institutions where people do research publishing and teaching.

I have always been a Democrat. I am interested in a more socialist organization of society, that is to say, at least interested in limiting capitalism in some way, although I am part of the capitalist system myself. I was active in the civil rights movement in the South when I lived in Chattanooga, Tennessee, and I was very active in the antiwar movement. I gave anti–Vietnam War talks around the state of Iowa.

On August 23, 1970, my two daughters, Lynn and Kathy Madden, and I went to Boston for the first big women's march. Similar marches were held in big cities all over the United States on the same day. My mother and my two sisters and two of our best friends also went. I still have the poster that I carried in that march. In fact, in class when I show pictures of suffragist posters showing how American and British women tried to win the vote, I always end up with this poster which shows Sojourner Truth saying, "Ain't I a Woman?" This shows how much more aggressive the women's movement has become. If you look at all the suffragist posters, the message is very mild, but if you look at the posters in the new women's movement, they are very aggressive. So in a way, I suppose we were much more aggressive. But don't forget that we had lived through the civil rights movement; we had lived through the antiwar movement, and as Sara Evans in her book on the American women's movement says, there is a connection there, at least in tactics (Evans 1989). In that way, the civil rights movement was very important.

In 1970 a group of us in Cedar Rapids started a consciousness-raising group but then we thought we should have a political arm to put some pressure on the community and that's one of the reasons we started the Cedar Rapids Women's Caucus in 1971, which then became a NOW organization. We eventually expanded to about twenty women but our newsletter got to many more people. There were a lot of things we wanted to change. They seemed like small things, but to us they were outrageous. For instance, the large Armstrong's and Killian's department stores had small restaurants in the back that were reserved for men only. We traipsed right down to Armstrong's and went in and sat down for lunch. (This is what blacks did in five-and-ten-cent stores in the South.) We were told that we couldn't stay. We told them we intended to stay. We ended up being called up into Mr. Armstrong's office and we told him why we thought that it was not proper to do this anymore. Within a few weeks the practice was stopped. People just seemed to need to be reminded. Very soon thereafter, the unspoken rule against women realtors having a license of their own was dropped. Then we started to work on the television stations.

I can't remember just how our group got started. I think somebody told Bev Mitchell about one of the talks I had given and she called me. I was on television in September 1970 with my two daughters talking about the women's movement, which the media in those days liked to call "women's lib." I think Bev saw that program and called me. That was a very nice call. You should have heard some of the calls I got from people who thought this was something that was quite improper for a lady. Of course, that always led up to my saying that we were not ladies, for obvious reasons. Politically, I think we were all Democrats. I have the sense that Republican women came in later, past the first phase of the movement, which was very radical. During the first phase of the movement I refused to let anybody sidetrack the movement by talking about lesbians in a negative way. I think that's been one of the chief virtues of this movement, that we did not allow anybody to divide us along any lines, whether they were political—Republican or Democrat—whether they were straight or gay, whether they were married or single, whether they had children or not. That was a mistake in the first women's movement, which was very narrowly conceived; they were going for the vote. We realized right from the beginning that we were going for political, social, economic, and sexual parity, because women are so defined by sex and by sex attributes that it really makes a difference in the end. So we refused to be divided and as NOW grew into a much stronger movement, NOW also refused to let that division take place.

That really was one of the brilliant moves on the part of NOW. There are people who were always angry at NOW for that but I think it was right and proper that women so crushed over so many years by differences shouldn't allow that to happen again within their own movement. This was one of the big successes of our movement, because once people can find a way to divide you, they can easily conquer. There are so many ways you can be divided—whether you're a Republican or a Democrat, whether you're rich or poor, whether you're white or black, whether you're a lesbian or straight, whether you're married or single. There are all kinds of ways that people can disrupt a movement. I think we were pretty good at preventing that.

I attended just about every NOW meeting and so did Lynn and Kathy, who both remained strong feminists. Another person who was in that group was Anita Terpstra, whose husband was a partner in a big law firm in Cedar Rapids, Terpstra and Terpstra and Epping. Anita works in this law firm now. She's a very interesting person and a good friend of mine. She was chair of the Linn County Democratic party in the early seventies and was also on the state Democratic Central Committee. But early on there were only about six or seven of us and we had a very hard time getting members because we were looked upon as radicals. In fact, I do have to admit that we did try to shock people into some kind of sensibility about the ways in which texts and books that we'd read all our lives, including the Bible and the Declaration of Independence, have been skewed historically as far as women are concerned.

For me, that was especially interesting because I had hopes at the time of being a historian. I was working on a Ph.D. and I did a classically oriented dissertation, which then turned into a book that is going into French translation now (Hanley 1983). My second project, which I am currently [1990] working on, turns more directly toward women in sixteenth-, seventeenth-, eighteenth-century France. This historical purview was always my main interest, and so when I went around giving talks I always pointed to the historical dimensions. We also tried to make fun of things, like ads about women that were supposed to appeal to women.

I remember two speeches I made. One had to do with Biblical injunctions about women, which are really quite abysmal, and reli-

SARAH HANLEY, 1971. *"We decided to be bold. It's harder to laugh at somebody who's bold than it is at someone who is sort of pleading for your attention."*

gious people were quite upset. The other had to do with a meeting of one those men's clubs that meet at noon to have lunch. Perhaps it was the Optimist Club, I can't remember, but it is the one that sells light bulbs. The program had two people, a young black woman was going to talk on the race issue and I was going to talk on the women's issue. When we stood up to salute the flag, which was part of their ritual, the black woman refused to salute the flag. I always find that ritual odious in any case. After Nazi Germany, you have to think about what saluting a flag might mean. Because the black woman refused to salute the flag, I didn't salute the flag either. This made these men absolutely furious. They actually came running up to the podium. The black woman then explained why she did not wish to say, "with liberty and justice for all." She was very articulate and I tried to back her up. In any case, this fit in with the themes we were going to talk about. It's the notion of difference, where the group who is different is defined as having negative values. That is the single worst concept that keeps western democracies from fulfilling their promise of being democratic states. As I think back on it, we forget how angry audiences were. I was in my late thirties at the time and it didn't make so much difference whether people my age or above were converted as that the young start thinking about it. So I liked going to Cornell College and Coe College and a lot of other places to talk to students.

Just the other day I met a woman who is the head of the Domestic Violence Shelter in Iowa City, now in her early forties or late thirties. She said to me, "I heard your talk at Cornell in 1972 and I never forgot it." I thought, I did have something to say and people did hear it. I was just astounded and I felt so good about that, it had been so long ago. I was thinking also of my daughters and their chances in the world and I was thinking also of my son and his chances, because it's too much in modern times for a man to be responsible for supporting three or four other people. A young man, too, stands to benefit by all of this. You have to have two people supporting a family. So I saw this as something better for a generation coming along behind me.

At the time we began we were consciousness-raising for the public and maybe that's why we adopted tactics that were a little bold. Otherwise, if we couldn't make people at least somewhat angry or upset, they tended to try to laugh us off the podium. It's very interesting. At one point, just before I went to Paris to do my dissertation research in 1972, the *Cedar Rapids Gazette* did a big article on me, because they considered this so odd—that I would leave my children and my husband and go to Paris to do research. However, they put an inflammatory headline on the story which I realize was not the fault of the person who wrote the article, but the headline was meant to embarrass and demean me as a person. It said, "This Mom Isn't Stuck with the Dishes." Now, here the article was about a professional person who would be on a university faculty within three or four years. So the next time I had an opportunity to give a talk at one of those men's luncheon groups, I think it was the Rotary Club, the editor of the *Cedar Rapids Gazette* was there. As I gave my talk I pointed out that the *Gazette* was supporting Dick Clark, who was running for the United States Senate, and that, in fact, Clark was being supported financially by his constituents while he campaigned because he did not have a job. Yet—as I pointed out to them—nobody ever wrote over one of his articles, "This Father Isn't Stuck with the Garbage." These inequities were galling because the media had a heyday with the women's movement, as they always have when women have ever tried to do anything, whether it was during the French Revolution or the woman-suffrage movement. It's always been easy to make fun of women. That's a very corrosive tactic because most people can't stand to be laughed at and they will remove themselves from those situations. Maybe that's one of the reasons we decided to be bold. It's harder to laugh at somebody who's bold than it is at someone who is sort of pleading for your attention.

Boldness was the temper of the times and that, of course, was partially a product of the experience of the antiwar and the civil rights movements. I know I had become very bold about disregarding the police and marching and things like that. If you think in terms of western civilization, here you have all of a sudden all traditional authority undermined—churches, the government, families—in the sense of father being head and mother being subservient. The temper of the times was antiauthoritarian, asking people to rethink forms of authority and what kinds of rules they would follow. The antiwar movement had a lot to do with that boldness, and the whole temper fed into the women's movement also. For U.S. history there are subtle linkages between those three movements: civil rights, the war movement, and the women's movement. So then you wonder where you are. You try to make a better world for those who come behind you. I think it's better, but of course I'm the eternal optimist. Lots of things have changed. While I do not subscribe to the notion of "progress," I do think change has been effected.

I've found that if you're bold, you may make people angry, but they will at least react to you in some way, especially as a woman. In a way, in our group in Cedar Rapids—the Cedar Rapids Women's Caucus, which later became NOW—I was a good person to do that because although people could be very angry at what I was saying, especially men but some women, too, they couldn't get at me in the way they could at some others. For instance, it was clear to them that I was an ordinary, white, middle-class woman, that I was married, that I had children, that I was not lesbian (at least not that anybody could imagine), and therefore they didn't expect to hear from me what they did hear. This was all the more shocking. In a way, now that I think of it, we did think about that as a good strategy, because audiences would come intending to listen, and then they would get angry, and then they would think. Of course, some liked what they heard. This was just a personal style of my own: to confront, sort of stamp my foot, and argue back and forth with people from the audience. I liked that. In some ways that is why I am a good teacher because I really like to get students thinking about things.[1] They get excited, and then I get excited, and there's a good back-and-forth exchange. I was able to make a crowd do that too. This was probably a fairly successful tactic.

I was active in the Cedar Rapids Women's Caucus for about three years while it was getting started. I left in 1972 to go to Paris to work on my Ph.D. dissertation. Not long after my return, I moved to Iowa City. All my activities spilled over into academic life with the beginning of the Women's Studies Program. That, in effect, became the main way in which teaching about women goes on in the university, and the universities have neglected that heretofore. I

---

1. Hanley received the faculty award (1982–1985), which allowed her a year and a half off for scholarship. She was the first person in the history department to receive this award.

chaired the Women's Studies Program at Iowa from 1977 to 1980
and again for a year two years later when a crisis occurred. I chaired
the program for the four years we were building it. We developed a
very fine program here. It has a very good reputation. I was followed
by terrific people—Florence Babb, Margery Wolf, and now Martha
Chamallas.

The Women's Studies Program started off as little groups meeting together. It was finally institutionalized by our wonderful vice
president, May Brodbeck, who is now deceased. It was institutionalized with a chair and an office in 1974. This was a very interesting
proposition because the thing one had to do was to keep separate
the academic and the political. One could not have people going into
classes and putting forth political views as I did in those speeches I
made around the state. I always kept those things entirely separate.
But we did get courses started. I still teach one called Society and
Gender in Early Modern Europe. It is a course that focuses on
women and so it ends up asking different questions, but it is an
academic course like any other course that I teach. Where Women's
Studies Programs became part of the political wing (i.e., the Wom-
en's Resource and Action Center), they just devoured each other.
We were very lucky because we had the Women's Resource and
Action Center at the University of Iowa, a student organization
which attends to the political issues.

The Women's Studies Program is like any other program such
as the American Studies Program or the African-American Studies
Program. In effect, they are departments where faculty have visiting appointments. But there are linkages from the NOW movement
and other organized groups that flowed into this business of education which is a very powerful thrust now. I think future historians
will see some linkage there, because most of us who are interested
in having a Women's Studies Program and in supporting an African-
American Studies Program, and so forth, are people who were also
ideologically concerned about this bifurcation; that is, the way difference is treated. And again, in Iowa City, in all of this, we refused
to let any division come between lesbian women and straight
women. We have always insisted that there could be no distinction
made on these grounds. It seemed to me in the beginning that this
is what a lot of very hostile men would like to have done. They
would have liked to make those women who were straight afraid of
being called lesbian. We refused to let that happen. Some faculty
members are lesbian and open about it; others are lesbian and quiet
about it.

So a lot of what began as consciousness-raising on the part of

The man over there says that women need to be helped into carriages and lifted over ditches, and to have the best place everywhere. Nobody ever helps me into carriages or over puddles or gives me the best place ...

...and ain't I a woman?

Look at my arm! I have ploughed and planted and gathered into barns, and no man could head me ...and ain't I a woman?
I could work as much and eat as much as a man— when I could get it—and bear the lash as well ...and ain't I a woman?
I have borne thirteen children, and seen most of 'em sold into slavery, and when I cried out with my mother's grief, none but Jesus heard me ...and ain't I a woman?

The Sojourner Truth poster that Hanley carried in the Boston women's march, August 1970.

individuals eventually became institutionalized as we took our concerns to the community, talked around the state, then actively built a Women's Studies Program. Then came the educational business of getting things going in the university. Now women in the university are speaking up very strongly about the way we want the university to be run. For instance, this year [1990] in the College of Liberal Arts, we have made it possible for new, untenured faculty who become a primary or coequal caretaker of children to request that an additional year be added to the tenure timetable. Ordinarily people come up for tenure in six years, now they can ask for a seventh year. This is for males and females. When we argued this to the Academic Affairs Office, they wanted the policy to apply to females only. I argued against the latter policy, noting that if you make it for females only, you are saying we not only give birth to children, but we are the primary caretakers, and we will not accept that role anymore. So the Academic Affairs Office did back down and are giving the same option to men and women.

It is part of our strategy here to make the university a better place for women to work in, because universities have been structured for men who have wives at home doing everything for them. The senior women who are my age are not willing to have young women come behind us and face the same hard times. We are just not willing to let that situation continue. In a way, we think of that as the best possible definition of feminism. One cannot forget how hard it was coming through the system as a woman. One must try to change the university, to provide the kind of working conditions to help young women, and remember how much harder it is for them. One has seen the women who won't do this. They sit, like queen bees. They like being surrounded by men and they do not really care about extending a hand to women behind them. They are male-identified women.

We are slowly but definitely changing for the better here at the university. We happen to be extraordinarily fortunate in the College of Liberal Arts, which is the biggest college in the university, with forty-two departments and 690 faculty, to have Dean Jerry Loewenberg because he appoints women deans and listens to them and to women faculty, and I am one of these deans. In fact, he has been instrumental in making some of these changes. It is not hard to convince him. For example, the university has no parenting policy. Women who have to go to the hospital to have a baby are supposed to do it on their sick leave. We are working on that now.

Other colleges are not as well governed—the medical college for instance, whence issued the *Jean Jew v. Robert Tomanek* case. It is a source of pain and shame for me to see the former vice president of the university (Richard Remington) and the university attorney (Julia Mears) testify in this case that the slander Robert Tomanek spread about Jean Jew over a twelve-year period (some of it real "gutter talk," as I noted in court) was "business-as-usual," "normal in the workplace," "within the scope of employment." In 1990 I testified against them, rebutting their testimony. I felt privileged to be able to do so! This case is a perfect example of how women and sexuality are linked even in the workplace. It would be inconceivable for a male faculty member to have been harrassed like that on sexual grounds. [The jury awarded Jean Jew $35,000 in her defamation lawsuit against Robert Tomanek.]

So then one wonders where you are. One tries to make a better world for those who come behind. I think it is better but, of course, I'm the eternal optimist. I think lots of things have changed. The women's movement is now at a different stage of evolution. Young women normally say things nowdays that they think are perfectly all right to say, for example, remarks about "sexism." They do not realize that twenty, thirty, or forty years ago they would have been laughed at or shunned for saying these things about the desired equality of women and men. Probably organizations like NOW and especially the NOW Legal Education and Defense Fund are important organizations because legally they have pressed many challenges through the years. That is a step that one could not have imagined being taken back in the late sixties or early seventies. Challenging the legal system has been very important. Of course, affirmative action policies have also been effective. This, again, is tied with race and gender. I can see, for instance, the difference there is now in the university in actively hiring women and blacks with potential to publish and teach. I guess the women's movement is in a more institutionalized stage now as we institutionalize knowledge and as we reform the law.

Yet despite all the efforts to make equality work, what we have been delivered in the 1990s are women and children who are the poorest of the poor. That shows that there is something not quite right in the way society is structured. That leads, of course, to the necessity for reform in marriage laws. I think it is absolutely necessary for young women to be able to earn their own living. They cannot think that they will be supported by a man forever, because given the divorce rate, too many of them will end up having to support themselves anyway. We are at a crossroads. The question now is whether this society will be structured so that women do not become the poorest citizens. In that way the times are very exciting because the possibilities are there to make such changes.

For instance, the Congress of the United States has never seriously attempted to pass a "parenting" bill (as in Europe, especially France); that is a bill that would guarantee a woman the right to her job while pregnant and for some time after. It would give her a proportion of the salary from her job while she is engaged outside the salaried work force in the politically important task of reproduction. Until Congress enacts such a bill, which is unlikely since women are not properly represented in either the House or the Senate, then we have an example of "structured inequality based on gender" that is legally built into the workplace and negatively affects women.

There is a kind of plateau we are on now. There is a steep rise in consciousness today about these inequities. Everybody knows what "sexism" is now, yet people used to laugh in the early seventies when we talked about sexist practices. That is part of our daily vocabulary now. Women do have to remember that there are a lot of male feminists on their side, because there are certainly a lot of women antifeminists who will never support our aims. In fact, there was a direct backlash as NOW and other organizations began to be organized. That seems to have sifted out on the prochoice/antichoice, abortion issue also. Maybe institutionalization at this point is good in that laws are being reformed, but I think a more general overhaul of structure is needed. The structure of society and this business of jobs needs to be addressed. Young women somehow have to understand that they need jobs. And most of all, they need to be bold and demand what should be theirs!

REFERENCES

Evans, Sara M., *Born for Liberty, a History of Women in America* (New York: Free Press, 1989).
Hanley, Sarah, *The Lit de Justice of the Kings of France: Constitutional Ideology in Legend, Ritual, and Discourse* (Princeton: Princeton University Press, 1983). French edition: *Le lit de justice des rois de France: L'idéologie constitutionnelle dans la legende, le rituel, et le discours,* trans. André Charpentier, 1991.

Epilogue

WHAT DO THE WOMEN I interviewed think of the status of the feminist movement today? First of all, they are discouraged by the current apathy among younger women who take for granted the gains that have been made and who are not interested in action to correct the many injustices that still exist. Barbara Mathias comments that "In the early seventies we at least knew that we didn't have it so good, and it seemed like more of the young women were in touch with that and willing to work for some changes. People can't see feminism as an issue now. It seems almost as if the younger women think that the women over forty were kind of foolish to have worked so hard when we were going to get our rights anyway. In fact," Mathias says, "we don't have them yet. We don't have equitable pay. We don't have equal earning ability. There are just many ways in which we are prejudiced against in our society." Irene Talbott also talks about the apathy among women today. "People don't see feminism as an issue now," she says. Ginny Benware agrees. "It seems that younger women have a sense that they have made it and they have no idea how recent the struggles were that got them the opportunities they currently have."

The one notable exception to this apathy is the increase in activism because of the threat to abortion rights, which have recently been severely limited by the Supreme Court. "Right now we are demonstrating for abortion rights," Talbott observes, "but it took this big scare to do it." Louise Swartzwalder also comments on the concern over abortion rights. "A lot of people have probably been sitting on their duff for years and now they are going to get geared up again," she says.

There is concern that women's activities are too narrowly focused. "The movement appears to be focusing strictly on elective politics," Benware says. "The grass-roots organizing, putting pressure on different points in the system that NOW was so great at seems to have been abandoned." Bev Mitchell is "especially anxious to get back to enforcing the employment laws that we have and putting some of them back that have been gutted in the last ten years."

Sarah Hanley notes the backlash which NOW and other women's organizations felt as they began to be organized. She speaks of the current situation as a "kind of plateau." Yet she sees improvement in women's situations. "Everybody knows what 'sexism' is now, yet people used to laugh in the early seventies when we talked about sexist practices. Maybe institutionalization at this point is good in that laws are being reformed," she observed.

And what about the future? Naomi Christensen firmly believes that "In time women will achieve equality . . . but it is a slow process." She once thought it would happen in ten years, now she realizes that it is not even happening in her lifetime.

Minnette Doderer believes that although each advancement becomes more difficult, women in the United States will never accept going back to being second-class citizens again. Talbott finds hope in the thought that history is a pendulum. "When times really seem tough you always know that probably the pendulum will swing back again." Mitchell expresses a similar concept. "This movement never stops," she says. "It rises and subsides just like waves, and like waves, it can erode what it cannot smash." Karen Johnson is both "fearful and encouraged by the possibilities that present themselves in the 1990s." She hopes "we can make them the 'Gay Nineties' in a truly celebrative and liberatory sense."

My own feeling is that we have to keep on fighting one battle at a time until a new wave of feminism rises, bringing with it a return of the hope and enthusiasm of the 1970s.

Index

Page numbers in italics refer to photographs.